# Management in Transitional Economies

This book examines the past, present and future of management in the transitional economies of East and Central Europe, Russia, the People's Republic of China, and the Socialist Republic of Vietnam. It discusses the nature of the transition process, identifies different transitional paths, highlights common features and outlines a number of theoretical approaches. Each chapter covers a wide range of management issues in the countries covered, including the details of the country's historical and cultural background, the transition process, external and internal factors, and its macro- and micro-economic contexts. This work should be of interest to both an academic, as well as a practitioner, readership, across a wide range of disciplines.

**Malcolm Warner** is Professor and Fellow, Wolfson College and Judge Institute of Management, University of Cambridge, United Kingdom.

**Vincent Edwards** is Professor and Director, Centre for Research into East European Business (CREEB), Buckinghamshire Chilterns University College, United Kingdom.

**Gennadij Polonsky** is a former academic and now management consultant, Moscow, Russia.

**Danijel Pučko** is Professor, Economic Faculty, Ljubljana University, Slovenia.

**Ying Zhu** is Senior Lecturer, Department of Management, University of Melbourne, Australia.

# Management in Transitional Economies

From the Berlin Wall
to the Great Wall of China

**Malcolm Warner, Vincent Edwards,
Gennadij Polonsky, Danijel Pučko
and Ying Zhu**

RoutledgeCurzon
Taylor & Francis Group

LONDON AND NEW YORK

First published 2005
by RoutledgeCurzon
2 Park Square, Milton Park, Abingdon, Oxon OX14 4RN

Simultaneously published in the USA and Canada
by RoutledgeCurzon
270 Madison Ave, New York, NY 10016

*RoutledgeCurzon is an imprint of the Taylor & Francis Group*

© 2005 Malcolm Warner, Vincent Edwards, Gennadij Polonsky, Danijel Pučko and Ying Zhu

Typeset in Times by
BOOK NOW Ltd
Printed and bound in Great Britain by
MPG Books Ltd, Bodmin

*British Library Cataloguing in Publication Data*
A catalogue record for this book is available from the British Library

*Library of Congress Cataloging in Publication Data*
A catalog record for this book has been requested

ISBN 0–415–33194–3 (hbk)
ISBN 0–415–33670–8 (pbk)

# Contents

# Figures

# Tables

# Contributors

**Vincent Edwards** is Professor of East European Management and Culture at Buckinghamshire Business School, Buckinghamshire Chilterns University College and Visiting Professor at the Faculty of Economics, University of Ljubljana. He graduated from Cambridge University and completed postgraduate studies at the universities of Reading and Warwick. He is a founder member of the Centre for Research into East European Business (CREEB) and was previously Director of Postgraduate Studies and Head of Research. His research has focused on management and corporate change in transforming economies and he has conducted field research in Germany, Hungary, Slovenia and Russia. His publications include articles in academic journals and a number of co-authored books. He has been actively involved in delivering a MBA programme in Central Europe and is a member of the editorial board of the *Journal for East European Management Studies* and *Economic and Business Review for Central and Eastern Europe*.

**Gennadij Polonsky** is a management consultant working in Russia and the CIS, specializing in corporate restructuring. He graduated from Volgograd University and was awarded a PhD from Moscow University of Finance in 1985. He was formerly Reader in Transitional Economics at Buckinghamshire Business School, Buckinghamshire Chilterns University College. He is Russian by origin and was born in Kazakhstan. His research interests include problems of countries in transition, especially the interplay between social, political and economic factors. He has authored and co-authored more than 20 publications and presented papers at a number of leading international conferences. He is a founder member of the Centre for Research into East European Business (CREEB).

**Danijel Pučko** is a full professor at the Faculty of Economics, Ljubljana University and Honorary Professor at Buckingham Chilterns University College. After gaining a bachelors degree in economics at Ljubljana University in 1968, he became a teaching assistant at the Faculty of Economics. He completed his masters in Business Administration in 1974 and his doctoral studies in 1978. He was a member of the Yugoslav Federal

Parliament and from 1988–90 the Vice President of the Slovenian Chamber of Commerce and Economy. In the mid-1990s, he was Dean of the Faculty of Economics and since 2001 he has been Vice Dean for graduate and doctoral studies. Danijel Pučko has been a co-editor of the *Economic and Business Review for Central and South East Europe* since 1999. His books in Slovenian are in the field of business economics, strategic management, business planning and business performance analysis. He is also co-author of a textbook on strategic management in Croat. He has had over 50 articles published in Slovenian and foreign journals.

**Malcolm Warner** is Professor and Emeritus Fellow, Wolfson College and Senior Research Associate, Judge Institute of Management, University of Cambridge. He took his undergraduate degree and doctorate in the Faculty of Economics and Politics at Cambridge. Professor Warner has written and edited over 30 books on management and over 200 articles and is the editor-in-chief of the *International Encyclopedia of Business and Management*, 8 volumes, London: Thomson Learning, 2002. He is also the co-editor of the *Asia Pacific Business Review*. He is on the editorial boards of half a dozen international journals. He has been a Visiting Professor at a number of Asia–Pacific universities and is a Honorary Professor at the Cass Business School, City University, London.

**Ying Zhu** is Senior Lecturer in the Department of Management, the University of Melbourne. He graduated at Peking University in 1984, then held the post of Economist at Shenzhen Special Economic Zone Development Company. He later completed a PhD at the University of Melbourne. His teaching and research interests include international human resource management and development, international business, economic development in East Asia (e.g., China, Japan, South Korea, Taiwan and Vietnam) and political economy of globalization. He has a large number of publications on the topics of international human resource management, employment relations in Asia, labour law and regulations in Asia and economic development in Asia.

# Preface

How management in transitional economies has been affected by the momentous changes that have taken place since the late 1980s is a subject of great importance. This book represents an international collaboration between management scholars in the United Kingdom, Eastern Europe, Russia and Asia-Pacific. The five co-authors of this work, expert in one or more parts of the world studied, worked on the manuscript for over two years. The work covers historical background, general trends as well as specific research-based data collected in the course of their individual research activities over recent years. We deal with both the macro- and micro-economic levels of analysis, as well as the cultural, managerial, political and social influences involved. The work is thus essentially interdisciplinary in nature and we hope it will have a wider appeal for this reason.

The countries covered in this book stretch from the now happily fallen Berlin Wall to the Great Wall of China. They cover a range of countries from the former socialist and command economies of Central and Eastern Europe, Russia, the People's Republic of China, and ending with Vietnam. We are indebted to many colleagues too numerous to mention in those lands who have over the years been both friends and colleagues.

We would also like to thank the University of *Ljubljana* which provided the back-up for a Working Seminar at *Bled*, essential for the completion of the final drafts of the book. We should like to acknowledge the assistance of several people who helped make this work possible, including Jenny Edwards whose help was invaluable in the preparation of the manuscript, Pia Jönsson of London Metropolitan University for illustrating Figure 1.1, Adnan Mujagić of Buckinghamshire Business School for extensive data collection, our commissioning editor, Peter Sowden, at RoutledgeCurzon and many others.

MW, VE, GP, DP, YZ
*London,*
*2 March 2004*

# Abbreviations

| | |
|---|---|
| AFTA | ASEAN Free Trade Area |
| APPOT | Asian Pacific Project on Tripartism |
| ASEAN | Association of South-East Asian Nations |
| ATUC | Albanian Trade Union Confederation |
| BoP | balance of payments |
| CCP | Chinese Communist Party |
| CEE | Central and Eastern Europe |
| CEFTA | Central European Free Trade Area |
| CIS | Commonwealth of Independent States |
| CITUB | Confederation of Independent Trade Unions of Bulgaria |
| CJV | contractual joint venture |
| CMEA | Council for Mutual Economic Assistance |
| CMRS | Contract Management Responsibility System |
| COMECON | Council for Mutual Economic Assistance (also CMEA) |
| CPSU | Communist Party of the Soviet Union |
| DPE | domestic private enterprise |
| EBRD | European Bank for Reconstruction and Development |
| EJV | equity joint venture |
| EU | European Union |
| FDI | foreign direct investment |
| FOE | foreign-owned enterprise |
| FSU | Former Soviet Union |
| FYROM | Former Yugoslav Republic of Macedonia |
| GDP | gross domestic product |
| GDR | German Democratic Republic |
| GNI | gross national income |
| GNP | gross national product |
| HR | human resources |
| HRM | human resource management |
| IJV | international joint venture |
| ILO | International Labour Organization |
| IMF | International Monetary Fund |
| ISO | International Standards Organization |

| | |
|---|---|
| JIT | just-in-time |
| JSC | joint shareholding company/joint stock company |
| JV | joint venture |
| MBA | Master of Business Administration |
| MBO | management buy-out |
| MEBO | management and employee buy-out |
| MES | modern enterprise system |
| MNC | multinational corporation |
| MTP | Managers' Training Programme (Tacis) |
| NATO | North Atlantic Treaty Organization |
| NEP | New Economic Policy |
| NIC | newly industrializing country |
| OECD | Organization for Economic Cooperation and Development |
| PPP | purchasing power parity |
| PRC | People's Republic of China |
| R&D | research and development |
| RID | Russian Institute of Directors |
| RMB | renminbi (Chinese currency) |
| SEZ | Special Economic Zone |
| SME | small and medium-sized enterprise |
| SOE | state-owned enterprise |
| SRV | Socialist Republic of Vietnam |
| TQM | total quality management |
| UITUA | Union of Independent Trade Unions of Albania |
| USSR | Union of Soviet Socialist Republics |
| VAT | value-added tax |
| WOFE | wholly-owned foreign enterprise |
| WTO | World Trade Organization |

# Part I

# System change

One feature of the history of old Russia was the continual beatings she suffered because of her backwardness. . . . All beat her because of her backwardness, military backwardness, cultural backwardness, political backwardness, industrial backwardness, agricultural backwardness. . . . That is why we must no longer lag behind.

Joseph Stalin (1879–1953)

# 1 Introduction

## From plan to market

### Introduction

By the end of the Second World War, and most certainly by the end of the 1940s, the 'command economy', based on the 'Soviet model' (see Kaple, 1994) had been implanted in a wide range of countries, with a combined population of over one billion people around that time, in the name of Karl Marx.

Up to then, the 'planned economy' had been *de rigueur* since the 1917 Revolution in Russia and had been partially copied in Fascist states like Italy from the 1920s and Germany and Japan in the 1930s, for example. Even Allied governments had introduced an element of planning to advance the war-effort. The Cold War had seen the apogee of the Soviet model. The system became elaborated in different national guises across the continents of Europe and Asia and elsewhere. But by the late 1960s, cracks began to appear in the edifice and weaknesses revealed themselves. Experiments and reforms came to light in a number of countries and by the 1980s, the 'transition' as it came to be known, was well under way.

In this book, we intend to discuss how economies in general and their managements in particular have evolved in the above mentioned 'transitional economies', defined as those moving from 'plan to market', many of which were in mostly former state socialist countries, all of which stretched from what was the old Berlin Wall to the even older Great Wall of China. In particular, in those countries that made up the former Soviet Bloc, as one source put it, 'we have witnessed the collapse of state socialism. One after another Communist Party lost power and the nascent democratic regimes that replaced the old party states struggled to make transformative economic reforms' (Wu, 1994:1). The economies concerned are thus often described as 'transitional', as they are deemed to be 'on the road' from or in 'transition' from communism to capitalism but in reality only a few may have, it seems as yet, fully made the journey. In terms of 'ideal types', it may be said, it is probably unlikely that some ever will in any absolute sense, although a number will come closer to the market-driven model than others.

It is also worth making clear at this point that we do not see the *status quo ex ante*, that is to say 'communist' economies as a homogeneous entity, either conceptually or empirically, any more than the *ancien régime* was before it was abolished. It is also likely to be the case that the transitional economies are differentiated, although they may have strong as well as weak 'family resemblances'. We will focus in this book on the 'transition' by looking at how institutional change (see Scott, 2001) has been introduced and how country and cultural differences have been prominent (see Warner, 2003).

The term 'emerging' economies is sometimes employed but often has been used to apply more to formerly 'statist' regimes in less developed (as well as in non-communist) countries. We restrict our coverage here not only to ex-communist ones but also some that still remain 'red' (as communist party states, that is) officially at least. Additionally, both capitalism and communism as systems have moved on in turn and what economies may be in transition to, may not be what it was when the changes got under way.

The demise of the 'command economies', we must note, predates the fall of the Berlin Wall by some years. The roots of the gradual transition from planned economies to market reforms go back to a number of pragmatic experiments almost three or so decades ago. In fact debates about improving the system began in Central and Eastern Europe (CEE) in the 1950s, shortly after the introduction of the Soviet model. But Marxist economists, even before the Second World War had produced decentralized models and a number midway during the Cold War years. The seeds of globalization may even have been planted when economies were in the Council for Mutual Economic Assistance (COMECON) via their international trade links and where the first international joint ventures (IJVs) between state enterprises and foreign corporations, in what were to become transitional economies, were started. For a general chronology of the Soviet model and its variants see Figure 1.1.

The major communist economies that were set to experience large-scale economic reforms were Russia and the People's Republic of China – we will call it China hereafter (Nolan, 1995; Buck *et al.*, 2000). The other countries in CEE aligned with the former Soviet Union (FSU) were less well-endowed in resources and population. Russia and China were probably quite similar in a number of ways in that they were both geographically extensive, with large markets, cheap labour, etc. Both had a Marxist–Leninist ideology, command economy and management legacy. Both had swollen government expenditures, over-manned state enterprises and so on, with resultant low productivity. But the destinies of these two economic systems were to prove very different as one, Russia, embarked on a 'shock therapy' (see Peng, 2000) in the early 1990s, while the other had earlier followed a 'gradualist' path in the early 1980s en route to 'transition'. The key dates to have to note were of the death of Mao Zedong in China in 1976, followed as it was by Deng Xiaoping's reforms in 1978, much before the break-up of the former Soviet Union and Mikhail Gorbachev's emergence as leader in 1985.

The way each evolved was dependent on their respective history; the social scientists call this 'path-dependence' (see Stark, 1992). The deep-seated,

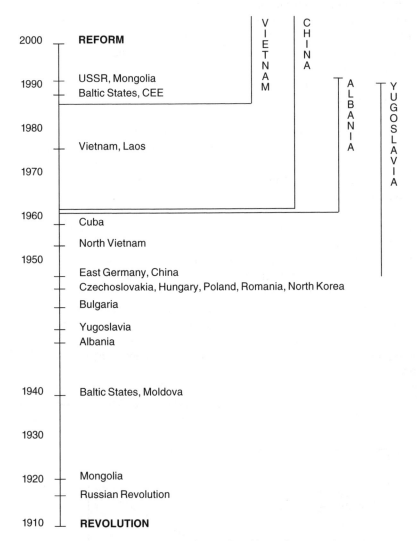

*Figure 1.1* Chronology of the Soviet model and its variants.

underlying cultural characteristics of each country help shape the way institutions are shaped and how the path of transition is constrained. Even within the 'Soviet model', there was room for deviation and variance. Managerial structures and behaviour have been found to differ between many of the countries of CEE and the FSU, for instance (see Kiezun, 1991). If we have an overarching theoretical framework in this study, it is the 'institutionalist' approach in both economics as well as management, relying on country or societal culture as a major theoretical variable (see Maurice *et al.*, 1980; Warner, 2003).

The institutionalist approach allows us to conceptualize the transformation as a complex process of institutional change in which formal and informal institutions interact with, influence and are influenced by the overall process of change. Within this the broad process of change can be sub-divided into three constituent processes of de-instutionalization, re-institutionalization and transition management (Clark and Soulsby, 1999).

To quote Lang and Steger (2002: 281–82),

> Institutions consist of institutional elements such as formal laws and rules, as well as informally reproduced social patterns like behavioural codes and norms, professional standards, roles, symbols, interpretative schemas, classifications, means, tools and procedures for categorization and classification.

While formal institutional elements may be relatively easily and rapidly changed, it may take longer periods of time for such new institutions to be generally accepted and effective. In particular, informal institutions may be especially resistant to change and undermine the introduction of new formal institutional elements (see Maruyama, 1993).

Transforming economies may thus be considered as sites of interplay between old and new institutional elements, with companies and their managements 'trying to understand how to react under two systems: the declining socialist system and the evolving market system' (Fogel, 1994: 232) (Figure 1.2).

The destruction of the formal institutions of the former system (de-institutionalization) may be carried out relatively quickly. However, the

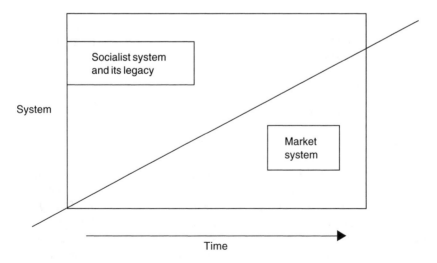

*Figure 1.2* Starting points.

elimination, or reform, of informal institutions (re-institutionalization) may prove particularly intractable. Institution building *grosso modo*, moreover, is not a quick process (van Brabant, 1998) and requires more time than either 'Big Bang' or gradualist approaches to transformation predicated. The easiest way to approach the problem is *historical* but this may be seen as merely descriptive, if highly useful. It is relatively easy to set out an account of formerly recognizably Marxist economies and their management and how these have changed over the last few decades. But it may be facile to merely say that one event or policy followed another in time. A narrative account, although sometimes helpful, is not sufficient. In order to fully come to terms with what has happened, we also must have an *analytical* approach. We present later (in Figure 1.3 on p. 11), our own schema, using two dimensions of 'marketization' and 'ownership' respectively, in the first instance (see Wu, 1994 for an earlier use of a similar schema). But it is worth noting that the discussion of alternative paths of organizing economic life had been going on for some decades preceding the start of the so-called 'transitional' process.

Indeed, the New Economic Policy (NEP) and the resultant debates in the Soviet Union after 1921 have been held up for comparison with later reforms (Wu, 1994); additionally, the 'socialist market' concept had been set out in the 1930s by economists like the Polish Marxist theorist, Kalecki for example, around the same time as Keynes was writing his 'General Theory'. Other contributors to the debate were the English democratic socialist economist Durbin as well as a number of contemporary economists like Lerner (United States), then Lange in Poland, Landauer (Germany) and Dickinson (UK). But the 'socialist market' model was not introduced in practice until much later and well into the post Second World War era.

### *Early period*

Among the first economies to introduce 'socialist market' reforms, before the big communist countries did so, was Yugoslavia as early as the 1950s. This experiment had a significant impact upon both theory and practice in the area of comparative economic analysis, as well as no mean political impact on socialist thinking. Much was spoken of in terms of a 'Third Way' between capitalism and communism with regard to the development of self-management and worker participation. After this came Bulgaria and the German Democratic Republic in the early 1960s, followed by Czechoslovakia and Hungary in 1968. Over the period, Poland also played its part in initiating experiments that helped this process along, first in de-collectivizing agriculture in 1956 and with the price reforms of 1970. These Polish, Hungarian and Yugoslav economic experiments above all others were to influence both the rest of COMECON and the Soviet Union, as well as reputedly having an impact on the Chinese reformers (see Edwards and Lawrence, 2000; Peng, 2000). But it would be rather hard to disentangle the weight of these influences and their ultimate effect very precisely.

### Middle period

As Edwards and Lawrence (2000:1) point out: '1989 was a watershed for the countries of Central and Eastern Europe (CEE) and subsequently for the countries of the former Soviet Union (FSU), as the all-embracing system of state socialism collapsed'.

The policy of decentralization had been encouraged in Russia, particularly by economists like Lieberman and others, before the transition took off (see Nolan, 1995: 31, 32). But significant reforms had only first occurred under Gorbachev, who launched his gradualist reforms from the earlier 1980s. Even so, from 1965 onwards, a significant degree of decision-making space had been left to enterprise managements. There was also a growing degree of informal market activity but the major reforms (see Hertz, 1997) were not to be clearly seen until the early 1990s when Gorbachev attempted to implement his '500–day programme', albeit with little success (1997:23). It was not until Yeltsin came to power in 1991 that we saw the onset of substantive liberalization.

China, somewhat earlier, had launched its economic reforms in 1978 under Deng Xiaoping's leadership and these continued for the next two and a half decades. China, unlike Russia, had a sizeable agricultural sector and it was here that major reforms were to be introduced in the form of *de facto* 'property rights'. But even in the industrial sector, reforms were at hand quite early, indeed as early as 1978, in the form of the 'Open Door' and 'Four Modernizations' (of Agriculture, Industry, Science and Technology, and Defence) policies that tried to confront the inefficiencies of key parts of the economy. In Vietnam, also a predominantly agricultural economy, the reform policy of *doi moi*, introduced in 1986, weakened central planning and sanctioned market-type relations, including small-scale private enterprise (Williams, 1992). As in China, Vietnam's agricultural sector took on a major and pioneering role in the transformation process. The pragmatic strategy behind these policy initiatives, if indeed there was one formally, was to shape the Chinese as well as the Vietnamese transitional process up to the present.

### Late period

The late period of economic transition was concerned with 'deepening' the reforms that had already taken place or implementing these where there had been superficial compliance but no robust application. In many cases, in most transitional economies, 'institution building' had been incomplete and organizational inertia common. Some institutional change allowed new forces to be unleashed but sometimes they enabled older ones to reassert themselves. A number of writers (see Buck *et al.*, 2000) have pointed to pre-reform characteristics in communist economies, for example, that may underlie economic life in a particular country such as its base *culture* which may have facilitated the change process and allowed market forces to successfully reappear.

However, the base culture may also contain elements that impinge on the change process in unexpected and detrimental ways (see Maruyama, 1993; Edwards, 2002). The consequences of the changing institutional context and its interrelationship with the base culture of a particular country may be either positive or negative. In some instances a country's cultural resources may support the process of transformation, whilst in others they may slow down or amend the achievement of outcomes. In the worst scenario elements of the base culture may be dysfunctional under the new circumstances and consequently outcomes may be unsatisfactory in terms of the transformation process.

Many other economies, including non-Communist ones, started to move from a state-directed model to a more market-based one in the 1980s and 1990s. Countries like Argentina, Brazil, Ghana, Indonesia and so on launched structural reforms. 'Structural reform' was the order of the day from the International Monetary Fund (IMF) and the World Bank.

## Defining 'transitional economies'

We now have to pose the critical question – 'transition from what to what?' Each of the so-called transitional economies and their managements would have been evolving anyway, as they adapted to changes in their internal and external economic environments. Child (1994) argues that the final destination of the changing economy cannot be known *a priori*, hence the term 'transformation' should be used. We thus have to try to define 'transitional' and the 'transition' from the *status quo ex ante* to the one *ex post* as carefully as possible.

As the World Bank in its *World Development Report 1996* points out, there are three central issues for economies in transition to confront:

1   liberalization, stabilization and growth in the economy concerned;
2   property rights and economic reform to be achieved there;
3   social policies to alleviate the transition for citizens adversely affected.

These issues impinge on our earlier analysis in a number of interesting ways, as follows.

* Liberalization and so on points to the 'marketization' dimension by which decision making is decentralized to enterprises, to be discussed shortly.
* Property rights and economic reform suggests the 'ownership' dimension which we will deal with soon.
* Social issues imply the creation of a 'safety-net' for those who are disadvantaged in the change process, which we will come to later.

We can see that the World Bank sees these as final goals that may be achieved by the transition. So in terms of the schema we have set out above, we could score economies and managements by the progress they achieved along each of three such directions.

### At what pace?

In this section, we look at how fast change may be accomplished along the dimensions we might choose to measure transition.

The pace of change has varied from 'evolution' to 'big bang'. Some changes have been from 'first principles' and others 'pragmatic'. While some regimes experienced the 'big bang' in Eastern Europe, China by contrast explored a gradual, adaptive path, proceeding by trial and error. There was no 'shock therapy' as advocated for the Soviet economy, with the projected dismantling of the Soviet planned economy in the shortest time possible. In the FSU, the communist state has mostly gone but in China and Vietnam with 'reform from above' it remains. The upshot was a smoother transition in China, compared with the economic and psychological collapse initially experienced in Russia: 'It involved, too, the deepest sense of national humiliation in this country, which for most of the twentieth century considered it to be the leader of the world's socialist nations' (Nolan, 1995: 19).

We could range the countries involved along the time dimension *vis-à-vis* the pace of change or rate of so-called transition. But faster change may not have resulted in better economic performance. While China was to evolve pragmatically through the 1980s and 1990s, it proved to have the faster economic growth rate.

### Which countries?

Some countries that underwent transition were Communist or Socialist but others were not, being a variety of developmental states with a variety of nationalist governments. However, in this book, we cover only most of the countries of Central and Eastern Europe, Russia, the People's Republic of China and Vietnam, that is, those which were formerly Communist and have mostly now formally shed this tag, as well as those that have stayed within the fold, focusing on China and Vietnam. We will deal with their past, present and future in terms of the transition process at both the macro- and micro-levels. We do not, on the other hand, include a number of other economies like the Baltic states (for example, Estonia, Latvia and Lithuania) nor those of Central Asia (for example the member nations of the former Soviet Union, nor Cuba, North Korea, the Ukraine and the Yugoslav republics other than Croatia and Slovenia – except in passing – partly due to the restrictions of space, as well as the relative competences and expertise of the co-authors of the book.

### Which regions within countries?

In many cases, the main reforms took place in the larger cities and/or in the central regions. We will largely concentrate on these. In some, like China, the changes were much slower in the inland provinces. Similarly in Russia, the pace of transformation was fastest in *Moscow*, *St Petersburg* and a few other areas, with some areas seemingly intent on resisting the implications of the system change.

### *Which sectors?*

In some cases, the reforms were in the state-owned sector that was based on heavy industry. In other cases, the reforms started first in agriculture. It is interesting to note that Poland had retained private agriculture to a considerable extent; the Chinese and Vietnamese had also introduced the *de facto* liberalization of this sector early in the transition.

## Characteristics of transitional economies

It is hard to generalize about 'transition' across the board. The historical and structural and institutional contexts of different national systems have varied from country to country and period to period. But there are some common features of the changes we have noted. For example, in the experiments in what were later to become known as transitional economies, it is clear that moves towards 'marketization' preceded those involving changes in 'ownership', the two most important dimensions of transition as we shall make clear below.

'Marketization' as well as 'ownership' changes may range from low to high in degree, as can be seen in Figure 1.3. In both dimensions of 'marketization' and 'ownership', we may measure changes across a scaled spectrum ranging from a low to a high degree of change. Both dimensions measure movement over time towards a point where the transition has been completed from low $x$ to high $x$, low $y$ to high $y$.

Systems that were state-Socialist, for example, had already experimented with new structures of 'marketization' (in the form of devolved decision making) in the post-Stalinist period, ranging from those that were modest as were even seen in the former Soviet Union (Nolan, 1995), to those much bolder ones such as those in the Hungarian economy in the late 1960s (Kornai, 1992).

<br>

**MARKETIZATION**

| | | Low | High |
|---|---|---|---|
| | Low | (–/–) | (–/+) |
| **OWNERSHIP** | | | |
| | High | (+/–) | (+/+) |

*Figure 1.3* Dimensions of marketization and ownership.

It is clearly easier to devolve decision making than to change ownership. Step-wise ownership changes took place before extensive 'privatization' took place. Even when limited liberalization took place in the early days, this took the form of allowing small businesses to expand. Even today, seamless 'transition' has not taken place at all levels, whether the macro- or micro-level. For example, the conversion of former state-owned enterprises (SOEs) into shareholding or joint-stock companies (JSCs) often left the state (or one of its representative bodies) as the sole or majority shareholder, especially in the early period of transformation. This has been described as state or political capitalism. A second widespread form of privatization was the transfer of former state-owned assets to so-called 'insiders', either existing company managers and/or members of the former '*nomenklatura*' or party apparatus. The third form of privatization involved the transfer of assets to outsiders. Such a combination of privatization types, to which must be added the establishment of new businesses, created a complex landscape of private firms which varied in proportions between individual transforming economies and over time. For an illustration of the complex mechanisms used by state organizations to transform state assets into private capital in Poland in the early stage of transformation see Stanizikis's (1991) presentation of six combinations of capital and political power.

In the early days of transition so-called, both sets of changes would have scored in Figure 1.3 as 'low' (top left-hand). The rarest cases were where both variables score 'high' (bottom right-hand). Russia may be the most important candidate here in terms of the scope of what has changed but the smaller Eastern European countries have done very well in transforming their economies and societies, such that some (we may note, a surprisingly high proportion of former COMECON member states) are now candidates to formally join the European Union.

In comparing transition processes, we have a number of conceptual problems we now have to confront, if we wish to fully understand what has taken place and satisfactorily explain it. If we try to establish what is common to these processes, we can identify a core of characteristics that define the *status quo ex ante*, that is what was the case before the reforms, compared with what was found in the *ex post* situation, after the reforms had been introduced (Figure 1.4). Outside this core, there are 'country-specific' traits that are relevant. Clearly all core characteristics can be compared across the board but only some are country-specific ones, as it is here we find what distinguishes one distinct case from another in both the economy and management within it.

### Similarities

All transitional economies have moved from plan to market but in varying degrees. The citizens of Eastern Europe, for example, were pleased to see the demise of the planned economy and its accompanying shortages, particularly

| PRE-REFORM | POST-REFORM |
|---|---|
| Command economy | Market forces |
| State ownership | Diversified ownership |
| Resource-constrained | Demand-driven |
| Technical criteria | Allocative efficiency |
| Enterprise cadres | Professional managers |
| Job security | Labour market |
| Jobs for life | Employment contracts |
| Work assignment | Job choice |
| Personnel administration | Human resource management |
| Egalitarian pay and perks | Performance-related rewards |
| Enterprise-based training | Outside-courses |
| Company flats | Rented housing-market |
| In-house social services | External social provision |
| Free medical care | Contributory medical insurance |
| Central trade union role | Weaker union influence |
| High institutional dependency | Low institutional dependency |

*Figure 1.4* Characteristics of pre-reform and post-reform frameworks.

of consumer goods. Most such economies have now moved well along the marketization dimension. There was the common phenomenon of 'system shocks' (see Edwards and Lawrence, 2000:10) both external and internal. Communist economies saw the linch-pin of the COMECON implode with the demise of the Soviet Union in 1991. The initial managerial and other micro-implications of such systemic changes have been analysed elsewhere (see for example, Edwards and Foster, 1994).

*Differences*

Many have moved well along the marketization as well as the ownership dimension but some have done so less than others. There are a number of differences to note. Some examples have moved faster and further over time than others (Figures 1.5 and 1.6). Some changes were exogenously inspired; others were indigenously so. Again, some reforms were 'top-down' and others 'bottom-up'.

*Contradictions*

Changes may involve contradictions and discrepancies, in spite of the general trend towards greater marketization and increased private ownership, as the outcome of the interaction between internal and external factors in the different countries will vary between countries.

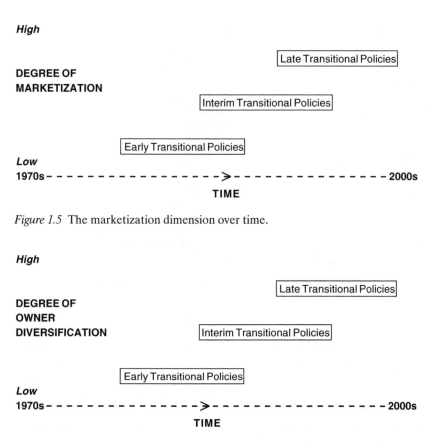

*Figure 1.5* The marketization dimension over time.

*Figure 1.6* The diversification of ownership dimension over time.

## Discussion

We must not, however, assume all change is uni-directional or uni-dimensional. Some books have been misleading such as Fukuyama's (1992) *The End of History* a work that argued that all economies were moving towards the 'free market' model. The 'globalization' thesis is equally *simpliste*. Change is complex and often piecemeal. Systems, nations and economies evolve in 'fits and starts'.

Nonetheless, the march towards WTO membership status for a host of countries clearly implies a movement towards a set of criteria that have to be met for inclusion and that these are 'market oriented'. Also the work of the World Bank and IMF seeks to impel economies and their management systems towards the 'Washington Consensus' as Stiglitz (2002) points out.

The interim, let alone 'final', outcome, may be a pragmatic compromise, more often than not. But the people of CEE and the FSU have concluded that the system change is irreversible and have found a way of accommodating *grosso modo* to the transition (Edwards and Lawrence, 2000: 131). In China, too, the reforms have been digested and accepted by most managers and workers but there are also losers as well as winners such that social discontent has been growing, especially with downsizing and the resultant unemployment (see Warner, 2003a).

We must be cautious in generalizing from a heterogeneous set of examples. Nonetheless, we will attempt to show how sets and sub-sets of country systems have experienced 'transition' in both their economies and management.

Here too, there are winners and losers and the metaphor of the 'Valley of Tears' (Peng, 2000)[1] vividly illustrates the position some transforming economies in CEE and the FSU find themselves in (Figure 1.7). Following the system change and the introduction of economic reforms all the former socialist economies in CEE and the FSU experienced a substantial drop in output and GDP.

The various economies were able to deal with this decline in output and GDP in various ways, more or less successfully. The more successful economies were with varying passages of time able to arrest the decline and regain and surpass the output and GDP levels pertaining at the beginning of the transformation process. In contrast, the less successful economies, even when arresting the decline, remained stuck at levels of output and GDP which were often considerably lower than those from before the system change.

The macro-economic context of the transitional changes is largely treated as background in this book but we will try to understand which kinds of macro-level policies are more likely to help micro-level change. The main emphasis throughout this book will mostly be at the micro-level, particularly the

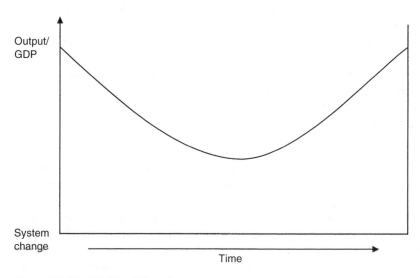

*Figure 1.7* The 'Valley of Tears'.

management level. We hope to look at the way in which management has been reformed, new management institutions and norms have been created and how a new breed of managers has evolved. We will set out in fuller detail a little later below the detailed agenda for this discussion.

We shall ask which kinds of management institutions and practices are appropriate to the 'transition' processes we have highlighted above. Additionally, we shall explore how different kinds of functional management are affected by transition.

To start with, management reforms are often likely to be related to changes in the external economic environment, as well as the internal consequences of such changes. With more open foreign trade, barriers against imports will fall in the transition period. This act will stimulate competition and enhance the linkages between the external economic environment and the internal one. The variable stimulating the latter may thus be dubbed exogenous. The second set of management reforms is likely to be related to major changes in the internal economic environment itself over the coming decade. An increase in internal competition may lead to reform in how enterprises respond to both demand and supply factors. This variable may be labelled *endogenous*. The third set of management reforms is likely to be linked to changes in business goals and how to achieve them, thus may be seen as strategic, that is, mainly changing organizational strategy and structure within enterprises themselves. The effect of the external and internal economic changes will most likely lead to a decisive shift from a strategy that is *'reactive'* to one that is *'proactive'*, although this is not to say some firms and their managers do not already adopt the latter stance already. The fourth is the effects of the above on enterprise managers and the development of a managerial culture at the level of the firm that may be initially 'transitional' after the initial wave of economic reforms and partly performance-based, evolving to one that is significantly performance-based. We may call this impact behavioural.

The changing roles of managements, in particular senior managers, have been explicated by Lang (1998), based on the work of Marr (1994) who applied Mintzberg's (1973) concept of managerial roles to different economic systems, namely the planned economy, the market economy and transformation. Although critical of some of the detail of Marr's exposition, Lang supports the general presentation of the evolution of managerial roles from the planned economy through transformation to the market economy. Without going into the detail of Marr's schema, in the planned economy managers had relatively few significant roles, of which the predominant one was to act as resource allocator. This is understandable in the context of resource-constrained economies.

The system change and ensuing transition increased the importance of management in general and of a number of roles in particular. While all of Mintzberg's roles were now significant, the pre-eminent ones became the interpersonal roles, the decisional roles (apart from resource allocation) and information monitor. With the achievement of functioning market economies, Marr reaffirms the importance of all managerial roles but identifies the particular significance of the leadership, information monitor and spokesman roles.

What Marr's application of Mintzberg's managerial roles indicates is that the demands on managers are firstly considerably higher in a market economy than in a planned economy and managers consequently suffer from 'overload'. More importantly, in the context of this book, the demands on managers involved in the transformation process are, as might be expected, even higher than in an established market economy. The system change and transformation thus placed particularly high demands on the capabilities and skills of managers in the former state-run economies.

These four factors – changes in the external economic environment, changes in the internal economic environment, changes in organizational strategy and structure, and the effects of the above on enterprise managers – may be seen as interrelated in a diamond-shaped relationship (see Warner, 2003a) and may have interactions with each other (Figure 1.8), perhaps mostly *one-way* in that the economic environmental changes will tend to be the *independent* variables. In the background of the diamond, we have placed the key influences of Tradition (encompassing Culture), Society (including Values), Economy (both External and Internal) and Polity (with the State/ Party). Although we emphasize economic environmental changes as the main

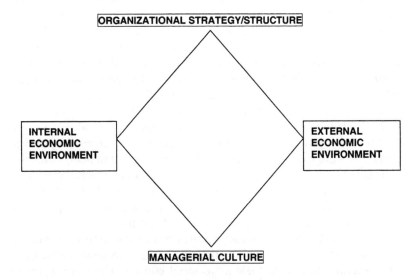

*Figure 1.8* Relationship between external and internal economic environments, organizational strategy, structure and managerial culture.

drivers of organizational and managerial behaviour, we do not underestimate the role of particularly the State/Party influence as the ultimate lever of macro-level policy, given the way some national systems like China's are still governed. Even in the transforming economies of CEE and Russia the Government/State decided on the nature and process of the transformation, selecting, for example, the mode and pace of privatization. The effects of changes in the respective main *dependent* variables in the diamond, such as organizational strategy and structure (we postulate the latter follows the former) as well as managerial culture, will not however be felt immediately but will occur *over time*, often unevenly. Similarly, there may already have been influences in train that have been causing change for some time. The external economic environment was becoming more 'open' anyway; the internal economic environment was already undergoing structural reform; the managerial culture had been evolving in order to adapt to the market forces that has been unleashed since the late 1970s. We hope to explore these themes in greater detail below.

There are a number of changes in the internal economic environment, we believe, that will affect management in the transitional process. One important strand, we would strongly argue, has been the 'marketization' of these economies. Most factors of production are now responsive to market forces to a degree unimaginable in the early days of the reforms. Broadly speaking, managers now have to respond to 'market signals'. Second, the extent of structural reform in many of the transitional economies has also been remarkable by any measure, although there still remain 'grey-areas'. Even so, much of the loss-making state sectors have been reformed and pruned but there is a way to go yet on this point. By and large, since the late 1970s, many have pursued an industrial policy of phasing out the ailing SOEs (the word 'privatization' had been used *vis-à-vis* CEE and the former Soviet Union but in China has been more or less taboo until recently) and have been able to hold their own in the global market. Third, the optimist would further point to the 'deepening' and 'widening' of the economic reforms in the last decade. Not only labour- but also factor-markets have been made responsive to market forces. 'Market efficiency' must now take precedence over political considerations – the role of the Party has been eliminated in many countries (or reduced as in China) in enterprise-level decision making – but even here not a few managers in the state sector still live in a world of government support and state direction. To beat the system, 'bureaucratic entrepreneurs' have set up new businesses to find new sources of revenue.

Next, the *diversification of ownership* in the economic structure has made a critical impact on both enterprises and their managers, through their business strategy, structure as well as their managerial culture. The state sector in China for instance underwent amalgamations in the 1990s, holding onto big firms but letting go of small ones. This policy was directly bound up with changing ownership structure. As a result, there is now a variety of new, often 'hybrid', ownership forms. In CEE and Russia, the state sector only accounts for a minority and still shrinking proportion of GDP, as it similarly does in China.

But in many cases, especially in the former COMECON states, the ex-managers of state firms acquired the ownership rights of the newly privatized enterprises, via the 'inside track', constituting a new phenomenon of '*Nomenklatura* Capitalism'. Here, managers were often seen as 'feathering their own nests' (Edwards and Lawrence, 2000:38). The result was a reaction against privatization in a number of countries. The state, as in Poland or Russia, often retained a 'golden share' of such enterprises to keep strategic control and to appease public opinion. In China, a number of giant state firms have been floated on the stockmarkets, both locally and abroad, as 'red chips' but the government has kept the lion's share of the controlling shares.

Human resource management (HRM) practices, in line with decentralized decision making processes in reformed enterprises, have day by day been slowly evolving towards something similar to those in Western firms, at least in large ones during this transition process; equally, the changing level of employee 'trust' within such firms may also depend on the nature and quality of these firms' reconstituted ownership. Last, the degree of competition in the internal economic environment may also be a major determinant not only of the firm's strategy and structure but also of managerial culture. More competition means managers have greater challenges in both manufacturing sector firms, as well as in the service sector, as this means more foreign businesses entering their markets.

The main effect of changes in both the external and internal economic environments on management will be on the latter's strategy, as well on its culture. As the new economic environments become more competitive, we can expect this to be mirrored in strategic responses at the enterprise management level. As organizational strategy – and no doubt structure – shift, firms and their managers may be under greater pressures to adapt better to the new market forces and to improve their performance.

In the transition, functional roles in the enterprise also change, as the internal environment of firms evolves, leading to accounting and finance becoming more important and as the change in the external environment of the enterprise requires greater emphasis on marketing and sales. With greater internal and external complexity, formalization, standardization and decentralization with a more systematic approach to transmitting and sharing information also have to become *de rigueur*. Organizational development has to be encouraged in order to build an appropriate corporate and managerial culture. Management has to become more professionalized, with greater management training and development a priority.

The post-reform strategy of enterprises will be more proactive than in the pre-reform ones but this may vary according to the ownership dimension (see Warner 2003a) (Figure 1.9).

**OWNERSHIP**

|  | State-owned | Non-state-owned |
|---|---|---|
| Reactive | ( + ) | ( − ) |

***STRATEGY***

|  | State-owned | Non-state-owned |
|---|---|---|
| Proactive | ( − ) | ( + ) |

*Figure 1.9*  Proactive and reactive strategy in transitional firms.

Strategy, structure and managerial culture may also be mutually inter-active, in that a change in the former may affect the latter and even vice-versa (Figure 1.10).

The main effect of changes in both the external and internal economic environments on management will be a recognizable shift from a culture that was not individually performance-based, to one that is ostensibly decidedly so. But this change may have already started earlier as we suggested above. We believe that there will be a spectrum of change over time, such that there will be the pre-reform model at one extreme and the post-reform one at the other, with one or more 'transitional' stages in between (Figure 1.11). The number of firms to be found in each category will depend on the rate of change and also the degree of *organizational inertia*. There is clearly also a need to evolve new *institutional norms* in both economy and management (see Scott, 2002).

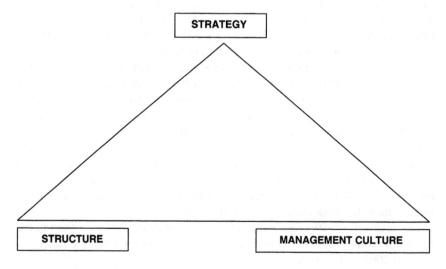

*Figure 1.10*  Interaction between strategy, structure and management culture.

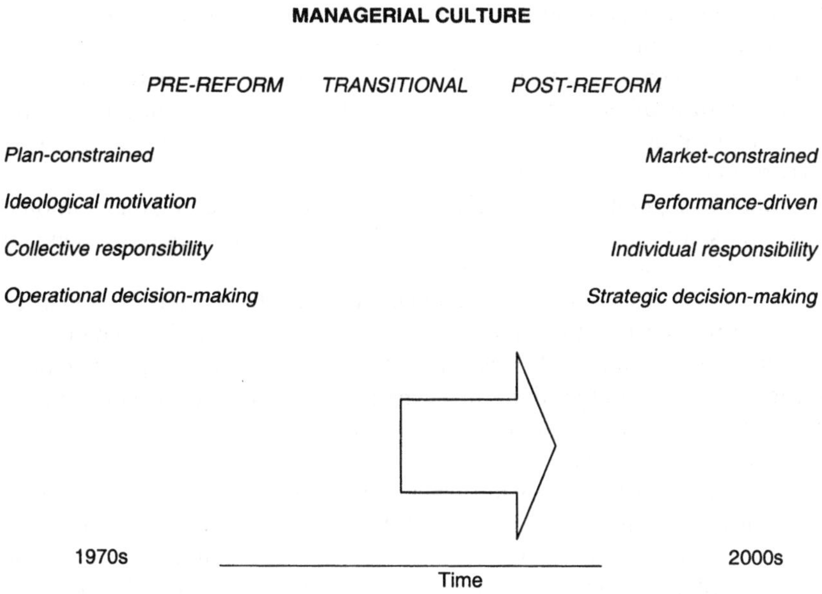

**MANAGERIAL CULTURE**

*PRE-REFORM    TRANSITIONAL    POST-REFORM*

*Plan-constrained*                                    *Market-constrained*

*Ideological motivation*                              *Performance-driven*

*Collective responsibility*                           *Individual responsibility*

*Operational decision-making*                         *Strategic decision-making*

1970s                                                        2000s
                                    Time

*Figure 1.11* Changes in managerial culture in transitional economies over time.

## Empirical propositions

From the above, we can derive the following empirical propositions.

The greater the degree of transition:
1    the greater the degree of marketization;
2    the greater the diversification of ownership;
[as well as]
3    the greater the salience of accounting;
4    the greater the salience of business strategy;
5    the greater the salience of finance;
6    the greater the salience of HRM;
7    the greater the salience of management development;
8    the greater the salience of marketing.

## Structure of the book

Each chapter will attempt to follow the following format, covering the main headings and subheadings we set out below.

*Introduction* to the region/country, the key issues related to theoretical debates in 'transition' theory, then the research questions individual chapters set out to tackle (in relation to the context of both country and theoretical debates).

*Historical background*, including the main historical influences of the economies involved, the ideological debate that occurred in different stages of transition and so on.

*Cultural background*: the main features and influences of the national/ societal culture of each economy; the implications for management and management practice, the mixed characteristics between cultural tradition and current political and economic systems.

*General background*: the development of each of the regional/national economies since the system change took place, including regional and global linkages, and economic development patterns.

*External/macro issues/factors* influencing organizations such as globalization (international) and economic reform (domestic) as well as changes in the institutional framework, government policies relating to privatization, restructuring and foreign direct investment (FDI); macroeconomic policies relating to the monetary system, prices, the labour market, foreign trade, industrial policy and small firms' development.

*Internal/micro issues/factors* influencing organizations and management – such as ownership and control, business strategy, and other functional areas, such as accounting, finance, HRM, marketing, operations and so on, as well as acceptance of and resistance to change, downsizing and the like; similarly, the impact of specific local conditions.

*Outcomes and performance*: corporate transformation and implications for management, that is, strategy development, organizational structures, managerial cultures and styles, management development; profitability, market orientation and sales; productivity and employment; as well as employee relations.

*Empirical evidence* relating to enterprise and managerial behaviour, based on research the co-authors may have carried out or which they have drawn on from secondary sources.

*Evaluation and discussion* of developments since the system change and possible future developments, responding to the theoretical debates mentioned earlier.

### Conclusions

The chapter order of the book is as follows. Chapter 1 presents the main themes, historical, theoretical and empirical appropriate to the transitional process (mainly Warner). Chapter 2 deals with evidence from Central and Eastern Europe (mainly Pučko), as does Chapter 3 (mainly Edwards). Next, the case of Russia and the Former Soviet Union is dealt with in Chapter 4 (mainly Polonsky). This is followed by an account of the transformation in the People's Republic of China in Chapter 5 (mainly Warner and Zhu) and in Chapter 6 Vietnam (mainly Edwards and Zhu). The final chapter attempts to sum up the findings of the contributions to the book (mainly Warner). Last, the Statistical appendix provides data on recent economic facets and, to some extent, an indication of developments since the early 1990s. The data on the countries studied in this book are complemented, for comparative purposes, by data on the United States and the United Kingdom.

## Conclusions

There has been enormous interest since the fall of the Berlin Wall in 1989, in the economic transformation of the former state-run economies of Central and Eastern Europe and the Former Soviet Union. Additionally, the Chinese economic reforms of the 'Open Door' Policy, initiated in the late 1970s, have attracted considerable attention. While 1989 was certainly a watershed for the countries of CEE, it would be wrong to regard 1989 as the starting point of transformation, even in CEE. The roots of transformation go back almost to the very beginning of the establishment of the command economies (indeed way back to 1917) as a consequence of the interplay of and friction between theory and practice. There is a need therefore to consider transformation in its broader context, in the attempt of seeking to understand the phenomenon as an ongoing process rather than a one-off event. At the same time the study of transformation would benefit from integrating the experiences of CEE, the Former Soviet Union and affected Asian countries, in particular China and Vietnam.

Much research and debate have already taken place regarding this topic. However, many studies in this area have of necessity been descriptive and partial. One aim of this book is therefore to make a contribution to the theory of the transformation, in particular with regard to transformation management. There is hence a focus on analysing and integrating insights from the various countries under study in the form of concepts and conceptual frameworks.

In terms of theory, the institutionalist approach has underpinned our analysis and interpretation of the range of studies comprising this book. The institutionalist approach allows us to deal with both formal and informal institutions, thus affording us insights into practices that may be masked by excessive focus on formal institutions. At the same time the institutionalist approach allows us to portray and analyse the transformation as a process of de- and re-institutionalization. This process of destruction and creation does not consist of discrete, sequential entities. Both destruction and creation of formal and informal institutions occur simultaneously, albeit with mismatches and time-lags, as institutions of the old system are destroyed, yet also survive, even if in a modified form. New institutions are created but often take time to establish themselves and become effective. They may even fail. Moreover, institutions predating the command economy may re-emerge in either weak or strong forms.

The process of transformation is thus complex as old and new institutions, both formal and informal, interact in a multiplicity of ways and combinations. In this respect transformation management is one such institution, drawing on and influencing the other institutions with which it interrelates. Management during the transformation from plan to market is consequently both an integral and active element of the transformation process as well as one of its outcomes.

A further aspect of our argument is that culture is a pervasive influence on the attitudes and behaviour of individuals and formal and informal institutions. Culture, moreover, can influence the transformation process in both positive and negative ways, in ways that, for example, facilitate and support, but also in ways that frustrate, impede and work against the achievement of expressed policy aims (see Warner, 2003b).

The pervasive influence of culture, in its various manifestations at the national, local and organizational levels, interacts with other elements of the transformation process. In so doing, culture too changes and develops, although this generally requires the passage of lengthy periods of time. Within the transformation therefore, there is also an interplay and sometimes clash of cultural elements, as the new interacts with the old, resulting in new cultural contexts over time.

At this point, it would be appropriate to reaffirm our conceptualization of management in transforming economies (see Figure 1.8). Management itself is at the heart of our conceptual framework. It is most closely bounded by and interacts with the four elements of management culture, organizational structure and strategy, the internal economic environment of the firm, and the firm's external economic environment. This interaction is contextualized within a setting comprising the four key elements of the polity, economy, society and tradition. All the elements of this conceptual framework influence each other, creating a complex interaction of factors whose particular influence varies between countries and over time.

We argue, furthermore, that the transformation process has increased the significance of management and managers, compared to the situation in the former command economies. The demise or even relaxation of central planning has placed a greater onus on managements and this new responsibility has been further increased by factors such as privatization. During the transformation managers are subjected not only to more pressures than under the command system but also are relatively 'overloaded' compared to managers in the established market economies. This 'overload' is due to a range of factors, including the move from plan to market, corporate restructuring, the development of functional specialisms, and so on. For many managers, the overall experience of transformation has created many tensions between the old and the new, the certainties of the past and the insecurities of the present and future. Moreover, it has put considerable pressure on managers' existing knowledge and on managers to acquire new knowledge.

In the preceding paragraphs, we have tried to develop a general schema of management in transforming economies. What we wish to do through the chapters of this book is to explore the conceptual framework we have developed in the context of various countries of CEE, the Former Soviet

Union and Asia which have been undergoing the transformation from plan to market. In this, we wish to assess the validity of our framework and at the same time explore both the general influences of transformation management (for example, globalization and the pre-eminent influence of the Anglo-American model of business and management) and the particular nuances of individual countries. By this approach, we would hope to identify common elements as well as differences in the management of the various transforming economies of this book.

## Note

1   The 'Valley of Tears' metaphor derives from the 'Vale of Tears' biblical phrase, in the Old Testament: Isaiah 24:1–2.

# Part II
# Country and regional studies

The socialist camp has become an independent world economic system, standing opposite the capitalist world economic system. It will soon surpass the gross industrial output value of all the capitalist countries put together.

Mao Zedong (1893–1976)

# Part II
# Country and regional studies

# 2 Central Europe 1

## Successful transformation

### Introduction

From a historical and cultural perspective, the Central European countries in transition may be considered to comprise Croatia, the Czech Republic, Hungary, Poland, Slovakia and Slovenia. The former East Germany also belongs to this group of countries in spite of the fact that it is no longer an independent country but nowadays the constituent part of a united Germany.

The above five Central European transitional countries plus the former East Germany have been developing in a comparatively satisfactory way after the transformation of the political, economic and social system. They have achieved similarly favourable transitional results. The only exception among them is Croatia. They all experienced a transitional crisis. Its result was a sizeable decline in production, consumption, wages and salaries, and the standard of living of the population. They have however already surpassed, with the exception of Croatia, the GDP level that they had had before the transition.

Croatia and the Czech Republic were the only two countries that experienced negative real growth rates at the end of the nineties because of macroeconomic policy errors. The former East Germany entered the European Union with German unification in October 1990. Other Central European transitional countries, with the exception of Croatia, joined the European Union in the first wave of enlargement in 2004.

### Historical background

The Central European area, from around the ninth century, formed part of Christendom and participated in European social, political and cultural developments. Independent kingdoms emerged in the ninth to eleventh centuries in Moravia, Hungary, Poland, and, albeit briefly, in Croatia. The area contributed to academic and scientific developments in Europe and universities were founded in Prague in 1348 and in Cracow in 1364. The states of the region were also on the front line of opposition to the advance of the Ottoman forces and contributed considerably to halting their progress. Furthermore, the region was deeply involved in the controversies of the Reformation and Counter-Reformation.

From the sixteenth century, however, the position of the national states was weakened and by the end of the eighteenth century they had been absorbed into Prussia, Austria-Hungary and Russia. This experience of 'interrupted statehood' (Wandycz, 1992:8) was of particular significance for the populations of the formerly independent kingdoms and nationalism and national identity became a key issue in the region in the nineteenth and twentieth centuries. The loss of statehood was felt particularly acutely by the Poles who lived in three separate states.

The conclusion of the First World War saw the re-emergence of independent states in Czechoslovakia, Hungary and Poland, while Croatia and Slovenia became part of the newly formed Yugoslavia. The conditions after 1918 were not especially propitious and the countries of the region were affected by the Economic Depression, ethnic disputes and the rise of Fascism. The outbreak of the Second World War was very much conditioned by Hitler's designs on Czechoslovakia and Poland.

The post-war settlement placed Czechoslovakia, Hungary and Poland in the Soviet sphere of influence, while in Yugoslavia under Tito an independent-minded model of socialism developed which differed in significant aspects from the Soviet model. Soviet control of its satellites in the region was, moreover, never absolute and, in spite of substantial use of repression, opposition to the communist régimes was always a feature of everyday life in the region. For a post-1945 chronology of developments in the region, see Figure 2.1.

## Cultural background

Cultural values in the region were strongly influenced by religious affiliation, national identity and level of economic development, although the influence of each factor and the interaction between factors varied from country to country. (For a more detailed discussion of national cultures in the countries of the region see Edwards and Lawrence, 2000.) Although Catholicism predominated after the Counter-Reformation, it was particularly significant in Poland where it was closely linked to national identity. National identity, moreover, was more influential in those states which had historically been independent kingdoms so that in Slovakia, for example, a distinctive Slovak identity did not begin to emerge till the middle of the nineteenth century.

The level of economic development, in particular industrialization and urbanization, played an important role in forming cultural values. Apart from the Czech lands (Bohemia and Moravia) there was limited industrialization in the region apart from certain areas in Poland (e.g. Silesia) and Hungary. The region was overwhelmingly agricultural and rural, a factor which tended to support conservative values. There was thus a considerable gap in the early twentieth century between the advanced industrial society of the Czech lands and the widespread rural areas.

However, one outcome of the policies of the communist regimes after 1945 was the promotion of heavy industry so that formerly predominantly agri-

| | |
|---|---|
| 1945 | Czechoslovakia, Hungary and Poland under Soviet control; Tito establishes communist régime in Yugoslavia |
| 1948 | Tito breaks with Stalin |
| 1949 | CMEA established |
| 1950 | Workers' self-management as basis of Yugoslav socialism |
| 1953 | East Berlin uprising |
| 1956 | Poznan uprising; collectivization of agriculture halted in Poland; Hungarian uprising |
| 1961 | Berlin Wall built |
| 1965 | Yugoslavia introduces market instruments |
| 1968 | New economic mechanism (guided market model) introduced in Hungary |
| 1968–69 | 'Prague Spring' (terminated by invasion of Czechoslovakia by USSR and other members of the Warsaw Pact) |
| 1970 | Gdansk riots and establishment of Solidarnosc in Poland |
| 1981 | Martial law imposed in Poland |
| 1989 | Collapse of communist régimes in Czechoslovakia, Hungary, Poland and East Germany |
| 1990 | Disintegration of Yugoslav Federation begins; German unification |
| 1991 | Slovenia and Croatia declare independence; CMEA collapses |
| 1991 | CEFTA founded by Czechoslovakia, Hungary and Poland |
| 1991–95 | Croat–Serb conflict |
| 1993 | Czech and Slovak Republics established (Velvet Divorce) |
| 2004 | Czech Republic, Hungary, Poland, Slovak Republic and Slovenia join the European Union |

*Figure 2.1* Post-1945 chronology of developments in Central Europe.

cultural areas such as Slovakia became the location of heavy industries. As a consequence such areas were introduced to practices of management in the guise of the Soviet model. Soviet-style management practices were therefore able to establish themselves strongly in areas with limited experience of capitalist industry.

## General background

The collapse of the communist regimes in the region in 1989–90 represented not only the demise of an ideological system but also reassertion of national identities, often the result of decades of opposition. Issues of ethnicity and national minorities regained considerable importance in the political sphere. Some could be resolved peacefully as in the case of the 'Velvet Divorce' between the Czech and Slovak Republics in 1993. In the case of Yugoslavia, the period since 1990 has been marked by brutal ethnic conflicts and foreign intervention, which affected all constituent republics to a greater or lesser degree.

The transformation from communism has thus been a complex process for the countries of the region and has affected far more than just the economic sphere. The experience, moreover, has varied from country to country, reflecting each country's distinctive heritage, its position at the outset of transformation and its approach to the new circumstances.

## External/macro issues/factors

All Central European transitional countries carried out market-oriented policy reform. Economic stabilization policy in different forms but in the majority of cases as 'a shock therapy' had a very important role in the early stage of the transition. Controlling inflation and maintaining an appropriate rate of exchange depended on the chosen stabilization policy measures.

During the transition, the industrial sector shrank and its share of GDP creation fell to about a third. The service sector grew to over half. There was moreover a dramatic increase in the private sector's share in the creation of GDP.

Real wages in Central European transitional countries, as compared to the European Union average, increased in the 1990s. If we take the European Union level as 100, then the average Polish wage (being at the lowest level among the countries) increased from 17.3 to 35.7 per cent and the average Slovenian wage (being on the highest level) went up from 56.6 to 70.0 per cent of this level (Pavlik, 2001:122). In spite of the dramatic improvements in the average wage levels, market reforms and structural changes in Central European transitional countries have produced a sharp increase in social inequality and in poverty for certain strata of the inhabitants.

*Croatia* became an independent country in 1991 but had to fight a war for her independence during 1991–95. Her relatively poor transitional achievements are also due to the loss of the previous large Yugoslav domestic market and serious errors of economic and general policy that brought Croatia in the mid-1990s into a position of international isolation. After the democratic changes of 2000, the international position of Croatia improved considerably. The new government put a stronger emphasis on the hard budget constraint, enterprise restructuring and selling state-owned enterprises to strategic foreign investors.

*Czechoslovakia* started its transformation with a shock therapy and by implementing a quick large-scale method of privatization of previously socialist enterprises. The break-up of Czechoslovakia at the beginning of 1993 did not represent a big obstacle for the Czech transformation. The Czech government tried to avoid bankruptcies of large enterprises almost at any cost as well as privatization of the strongest Czech banks up to November 1997 (Pavlik, 2001:110). Such policies enabled the development of special interlocking relationships between Czech banks, investment funds and large non-performing companies. The policies implemented by the Czech government after 1997 brought needed changes.

The transition of *East Germany* is a unique case among transition countries. This is so because the West German economic, social and political system was implemented by the treaty of unification. A true shock therapy took place. The exchange rate of East to West German marks was inappropriate, vastly overvaluing the East German currency. The East German transition produced a quick and drastic improvement in the average wage and GDP per capita level on the one hand, but on the other hand saw a deeper initial economic decline than in other Central European transitional countries, the lowest GDP growth rate among transitional countries, a very high unemployment rate (17.6 per cent officially in 1999; by adding persons on government employment programmes and retraining it reached 25 per cent (Brezinski, 2001:9)) and an anaemic growth of new enterprises.

*Hungary* started to implement transition quickly and rather successfully. A gradual but fully credible trade liberalisation opened the Hungarian economy to foreign investors and provided restructuring incentives without decimating the domestic manufacturing sector (Lieb-Doczy, 2001:151). Therefore the first wave of privatization was heavily based on foreign direct investments. Hungarians also achieved quite positive results in developing new small and medium enterprises. Hungary achieved the highest growth of labour productivity and of industrial output in the nineties among all Central European transitional countries. The Hungarian level of unemployment is the lowest among the Central European transitional countries. It amounted to 5.8 per cent in 2002 (*Cestat Statistical Bulletin*, 2003/4).

The Polish government adopted early in the transition a predominantly neo-liberal and *laissez-faire* approach and policy (Gorynia and Wolniak, 2001:90). Market discipline was established for state enterprises too, with sufficient transparency of corporate governance to prevent large-scale asset stripping before privatization. Governments undertook needed structural reforms and generated an investment climate favourable to the creation of new small and medium-sized enterprises. Polish privatization was predominantly based on large-scale methods. The country did not achieve until 1995 a boom in domestic investment. Early transitional results were not linked to a huge flow of foreign direct investment. The Polish unemployment rate was rather high and amounted to 19.9 per cent in 2002 (*Cestat Statistical Bulletin*, 2003/4).

*Slovakia* became an independent country in January 1993. Her transformation in the early transitional phase had the same characteristics as were already described for the Czech Republic. The split of the Czechoslovak Federation had more serious effects on the Slovak than on the Czech economy. Slovakia changed the dominant mass-privatization method used in the privatization process after becoming independent. The government did not implement hard budget constraints in the mid-1990s. Therefore large enterprises did not restructure much. Porvaznik and Stanek (2001:132) states that 3,000 of the total number of 7,000 medium and large-sized companies in the country are still unprofitable. The logical consequence was a big increase in Slovakian debt and a drastic jump in the proportion of dubious and non-performing loans in the country (Pavlik, 2001:111). In spite of such a policy, the Slovak unemployment rate reached nearly 18.5 per cent in 2002.

*Slovenia* has been in the forefront of reforming its macroeconomic structures among Central European transitional countries. Economic growth has been mostly due to the growth in foreign companies and newly founded small and medium-sized enterprises (SMEs). The rate of unemployment according to the International Labour Organization (ILO) definition was no more than 6.4 per cent in 2002. The apparent weakness of Slovenia is its high level of foreign indebtedness which amounted to US$3,370 per capita at the end of 2001 (see Table 2.1) which is the highest level among the Central European transitional countries (*Cestat Statistical Bulletin*, 2003/4).

### Privatization

Governments in transitional countries created very different approaches to privatization. *Croatia* started to privatize SOEs in mid-1991. Sales methods with the preferential treatment of privileged buyers were the dominant approach. The transformation project included at the beginning 2,867 enterprises (Benić, 2000:32). The privatization of the large state-owned companies was carried out more slowly than expected and more slowly than in other Central European countries.

During 1997, Croatia started the second phase of its privatization using a voucher method. Observers of the privatization process reported that the state maintained share ownership in many of the privatized companies, even retaining majority stakes (Collin and Cesljas, 2002:176). The large-scale enterprises and state owned systems (like the energy sector, shipbuilding, some areas of metallurgy, a major part of telecommunications, etc.) have remained unprivatized. They employ a great number of workers and create mostly huge losses (Benić, 2000:34–5). Their privatization is being processed in a case-by-case manner.

In the *Czech Republic* the large-scale privatization used several standard methods, but so-called voucher privatization was the most important. This mass privatization affected about 1,800 companies and covered about 40 per cent of the book value of state property divested (Bornstein, 1997:334).

*Table 2.1*  Foreign direct investment and foreign debt position in 2001 (end of period) of Central European transitional countries

| Country | FDI stock (US$ m) | Inhabitants (millons) | FDI per capita (US$) | Foreign debt per capita (US$) |
|---|---|---|---|---|
| Croatia | 6,398 | 4.4 | 1,069 | 2,572 |
| Czech Republic | 38,450 | 10.2 | 2,656 | 2,112 |
| Hungary | 30,934 | 10.2 | 2,293 | 2,412 |
| Poland | 33,563 | 38.6 | 870 | 1,857 |
| Slovakia | 4,728 | 5.4 | 876 | 2,053 |
| Slovenia | 3,209 | 2.0 | 1,604 | 3,370 |

Source: *Cestat Statistical Bulletin* 2003/4; www.hnb.hr/statistika, 23.7.2003.

Investment privatization funds acquired more than 60 per cent of this value (Ondrcka, 2001:90). Thirty-three per cent were privatized by 'direct sales' and management buy-outs (MBOs). The rest was left for restitution (7 per cent) and competitive bidding (3 per cent) (Benaček, 2002:64). Although much of the large state-owned or semi-state enterprises have been privatized, there remain still several large SOEs, mainly in the energy sector, telecommunications, steel industry and coal-mining, that need to be privatized and many even radically restructured (Pavlik, 2001:125).

*East German* privatization was completed by 1994. The *Treuhand* agency led the whole process. As a privatization method MBOs were hardly used. More than 60 per cent of enterprises were sold to West German and about 10 per cent to foreign investors (Brezinski, 2001:7). Out of the 12,370 East German SOEs 7,853 were fully privatized (i.e. 63.5 per cent of the total, 3,713 were closed (i.e. 30 per cent of the total), 563 were transferred to municipalities or majority private shareholding (i.e. 4.3 per cent of the total) and 268 remained (i.e. 2.2 per cent of the total) (Wei, 2003:105).

In *Hungary*, the privatization policy preferred real owners (Balaton, 2001:11). Therefore in the first two years of transition, over 70 per cent of privatized property was acquired by foreigners (Bornstein, 1997:331). Small investors were able to buy on favourable terms shares of smaller state-owned companies from 1992 on. This approach actually meant management–employee buy-outs. The Hungarian government excluded from privatization a number of so-called strategic SOEs in the early stage of transition. The result of the privatization process is that some 1,700 of 2,000 state-owned companies were privatized between 1989 and 1999; another 44 were still on the list as candidates for privatization at the end of the year 2000 (Illes and Pataki, 2001:407). Foreign owners control 90 per cent of telecommunications, 70 per cent of financial institutions, 66 per cent of the industrial sector, 60 per cent of energy production and 50 per cent of the trading sector (Illes and Pataki, 2001:407).

The *Polish* privatization model was strongly influenced by the tradition of workers' councils in the country (Edwards and Lawrence, 2000:38). In 1990, the state Law on Privatization of SOEs enacted two main privatization methods: capital privatization (the commercial method) and 'liquidation privatization' (Bornstein, 1997:328). The first method required an SOE to be transformed into a JSC whose shares are sold to private investors through public offerings, tenders, or direct negotiation. Workers got the opportunity to buy up to 20 per cent of the JSC's shares at half price. The 'liquidation' method meant the liquidation of the SOE whose assets are leased, sold or otherwise 'contributed' to a new private company. Leasing to management and employee buyouts (MEBOs) was the major form of liquidation (Bornstein, 1997:328). From August 1, 1990 to the end of January 2002, 2089 applications for direct privatization (i.e. capital privatization) and 1752 applications for 'liquidation' were approved (http://www.mst.gov.pl/en/prywat/estat.htm). The share of non-managerial employees in ownership has steadily decreased in employee-leased companies, while the number of shares in the hands of outsiders (i.e. predominantly domestic investors) increased five-fold by the end of 1999 (Woodward and Kozarzewski, 2003:83). Insider and dispersed ownership are not of great significance in Poland.

The first new independent *Slovak* government pushed the commercial privatization approach. It was based on the possibilities of instalment-based sales. The Slovak banks supported purchasing of the economic assets by private domestic investors and managers too. Domestic owners have been formed in this way. By the end of the year 1996, around 92 per cent of all Slovak manufacturing firms were privatized. Foreign investors started to buy 'majority stakes' in privatized Slovak companies after 1995 (Djankov and Pohl, 1998:74). Therefore, the period 1995–98 is known as the second privatization phase in Slovakia.

Slovakia recently privatized state monopolistic enterprises in the energy and telecommunications sectors. The country is currently experiencing the privatization of its financial and banking sector (Porvaznik and Stanek, 2001:136). Foreign banks will mostly overtake the Slovakian banks.

The *Slovenian* gradualist privatization approach was based predominantly on mass-privatization approaches giving a certain advantage to internal forms of enterprise privatization. Employees and retired former employees were eligible to sizeable discounts. By the end of 1997, 1,329 social (state) enterprises were privatized out of 1,345 enterprises that were earmarked for privatization (Pučko and Edwards, 1999:73). At the end of the formal privatization process, 76.7 per cent of companies had a majority of internal owners and less than a quarter of the privatized companies with predominantly external owners held 56.3 per cent of privatized former social (state) capital. The energy sector, telecommunications, the iron and steel industry and most other utilities have not been part of the formal privatization process. They will be transformed into private ownership gradually on a case-by-case basis. The financial and banking sector have also yet to be privatized. The biggest domestic commercial banks started to be offered for sale from 2001.

### New firm development

Whilst there are many similarities in the national SME development policies and their results in the Central European transitional countries, there are many differences too. Some of the countries, like Croatia, Hungary, Poland and Slovenia, had developed a certain SME sector already under the socialist regime; on the other hand, Czechoslovakia started transition almost without SMEs. In spite of the stated difference, nearly all countries met with an explosion of entrepreneurship in the early stage of transition. In the mid-1990s, the number of SMEs somehow stabilised practically in all countries.

Croatia had a dynamic growth of new small businesses in the first half of the 1990s. The SME sector employed 54.9 per cent of the total workforce in the economy in 1998 (Benić, 2000:35). The Czech Republic created a sizeable number of new small business firms by small-scale enterprise privatization at the beginning of transition. By the end of 1994, an estimated 2,200 SMEs had been created as a result of large enterprise privatization and 23,000 from small-scale enterprise privatization (Fadahusni and Smallbone, 1998:155).

East Germany gained most new business firms in the first five years after the Berlin Wall had fallen. During 1990–94 184,200 new firms were founded, and in the next five years an additional 110,600 firms (Brezinski, 2001:4). This achievement was still far from being able to compensate for the decline of employment in former state enterprises.

The Hungarian experience was a dramatic rise in numbers of new small business firms —there were more than 500,000 in existence by 1993. Poland was rather successful in creating new small and medium businesses too. The number of sole proprietorships and partnerships increased by 42 per cent in 1988–89 and 40 per cent in 1989–90 (Fadahusni and Smallbone, 1998:150). The number of SMEs increased from 1.2 million to nearly 2.8 million during the period 1990–98. The ratio of SMEs to the total number of economic units in Poland is comparable to that in the European Union now (Smallbone and Rogut, 2003:209).

Around 50,000 small-sized enterprises were founded in Slovakia during the nineties, but they did not have a significant impact either on employment or government budget revenues (Porvaznik, 2001:134). Small and medium-sized enterprises started to be rapidly founded in Slovenia from 1990 on too. At the end of 1996, there were already 35,655 such enterprises accounting for 99 per cent of all business firms. In 1996 the SME sector already employed 66.3 per cent of the whole workforce of the Slovenian economy (Pučko and Lahovnik, 1998:40).

Small and medium-sized enterprises employed about 50 per cent of the workforce in 1998 in Croatia, the Czech Republic, Hungary, Poland and Slovenia. Such a level is quite comparable to that of the European Union (World Bank, 2002:39). The respective East German and Slovakian achievements were not so favourable in this regard.

### Capital and labour

If a high level of egalitarianism among workers prevailed in the former communist countries, a stronger support for strong trade unions and state intervention in the job market than in the Western market economies might have been expected after the system change. Moreover, workers would be inclined to active unrest and to support even more strongly their labour unions. In general, this has not happened. Taking into account the strong tradition of workers' self-management in Slovenia and Croatia, as well as in Poland and to a certain extent in Hungary this is surprising. The role of labour unions in the management of firms and their involvement in the change process have been insignificant. In the vast majority of cases, the former unified 'socialist' labour union split into a number of labour unions in the transitional period. Moreover, new labour unions were established. These new organization have even initiated politically motivated tensions between themselves, but their main activities have been limited to wage claims and very rarely have their representatives put forward serious initiatives regarding the direction of the firm's development (Stepien and Robinson, 2001:50). Labour unions have generally co-operated with (or at least tolerated) the transition process. Lieb-Doczy (2001:105) found in her case studies that in 61 per cent of the East German companies and 54 per cent of the Hungarian ones, the trade unions co-operated in the restructuring process. Co-operation was usually broken only if local managers or investors did not behave in accordance with the agreements made concerning investment or the firm's restructuring plans.

### *Regional and global links*

The reunification of Germany restructured completely and rather quickly all former East Germany's regional and global links. Other Central European transitional countries have also restructured their political and economic relationships in a relatively short period of a few years. All became members of the Council of Europe and the World Trade Organization (Croatia as the last one in 2000). All except Croatia were members of the Central European Free Trade Agreement (CEFTA) already in the 1990s. All except Slovenia and Croatia joined the Organization for Economic Cooperation and Development (OECD). The Czech Republic, Hungary and Poland became North Atlantic Treaty Organization (NATO) members in 1999. The last three countries, Slovakia and Slovenia were accepted in the European Union in 2004.

Economic relationships of all Central European transitional countries have been radically remodelled. The average East German state enterprise sold 85 per cent of its output on the home market and not more than 2.5 per cent in the European Union in the 1990s. Its 1996 EU share already amounted to 32.9 per cent and the domestic market share was reduced to 61.6 per cent (Lieb-Doczy, 2001:166). An average Hungarian enterprise exported 35 per cent of its output in the 1990s; 19 per cent of its sales were achieved on Eastern European markets. Slovak enterprises sold 46 per cent of their output on Council for Mutual Economic Assistance (CMEA) markets in 1991 and 9 per cent in Western Europe or other markets (Djankov and Pohl, 1998:77). Enterprises from other Central European countries had a similar structure of regional sales. Already by 1996, the Czech Republic (35.6 per cent of all exports), Hungary (29 per cent), Poland (34 per cent) and Slovenia (30.6 per cent) had Germany as their strongest export partner, while Slovakia had the Czech Republic (31 per cent of all exports) and Croatia Italy (21 per cent) as the strongest partner. The import structure was also very similar. Later in 2000 Slovakia joined the group, which had Germany as the biggest foreign trade partner. For Croatian foreign trade, the German market was still second by importance (*Statistical Yearbook on Candidate and South-East European Countries*, 2002).

*Foreign direct investment*

Foreign direct investment has been a key factor in the speedy transformation of economies and firms in a number of Central European transitional countries. Because of the persistence of historical values and other reasons all countries did not open themselves completely to FDI. Theoretical arguments and empirical evidence support in general the thesis that companies with FDI out-perform those with other enterprise restructuring strategies. Some researchers warn us that this is not true in all countries (Lieb-Doczy, 2001:123). Others raise the issue of 'national interest' (Senjur, 2002:4), which is a concept not known in macroeconomics, but worth considering.

The behaviour pattern of FDI is fairly clear. Foreign owners usually implement a major investment programme and transfer technology and commercial knowledge. They make considerable changes in senior management structures and reallocate 'creative' business functions to more developed regions. They open the access to markets (Carlin *et al.*, 1995:449).

On the other hand, one should not forget that there is not an unlimited supply of FDI. Countries must create a stimulating environment for attracting investors. A combination of all these factors (and many more) might explain FDI's achievements in the Central European transitional countries in their first decade of transition.

If Hungary had the highest inflow of foreign direct investment from the very beginning of the transition period, the Czech Republic held the second place in this regard (Holland and Pain, 1998:304), Poland and Croatia intensified such an inflow more recently. The Czech Republic overtook Hungary in the extent of FDI per capita in recent years (*Cestat Statistical Bulletin*, 2001/4). In the period 1995–2000, the Czech Republic attracted the most FDI per capita, with Hungary following. Poland and Slovakia were the lowest achievers in this regard at the end of 2001 (see Table 2.1, p. 34).

## Internal/micro issues/factors

Structural changes in the *rules of the game* as well as in *parameters of the game* meant a radically new micro environment for the former socialist enterprises at the start of the transition period. They met with a kind of strategy shock resulting from:

- the withdrawal of protection for the domestic competitors in the home market;
- a sudden loss of the markets of the former socialist bloc countries;
- the loss of the former big domestic market because of the split of the former socialist country into more new states (i.e. the Yugoslavia Federation, Czechoslovakia);
- the introduction of market criteria for allocating resources.

Enterprises were faced with new market institutions, which have been developed, step by step.

While confronted with the new macro and micro-environment 'old' enterprises' survival depended on their ability to adapt. A well-known principle that an enterprise has to be co-ordinated with its external environment could not be disregarded therefore.

### Corporate restructuring

The new macro and microenvironment demanded from the 'old' enterprises their restructuring. Researchers of corporate restructuring in transitional economies classify it into two types: strategic or deep (radical) and reactive or ambiguous (Lieb-Doczy, 2001:125; Stepien and Robinson, 2001:40). Strategic or deep (radical) restructuring is interpreted as the development of new capabilities and final products, which improve an enterprise's performance. It means that the enterprise will have once again a sustainable competitive advantage. Reactive restructuring is generally seen as survival oriented behaviour which aims at maximizing enterprise performance within its existing resources and capabilities.

There have been 'old' enterprises in the transition countries that went through a restructuring process. Companies taken over by foreign direct investors carried out in the majority of cases a strategic restructuring quickly. A foreign investor has usually provided additional capital, needed for new investment in fixed and current assets, introduced new products and production methods, enabled access to new markets and transferred managerial knowledge, which was lacking in the enterprise. The final result is a financially well-performing company, which had been turned around in a relatively short period.

Domestically privatized enterprises have been meeting with a shortage of needed additional resources and managerial knowledge. Therefore, they intended to carry out strategic restructuring, but many were forced to implement for quite a period a reactive restructuring before needed 'fresh' capital was provided or created for making radical strategic changes in their product portfolio, fixed assets, suppliers and customer networks, human resources, management systems, etc. The restructuring of the enterprises in this group has usually required from five to ten years (Pučko, 2001:22; Stepien and Robinson, 2001:40).

The restructuring of unprivatized enterprises was mostly of the reactive or ambiguous type. It meant a rather prolonged period of crisis management with the focus on enterprise survival and retrenchment by reducing output, work force, cost, assets and asking for government subsidies. Such enterprises have been finally sold to private owners or undergone bankruptcy. Some are still fighting for their survival.

The vast majority of 'old' enterprises were exposed to the corporate recovery process based on domestic resources (combined in some cases with foreign consultancy services). Therefore, it is worth considering what characterized those corporate recovery processes. Different authors who have been researching empirically the restructuring of 'old' enterprises in Central European transitional countries suggest slightly different segmentations of these processes. Edwards has identified two main stages: the inwardly directed as a first stage when managers implemented internal changes in their enterprises and the outwardly directed second stage when managers started to make changes regarding the enterprise's market and competition (Edwards and Lawrence, 2000:39). Stepien and Robinson suggested the process as segmented in two main phases: a phase of 'rescue' transformation (i.e. solving a latent or acute crisis situation) and a phase of developmental transformation (Stepien and Robinson, 2001:43). Pučko developed a model with four main stages of the corporate recovery process (2001:18–21). He argued that the typical enterprise met with a latent or acute crisis at first. It required a crisis management approach.

The second phase is called revitalization. Firms started to implement mainly a consolidation strategy at this stage. Most enterprises still operated at a loss but no longer with a negative cash flow. Their debt level, because of a swap of debt for equity, improved. The duration of this phase varied in different enterprises between one and three years.

The third phase is linked to making real strategic changes in the enterprise. Firms become outward directed. Some firms still implement a stabilization or consolidation strategy. Many firms choose an external quality development strategy at this stage. The typical enterprise operates again with a modest profit during this phase, which lasts typically from two to four years.

The fourth growth phase of corporate recovery begins at the moment when an enterprise has rebuilt its competitive advantage and is able to operate as a viable market unit again. Profitability levels move in line with the owners' demands. As many 'old' enterprises have not achieved this stage yet, it is not possible to give it any time dimension.

It is difficult to explain all the specificities of the enterprise restructuring process in Central European transitional countries with a common model. The output and workforce reduction in enterprises were two of the main common characteristics of the early stages of the restructuring processes. The intensity of workforce shedding was different in different transitional countries and periods.

### *Corporate strategies and alliances*

According to the four-stage corporate recovery model described in the previous section, the most frequently prevailing corporate strategies in individual stages can be identified (Table 2.2). The most economically important enterprise segment, i.e. domestically privatized 'old' enterprises, implements typically such strategies. Certainly, no one is able to argue that such an overview of corporate strategies describes enterprises' strategic

*Table 2.2*  Typical corporate strategies in individual stages of the corporate recovery process in Central European transitional economies

*Strategy*

| Stage I: Latent or acute crisis | Stage II: Revitalization | Stage III: Strategic changes | Stage IV: Growth |
|---|---|---|---|
| Output reduction | Focus on core | Product | Growth |
| Work force reduction | business areas | improvement | Product |
| Finding new markets | Divesting | Market | development |
| Co-operation with | peripheral areas | development | Partner |
| foreign partners | Product | Product | selection |
| Cost reduction | improvements | development | Diversification |
| Management buy-out | Marketing | Growth | Acquisitions |
| Joint ventures | improvements | Stabilization and | Human resource |
| Organizational | Subcontracting | consolidation | development |
| changes | Training | External quality | Organizational |
| New recruitment | Productivity | development | culture |
| | improvement | Co-operation | development |
| | Assets divestment | TQM | |
| | Organizational | Generic business | |
| | changes | strategies | |
| | Preparation for | | |
| | and privatization | | |

Source: Pučko, 2001:19.

behaviour in each Central European transitional country perfectly. There have been too many differences in the macro and microenvironments in different countries which have produced specific features in implemented corporate strategies and which make any generalization difficult.

Pavić and Vidučić (1999:29) assessed that many large Croatian enterprises were characterized by a lack of a clear vision and blamed this fact for the poor achievement in Croatian corporate recovery. The enterprise fragmentation strategy seems to be important in the Czech environment. Many previously vertical Czech conglomerates were transformed into systems of satellite firms around a new technological core, which were effectively re-integrated in an industrial conglomerate later (Clark, 2000:178).

East German enterprises were forced to implement retrenchment strategies in the most direct way among all Central European transitional countries. The fragmentation strategies were also very popular in the German environment, but they did not result in systems of satellite firms. The majority of the German firms that survived quickly adopted a product quality and a punctuality of delivery strategy, trying not to compete on a low cost basis because East German wages had increased too much after German unification.

'Old' Hungarian enterprises mostly applied retrenchment strategies in the early stage of the transition. Joint ventures and foreign-owned firms focused on realizing first mover advantage, exploiting cheap but skilled Hungarian labour and being cautious in making larger investments. Private Hungarian enterprises already implemented growth strategies based on innovation and diversification (Balaton, 2001:11). State-owned firms mainly persisted in the latent or acute crisis stage, fighting for survival and preparing for privatization.

'Old' Polish firms mostly implemented a 'wait and see', cautious strategic approach in the early stage of the transition and then started to implement a proactive strategy in the second half of the 1990s. Empirical research findings (Stepien and Robinson, 2001:37) show that FOEs implement product development and market development kinds of growth strategies most frequently in recent years, domestically privatized firms apply mostly product development or product specialization kinds of growth strategies while state-owned firms have been oriented to modernization and introduction of a few new products as well as to a slight expansion of their markets.

Foreign-owned and private Polish-owned firms invest much more frequently than SOEs. Therefore, the first two groups of firms have already reached the strategic change phase in the corporate recovery process while state-owned ones are still mostly in the first or second stage (i.e. crisis or revitalization phase).

Large Slovak firms have implemented mainly a product development strategy. According to Djankov and Pohl's (1998:79) research findings 35 per cent of all product lines were introduced in their product range after 1991. Investment strategies were more in use in the second half of the nineties while product quality orientations were evident mostly in the form of providing ISO 9001 certifications in the mid-1990s. Large Slovak enterprises are more oriented to cost effectiveness than product differentiation strategies (Slavik, 2001:76). The firms have implemented intensively in the last part of the previous decade co-operation strategies. Thirty-six per cent of enterprises in the Djankov and Pohl sample were subcontractors of foreign partners.

The 'old' Slovenian firms mostly during the early stage of the transition also implemented crisis management and a kind of corporate retrenchment strategy. The second stage started after 1993 and lasted to the middle of 1997. It was the period of the 'old' firms' privatization. The majority of 'old' firms started to implement a growth strategy again. Market development, market penetration and product improvement strategies were the most frequently implemented in the enterprises. Product development strategies were not much in use nor diversification and acquisition strategies until recently (Čater, 2003:2264). It was noted that enterprises started to invest more in R&D activities during this period (Pučko and Edwards, 1999:81), but R&D results were still very modest.

Most Slovenian firms compete on a product differentiation basis. Primarily by developing and implementing collaboration strategies, they achieved a rapid market reorientation. Collaborative strategies were already implemented by 65 per cent of the 'old' Slovenian firms by 1996. This share increased further later. The acquisition strategy became an interesting one for firms – at first domestic and then foreign – after the conclusion of the privatization process.

### *Functional strategies*

It is evident that managerial attitudes and behaviour which had become established under the communist system in the transitional Central European countries are still manifest in enterprises and that the achieved quality levels of functional management differ significantly between individual enterprises and not just between various groups (i.e. foreign-owned, private domestic and state-owned enterprises).

Research findings (Pučko, 2002:78) offer evidence that among all enterprises newly founded ones are the most market oriented in Slovenia. Foreign direct investments have not made a significant move towards a marketing orientation, while 'old' enterprises are the most lacking in a marketing orientation. In marketing terms, enterprises are focused predominantly on products, offering 'the best products', instead of on customers. Enterprises carry out mostly quantitatively oriented market research and still neglect qualitative approaches. Enterprises still expect the market research to produce an answer to 'how much' instead of the answer to 'why'.

Many similar characteristics have been identified in the enterprises in other Central European transitional countries. Czech firms have not been able to shift fully to a market orientation and shake off old practices (Savitt, 1998:347). Management frequently set up a marketing department, but it has rarely become more than a staff department that collects and analyzes marketing data and prepares sales forecasts. According to research findings (Sysko-Romanczuk and Lozano, 2002:1509). Polish enterprises have concentrated on the expansion of their product range, promotion and advertising and design of a new logo within their marketing. The majority of the Polish firms still do not segment their markets and still generates ideas for new products within the company.

The production-focus approach is still strongly present in the mind of managers as their heritage from the past (Edwards and Lawrence, 2000:29). The management of operations is confronted with many weaknesses nowadays. The enterprises' restructuring processes made evident a long lasting problem of poor production capacity usage in many enterprises. Apart from a low volume of production, production managers are meeting with too low a degree of automation. Information technology has been penetrating the production management processes relatively intensively. In spite of this, the production managers share the prevalent opinion of inadequacy of current information systems in production. There are many firms which have introduced ISO standards and even total quality management (TQM) approaches, just-in-time (JIT), business process re-engineering and programmable, flexible automation, outsourcing, lean production, etc., but in the majority of cases they have not yet had any significant achievements in this regard.

The area of financial management is probably one of the areas where the differences between the quality level in the enterprises in the developed market economies and the transitional context are the biggest (Pučko, 2002:79). There will be many financial experts in transitional countries that will never adapt to new demands. The main criteria for financial decision-making are still not very clear (it is still not the maximization of the owners' value). Capital budgeting methods are in use, but weaknesses are linked to neglecting the proper cost of own capital and not taking risk explicitly into account in the relevant decision making. There are just a few enterprises that analyze the issue of optimal capital structure. Financial planning in the firms still has serious weaknesses. Financial managers are not very familiar with the analytical methods known in the financial management theory and therefore they are not in use.

The HRM function has not yet been developed satisfactorily in the enterprises. One can still find in the firms predominantly approaches to personnel management that consist of carrying out traditional legal and administrative activities connected with employees, of developing traditional reward and communication methods, of dealing with working conditions, and other tactical issues. It is fair to say that elements of the leadership model are present too (Pučko, 2002:80). An orientation to leading, solving work problems, productivity and training are emphasized in these approaches. The enterprises, which are more market oriented, already try to implement reward systems based on work measurement instruments. The approaches of real strategic HRM which focus on strategic issues, changes, comprehensive problem solving, developing different reward systems that stimulate creativity and work performance, developing labour flexibility, and the individuals are still not a management reality.

Sysko-Romanczuk and Lozano (2002:1510) found that Polish firms do not apply HRM tools in the majority of the firms in their survey, while Stepien and Robinson (2001:51) found highly differentiated HRM practices in various types of Polish firms. Differences exist in respect of employee training, multi-skilling and the role played by employees within the firm. Foreign-owned firms place a noticeably greater emphasis on regular and comprehensive staff training as well as paying attention to the needs of employees to feel valued and well-informed.

### *Organizational structures and cultures*

Actual organizational change within enterprises in the Central European transitional countries has been somehow limited. This statement is not valid for enterprises, which were taken over by foreign owners. The main changes in 'old' enterprises were carried out by introducing hierarchical functional organizational structures and by abolishing previous rather egalitarian structures. Firms most frequently implemented modifications affecting the organization of work and adopting ISO 9000 system requirements.

Research findings show us that functional organizational structures dominate in enterprises. Galetić and Tipurić (1999:151) found that as many as 73.1 per cent of large Croatian enterprises apply such a structure and that 26 per cent of large enterprises had a completely unsuitable organizational structure in terms of their strategy, which makes them slow and inflexible. Clark (2000:181) identified that Czech managers still draw heavily on old practices and contacts, employ a simple functional structure and ignore institutional pressures to decentralize. The fragmentation of previous Czech vertical conglomerates has contributed to a certain degree to less hierarchical relationships and a higher level of decentralization.

Previous East German enterprises have introduced more organizational changes in the sense of flat structures and lean organization than Czech or Polish enterprises because East German enterprises were forced much more because of higher wages to find organizational solutions that reduce cost. Hungarian enterprises also did not make radical organizational changes in the early 1990s (Edwards and Lawrence, 2000:29), but they have changed later toward decentralized divisional structures according to Balaton (2001:16). In Poland, firms modified their organizational structure, trying to simplify communications' channels within the firm and to decentralize management. In spite of these changes organizational structures found are still in the majority of cases used as a tool for the division of authority, not as a mechanism of coordination and control (Sysko-Romanzcuk and Lozano, 2002:1509). Slovak and Slovenian enterprises do not differ much regarding organizational solutions in the comparison with other Central European transitional counterparts.

Organizational cultures in enterprises have been transforming, but it is difficult to find many common denominators. A great stress on individual rather than collective responsibility and on strategic decision making, globalization and regional economic integration might be common change features. Many specific characteristics of enterprise cultures in individual countries can be more easily identified. Czech managers are inclined to take a short-term rather a long-term view. They tend to prefer self-sufficiency and passive resistance behaviour. They believe in a Czech approach in management and they do not trust in superior foreign management expertise. They still strongly feel their social responsibility to the community (Clark, 2000:177).

Polish managers prefer formal organizational structures and systems. They show a marked tendency to individualism combined with more egalitarian and paternalistic approaches than their counterparts in neighbouring countries. Families and friends are important for Polish managers; therefore they are inclined to build on extensive informal networks. Because of predominantly historical reasons, they lack an entrepreneurial tradition.

Slovenian managers are seeking a 'middle' way regarding organizational culture issues according to Edwards and Lawrence (2000:139) among their counterparts in Central Europe, while Croatian managers differ the most in this regard. In spite of the stated difference, managers in these two countries have a strong orientation to Western European values.

## Management styles

The old system of management has been swept away after the radical changes in socio-economic systems in transitional countries. It does not mean that all old management attitudes and practices have been erased. The old authoritarian and paternalistic managerial approaches cannot be abolished as long as the same persons hold managerial positions. The old technocratic and bureaucratic management behaviour cannot be substituted in a short period of time with completely different behavioural manners. The inclination to a rather slow managerial decision-making and relatively a high level of inflexibility, strong relationships with the local communities, a low degree of managerial mobility and strong interpersonal ties are firmly rooted in the experiences of past managerial behaviour. They cannot be simply substituted by taking away 'the outmoded software program' and by installing 'the most modern one'.

Czech and Slovak managers are characterized by three main features which are rooted in Czechoslovak tradition: autocracy, a technical bias and paternalism (Edwards and Lawrence, 2000:65). They are under the influence of the old successful experiences of the *Bata* management system from the early part of the twentieth century. Czech and Slovak managers prefer to follow a short-term orientation. Czech managers repeatedly refer to the uniqueness of their environment and are not willing to accept support from foreign management consultants. The former Slovak managerial elite has retained its power. Slovakian managers are inclined to use heavily family and personal connections in achieving their goals. It is well known that a real ethical crisis has developed in the Czech Republic and Slovakia, which is characterized by a high level of corruption and even criminal practices.

The managers in the former East Germany do not possess attitudes, values and leadership styles, which would be significantly different from those of their Western counterparts, but they are also not promoters of new Western style management behaviour (Lang and Müller, 2001:401).

Senior Polish managers still have many attitudes and behaviours, which appear typical of the former system. The co-existence of old and new management practices describes the recent Polish environment the best. The enterprises whose ownership has passed into the hands of the pre-transition top managers are still managed by 'old-style' managers. A paternalistic managerial style is heavily in use (Sysko-Romanczuk and Lozano, 2002:1510). Managers frequently demonstrate a lack of clarity of enterprise goals and strategic direction. Enterprises often do not have any serious control and motivational systems which facilitate a continuation of a somewhat *laissez-faire* approach to work discipline (Robinson and Tomczak-Stepien, 2000:148).

It seems that Polish firms plan strategically. Private firms have strategic plans which are often only 'in the boss's head'. Written strategic plans are found in almost all foreign-owned and state-owned firms. In state-owned firms, however, strategic plans are simple extrapolations of past tendencies combined with a limited amount of information regarding changes in the external environment. Polish managers favour clear organizational structures, support formal systems and planned approaches.

Western managerial approaches are not sufficiently 'similar' for the Hungarian environment (Lieb-Doczy, 2001:123), but they could be sufficiently 'similar' to the Slovenian and Croatian environment. The workers' self-management system in the former socialist Yugoslavia, of which Slovenia and Croatia were a part, contributed to the inherited slowness in managerial decision-making processes in Slovenian and Croatian enterprises. In spite of that the overall quality of management in Slovenian enterprises seems to be quite close to Austrian managerial practice (Langer, 2001:1108). Top management teams practice strategic planning approaches in a great majority of enterprises. Annual planning or budgeting is also well in use in the stated Slovenian firms (Pučko, 2002:76).

Organizing as a management function is not a source of competitive advantage of Slovenian and Croatian enterprises. Modern organizational structures are applied in a marginal number of larger companies. It seems that managers often still lack managerial knowledge in this management field. Leadership has changed significantly in spite of the fact that managers' value systems have been changing constantly but slowly and they still differ noticeably from the value systems of Western European entrepreneurs and managers.

Controlling as a management function is not neglected in enterprises. According to research findings nine tenths of the top management teams in Slovenian enterprises use a certain system of tactical feedback control and a quarter even the feed forward type of control. Fifty per cent of large Slovenian firms have a controlling (in the German sense) department (Pučko, 2002:78). However, their control systems are still not timely. They are frequently not based on the responsibility centres concept and only a minority of firms has defined so called controllable variables in the existing responsibility centres.

### Management development

Central European transitional countries inherited a major part of their managers from the previous communist system. The majority of those managers had a university education mostly in various technical fields. The transition to a market economy confronted managers with radically new demands like business opportunity seeking, risk-taking, bearing individual responsibility, possessing knowledge of modern management concepts and techniques, having entrepreneurial creativity and capabilities for political lobbying, etc.

The new political elites felt a need to install their own cadres in the executive positions in SOEs because they did not trust the 'old' managers (i.e. those that had already held managerial positions in the previous system) and their abilities to adapt to new demands. The Czech government even passed the so-called Lustration Act in 1992 to get rid of 'old' managers. In reality, the Act had only limited impact. Between a quarter and a third of managers gave up their positions after 1989 in the Czech Republic according to one assessment and that was due to various reasons, not just because of the Lustration Act (Edwards and Lawrence, 2000:68–70).

Similar political pressures, but not supported by any legal act, have been present in other transitional countries. 'Old' managers that 'survived' the socio-economic system change still represent an important share of the new managerial elite. Their skills and experiences have simply been needed, as new political elites were not able to find many new ones for the demanding job of management. New managers – in the majority of cases they were relatively young – have been taking over executive posts in many 'old' enterprises. Foreign-owned firms brought foreigners or expatriates into executive positions in enterprises, at least for a certain period of time.

Kozarzewski (2001:2059) found that 74 per cent of the executive board members in his sample of Polish enterprises had already worked in managerial positions before firm privatization. On the other hand, foreign owners included in almost 80 per cent of the enterprises which are under their control at least one member of the executive board with experience of working abroad (Kozarzewski, 2003:2233). Therefore new, younger managers, many aged between 30 and 35, have found business opportunities for themselves, mainly in newly founded enterprises where they predominate (Edwards and Lawrence, 2000:40).

The restructuring of Slovak enterprises was not led by many new, better skilled managers, but by the 'old' *nomenklatura* (Djankov and Pohl, 1998:75). Slovenian managers had been in the forefront of introducing Western-style management in the Central European transitional countries. Bodenhöfer and Stanovnik (Edwards and Lawrence, 2000:120) investigated already in 1992 how Austrian investors viewed the capabilities of Slovenian managers. They found that their respondents acknowledged the higher level of management abilities of Slovene managers, when compared with those of other transitional countries. A majority of respondents believed that most Slovene managers in Austrian direct investment projects were as capable as managers in Austrian enterprises. Langer (2001:1108) obtained similar results in his 1998 research, which was dedicated to differences between organizational cultures in Slovenian and Austrian enterprises.

There were no systematic, politically forced changes in the top managerial positions in the 'old' Slovenian enterprises in the early transition period. Nevertheless, changes in executive positions were quite extensive. According to one survey (Pučko, 2001:15) 80.8 per cent of them were replaced in Slovenia in the period 1990–93 in medium and large-sized 'old' enterprises, which fell into crisis, and a rather high 65.5 per cent on average regardless of their enterprise situation in the period 1990–93. These changes contributed to a significant rejuvenation of the Slovenian managerial class. In 1997/98, fewer than 10 per cent of the top managers were in the over 56 years age bracket (Pučko and Edwards, 1999:76). Most top managers were in the age bracket between 36–45 years. Research results (Jaklič and Zagoršek, 2002:17) show that Slovenian managers are extremely powerful in their environments because they are able to disregard enterprise owners.

Croatian managers had very similar historical roots to Slovenian ones, but they have come to differ in their attitudes and values from their Slovenian counterparts in the transition period because of the different macro environment in which they have lived and worked. Case studies show (Collin and Cesljas, 2002:181) that the Croatian managerial elite is well educated. Their starting point appears to be the University of Zagreb, and especially the Faculty of Economics within it.

An enormous volume of managerial learning has taken place in Central European transitional countries in the last decade. Managers and would-be managers have been 'hungry' as far as management knowledge and skills are concerned. This has changed radically the level of relevant managerial skills when comparing the recent position with the level existing at the beginning of the transition. Despite that, managers are still lacking in relevant education and training.

## Outcome and performance: empirical evidence

As discussed and noted in the preceding sections there has been extensive empirical evidence on developments at both the macro and micro level in the region. An interesting feature of this evidence is the considerable diversity in approaches and outcomes both between and within countries.

This diversity reflects in part the different initial positions in the respective countries following the collapse of the former regimes, variations in policies at the macro level and different approaches at the micro level. Such factors have interacted to allow different outcomes and types and levels of performance to emerge, for example, with regard to company survival and restructuring.

Overall, it could be argued, much has been achieved and much still remains to be done. Clearly, foreign ownership and competition have been driving forces but the countries of the region have also demonstrated considerable energy, for example, in the area of new firm development. The drive to join the European Union has, moreover, proved to create an impetus to transform the institutional framework and improve organizational efficiency.

## Evaluation and conclusion

The Central European transitional countries have been among the most successful in implementing transition with as few painful effects for their inhabitants as possible. Many of them have already almost arrived at a point where they will start to say that their transition is over.

The privatization of the state-(or socially-)owned enterprises in Central Europe has been basically completed. It has enabled a new enterprise governance system to be now in place. Its influence on enterprises' performance is still ambivalent and depends on a set of factors (Kozarzewski, 2003:2223). In spite of this finding, the new governance systems potentially mean that a new system of economic motivation is now in place and that the possibilities for higher economic efficiency are present. The private ownership of the means of production is still quite dispersed, but the ownership concentration process has already been evident for a few years. There is no doubt about the intense need to develop and strengthen further legal and regulatory institutions to oversee the transfer of private ownership and corporate governance rights.

The birth and growth of new small firms have been of utmost importance for the successful transformation of the Central European transitional countries. New firms have created economic growth and new employment. All transitional countries will have to continue demolishing existing obstacles in order to promote a well performing SME sector.

Sectoral and regional structures of Central European transitional countries have been adapted to new realities and the demands of market economies. However, a slightly larger regional dispersion of the transitional countries' foreign trade will still be needed in the future.

Foreign direct investments and raising foreign debt have been very important sources for financing investments in the Central European transitional countries in the past decade. The Czech Republic and Hungary have preferred foreign direct investments. Slovenia and Croatia have financed investments much more by raising foreign debt. Some reversal of this behaviour should be expected, most probably in the current decade.

'Old' enterprises have already adapted to the new macro and micro-environment in the majority of cases. The exceptions are most probably Croatia and Slovakia. Unemployment levels, especially in Croatia, former East Germany, Poland and Slovakia, are unacceptably high socially. Policies for their effective improvement will probably be in the forefront of economic policies in those countries in this decade. Inflation is still a problem in the Central European transitional countries, but one must recognize that its trend is encouraging and rather promising.

Half of the transitional countries analyzed here have met with a widespread moral and ethical crisis. It is most pronounced in the Czech Republic, Slovakia and Croatia. The assessments of the quality of judicial systems show that Poland and Slovakia are the worst achievers in this regard. Their governments will not be able to disregard these weaknesses much longer. Enterprises as state monopolies still exist to a minor extent but their destiny will finally be, in the majority of cases, a de-monopolization and privatization.

'Old' East German and Slovenian firms have typically implemented mainly product differentiation strategies; Slovak and Polish firms have been more inclined to implement a cost effectiveness strategy. Such differences will persist in the near future too, despite a recent tendency that domestically privatized enterprises have begun to pay even more attention to factors of total quality management. Enterprises in the region will be forced not just to export but also to develop higher forms of internationalization if they want to compete successfully with foreign competitors.

Enterprises will still have to learn how to upgrade their marketing capabilities. The clear perspective of these enterprises is that they will have to increase radically their R&D and marketing outlays if they intend to compete successfully with their foreign competitors. The financial managerial capabilities are still on a relatively low level and they can be changed only gradually over the long term. The human resource management area has been changing radically and has been moving away from predominantly legal and administrative approaches, but it still has a long way to go before a real strategic HRM will be introduced in enterprises.

Actual organizational change within enterprises has been somewhat limited. Organizational structures in medium- and large-sized enterprises will demand radical adaptations in the near future.

Enterprise organizational cultures have been transforming continuously during the transition. Individuals have been taking on even more individual responsibilities, strategic decision-making and international (global) thinking, which may be considered as very positive changes. On the other hand, there are many specific national characteristics present, from preferring self-sufficiency and a nationalistic orientation to more open and international inclinations, from preferring formal organizational relationships to informal ones. Differences in managers' values and attitudes also persist even though they are tending to diminish constantly but slowly.

In spite of radical changes in management styles that have been implemented in the last decade, a number of pre-transition management features continue to be present and influential in organizations. Authoritarian and paternalistic styles, technocratic and bureaucratic management behaviour, a rather slow managerial decision-making, relatively inflexible behaviour, a low degree of managerial mobility, the practice of intensively using interpersonal ties and contacts have still not completely disappeared. A lack of management knowledge has been significantly diminished, but it has not been abolished. Strategic managerial thinking still does not prevail. Business ethics has been heavily disregarded in many environments. Western managerial approaches are not attractive to all managers in the region. Polish, Slovenian and Croatian managers seem to be much more inclined to the American management model than Czech, Hungarian and Slovak ones.

Planning and control as management functions are rather well in use in Central European transitional countries and their quality is not unacceptably poor. On the other hand, organizing and leading as management functions, despite having changed significantly, still display many weaknesses, mostly based on the lack of appropriate managerial knowledge and the persistence of old managerial values, stereotypes and mentality.

The transition has apparently produced a significant rejuvenation of the managerial class in the Central European transitional countries. It means that, even though less managerial experience is present in the region, there is a greater potential for learning, creating and innovating. In spite of the enormous volume of managerial learning that has taken place in the analyzed transitional countries in the last decade, managers are still not so well equipped with managerial knowledge as their Western counterparts. They will still have to 'run behind' their Western colleagues and try to close the relevant gap in the future.

# 3 Central Europe 2

## 'Valleys of Tears'

### Introduction

South-Eastern Europe comprises the countries of the Balkan peninsula that were historically part of the Ottoman Empire and whose populations adhere predominantly to the Orthodox and Moslem religions. The following countries may be considered as constituting South-Eastern Europe: Romania, Bulgaria, Serbia and Montenegro (the two remaining components of the former Yugoslavia), Bosnia-Herzegovina, the former Yugoslav Republic of Macedonia (FYROM) and Albania. Internal and external conflicts have seriously hampered the transition process in many of the countries of the former Yugoslavia and have also influenced developments in neighbouring countries. Overall, the outcomes of transformation have been slow to materialize so that the countries of South-Eastern Europe are generally regarded as slow achievers in effecting the transformation of their economies from a command to a market system.

The transformation of the former communist economies of Central and Eastern Europe (CEE) has not involved a uniform experience. The collapse of the communist regimes presented the successor governments with a range of problems and, in some respects, opportunities which varied in their nature from country to country. Within CEE, Albania, Bulgaria and Romania can be considered as belonging to a group of countries which experienced a high degree of difficulty in facing the transformation process. Exploring the nature of and reasons for this difficulty is one of the objectives of this chapter. One perspective, 'path dependence' (Stark, 1992), places particular importance on inherited factors and the starting position of countries at the beginning of the transformation process. Another perspective (World Bank, 2002) highlights concepts such as discipline and encouragement (contrasted with protection and discouragement) as underlying principles of the transformation process, with discipline and encouragement contributing to positive developments in the countries concerned. The introductory section of this chapter, moreover, investigates similarities and differences between the three countries as a basis for understanding their post-communist development.

**Historical background**

Following the partition of the Roman Empire in 395, South-East Europe (often referred to as the Balkans) became part of the Byzantine Common-wealth, a term used by Obolensky (1971) to denote the area of Byzantine political and cultural influence. This area stretched beyond the Balkans to include Romania, the lands on both sides of the middle Danube and Russia. For over a thousand years, Byzantine influence predominated although it was challenged both in the religious and political spheres, for example by Bogomilism in the case of the former and the First and Second Bulgarian Kingdoms (852–1018 and 1185–1396) in the case of the latter.

Byzantine rule was ultimately broken with the Fall of Constantinople to the Ottoman Empire in 1453 and the advance of the Ottomans into Europe was not halted until 1683 at the gates of Vienna. The subsequent period up to the early twentieth century in the Balkans was marked by Ottoman domination and the attempts of various territories to extricate themselves from Ottoman rule. Romania had been ruled by the Ottomans from 1526, even though this rule was mediated in the eighteenth century by Phanariots, Greeks loyal to the Ottoman Empire. An independent Romanian state did not emerge till 1878.

Bulgaria had become part of the Ottoman Empire in 1396. It was only in 1878 that Bulgaria gained a measure of independence by becoming a principality subject to the Sultan, although even then southern Bulgaria (Eastern Rumelia) remained an Ottoman province. Full independence was obtained in 1908. Albania was occupied by the Ottoman Empire in the latter part of the fifteenth century and did not become an independent state until 1912.

The period after the First World War confirmed a reduction in the presence of Turkey, the successor to the Ottoman Empire, in Europe to a small area around Istanbul and raised the profile of the other states in the Balkans. Romania benefited in particular from the defeat of the Austro-Hungarian Empire and Russia's capitulation. Its territory expanded to include Transyl-vania (from Hungary) and Bessarabia (from Russia) and nearly one quarter of its population consisted of other nationalities (Wiskemann, 1966:267).

The countries of the region were strongly influenced and affected by the rise of Fascism and Nazism. Albania was annexed by Italy in 1939, although the country succeeded in liberating itself in 1944 under the leadership of the communist Enver Hoxha. Romania and Bulgaria, in contrast, were occupied by the Soviet Union and were incorporated in the so-called Soviet bloc. For a chronology of developments since the 1940s in the region (Figure 3.1).

**Cultural background**

The Byzantine heritage and Ottoman rule had a profound and lasting influ-ence on culture in the area. However, the context in which culture operates is extremely complex. Even today, the pattern of culture is characterized by

| 1944 | Liberation of Albania from Axis forces by communists under Hoxha |
|---|---|
| 1948 | Albania severs ties with Yugoslavia |
| 1954 | Zhivkov becomes First Secretary of the Bulgarian Communist Party |
| 1961 | Albania severs ties with USSR |
| 1965 | Ceausescu becomes General Secretary of the Romanian Communist Party |
| 1977 | Albania severs ties with China |
| 1980s | Ceausescu's 'shock therapy' to repay foreign debt |
| 1985 | Death of Hoxha |
| 1989 | Zhivkov deposed; Ceausescu executed |
| 1990 | Collapse of communist régimes in Bulgaria and Romania |
| 1991 | Collapse of communist régime in Albania. Bulgaria launches 'shock therapy' |
| 1992 | Start of reform process in Albania; Black Sea cooperation in form of loose association |
| 1996–97 | Economic crisis in Albania, Bulgaria and Romania |
| 1997 | Collapse of Albanian pyramid schemes |
| 1998 | Black Sea Economic Cooperation Organization (BSEC) established |

*Figure 3.1* Developments in the region since the 1940s.

great variety. For example, while states differentiate themselves from each other by reference to ethnic and historical origins, there is still considerable internal diversity both in terms of ethnic origin and religion, although ethnic diversity has tended to diminish (see Magris, 1997). Romania, for example, has a sizeable Hungarian minority and Bulgaria a Turkish minority. While predominantly Muslim, Albania has Orthodox and Catholic communities. Furthermore, the Jewish and Protestant communities had also influenced the cultural situation of the region. Ethnic and religious differences often, but not always, align.

Furthermore, the countries of the region were until the middle of the twentieth century largely agricultural and relatively poor. Cultural values were thus also influenced by economic activity. Largely agricultural communities, characterized by a relatively high degree of religious and ethnic diversity and having experienced centuries of occupation, tended to display '*Gemeinschaft*' values (Tönnies, 2001 [1887]) which were focused on circles of family and close friends. The legacies of the Orthodox Church and Ottoman rule have supported autocratic, patriarchal styles of leadership, which were often consonant with the style of management adopted by the communists after the Second World War.

## General background

Whilst Albania, Bulgaria and Romania may be regarded as laggards among CEE countries undergoing transformation, each country has had its own distinctive experience of post-communism as it had of the communist era. Albania was for decades one of the most idiosyncratic and reclusive communist regimes. Albania managed to form close relations and then break with a series of communist states: Albania abandoned its links with Yugoslavia in the late 1940s; the Soviet Union in 1961; and China in 1977. Albania was a totalitarian regime which after the break with China became almost entirely introspective and autarkic. Bulgaria in contrast was the Soviet Union's most loyal and placid ally and a 'byword for acquiescence and conformity with the Soviet model' (Crampton, 1997:241). Throughout the communist period, Bulgaria gave the Soviet Union very little cause for concern.

Romania, on the other hand, while remaining a member of COMECON, pursued nationalistic policies not always approved by nor agreeable to the Soviet Union. Especially from the late 1960s under Nicolae Ceausescu, Romania pursued foreign policies which challenged the demanded subservience to Moscow, for example, by cultivating closer links with the West and China. In the economic sphere too, Romania resisted Soviet proposals to remain predominantly a producer of agricultural products and created its own base of heavy industry. Moreover, in the 1980s Romania pursued a policy of repaying all its foreign debts which caused considerable hardships to the Romanian population. Not surprisingly at the beginning of the 1990s, Romania was one of the most impoverished countries in CEE, although not as poor as Albania.

In spite of differences in the nature and orientation of the respective regimes, Albania, Bulgaria and Romania under communism underwent similar processes of economic change involving such factors as the imposition of the pre-eminence of state-owned property and assets, the collectivization of agriculture and the promotion of heavy industry. All three countries exhibited the general features of a centrally planned command economy, with economic decisions taken by governmental bodies responsible to the leadership of the respective communist party.

All three countries were also characterized by continuity of political leadership. Enver Hoxha ruled Albania from 1944 to his death in 1985. After 1985 Hoxha's policies were maintained by his successor Ramiz Alia and Hoxha's widow (Brogan, 1990:182). In Bulgaria, Todor Zhivkov had been the *de facto* ruler from 1954 until his removal in a 'palace coup' in late 1989, whilst in Romania Ceausescu had been in power from 1965 until his execution at the very end of 1989. It was not until December 1991 that the communist regime in Albania actually collapsed. Even in Romania and Bulgaria, the demise of the regimes did not occur until 1990. In this respect the three countries were very much late adherents to the transformation process.

What was the legacy of the communist regimes in Albania, Bulgaria and Romania? The economic policies pursued under communism had left Albania and Romania in particular severely impoverished. All three countries, moreover, showed signs of distorted economic structures. The push for industrialization in countries which had been overwhelmingly agricultural before the communist take-overs often led to the creation of industries and enterprises with a political rather than an economic justification. Policies of full employment, moreover, encouraged an inefficient use of human resources. Signs of a fundamental economic crisis began to emerge in the 1980s. In Albania, economic difficulties were aggravated by lack of investment, reliance on outdated technology and a backward agricultural sector as well as the overarching isolationist position of the regime (Kume and Llaci, 2000:106).

Bulgaria, among the CEE economies, was the most highly integrated within COMECON. As well as being a major supplier of food products, Bulgaria also specialized in the production of items such as fork-lift trucks and some computer products. Overall, Bulgaria was a major beneficiary of the mechanisms developed by COMECON, including its specialization schemes. According to official statistics, Bulgaria in the late 1980s was reported as having the third highest GDP per head in CEE after the former German Democratic Republic (GDR) and Czechoslavakia (Lavigne, 1999:48). Whilst, at least for the first 25 years of its existence, it is widely accepted that the regime improved the living standards of the vast majority of the population, this was achieved by strict adherence to the Soviet model. Unlike in other COMECON countries, such as Hungary and Czechoslovakia, there was little experimentation with economic reforms. Considerations of the increasing decentralization of industry were dropped following the crushing of the Prague Spring in 1968. Proposed enterprise reforms in the 1980s, involving workers' self-management and the election of directors, caused only 'massively destructive dislocation in economic administration' (Crampton, 1997:213).

The communist regime transformed Romania from an agricultural to an industrial economy and by the 1970s the population enjoyed relative prosperity. The economy, moreover, had been a net exporter of raw materials and energy. The situation changed dramatically with Ceausescu's decision to pay off all of Romania's foreign loans by increasing exports. The 'export drive' of the 1980s required the import of raw materials and energy in order to meet industrial demand. At the same time, domestic demand for products and energy was strictly rationed in order to maximize exports. This policy placed the population under considerable hardship and the 1980s have been described as the decade of Ceausescu's 'shock therapy' (Shen, 1997).

At the time of the collapse of the communist regimes, the economies of Albania, Bulgaria and Romania were already experiencing considerable difficulties. These difficulties would, moreover, be exacerbated by the change of system. Neither the national-communist policies of the Albanian and Romanian regimes nor the heavy reliance on COMECON of the Bulgarian economy represented an adequate basis for the change to a market economy.

## External/macro issues/factors

### Economic policy and structural reforms

Following the collapse of the communist regimes and the consequent change of system, all countries implemented policies to develop market economies.

Such policies included policies relating to prices, competition, trade, public spending and monetary policy. Key issues related to the speed of implementation of these policies, i.e. whether the country should be subjected to 'shock therapy' or a more gradual transformation, and the sequencing of particular aspects of the policies. Irrespective of these issues the system change in itself represented a kind of shock therapy as the fundamental elements of the command economy were abandoned and a market system was introduced.

The stabilization packages introduced in CEE to carry out the transformation comprised a number of elements including the liberalization of prices and domestic trade; balancing of the government budget; a restrictive monetary policy; an incomes policy; and a liberalization of foreign trade (Lavigne, 1999). Price liberalization was intended to introduce transparency of costs and eliminate subsidization and cross-subsidization of goods and services. The aim of balanced governmental budgets was to contain inflation and promote efficient administration. Through restrictive monetary policies it was intended to re-establish a positive real interest rate, while incomes policies sought to inhibit wage inflation caused by employees resisting the establishment of market wages. Finally, foreign trade liberalization was proposed as a means of promoting competition and engaging in the international economy; furthermore, it assisted the determination of real exchange rates, generally by devaluation of the domestic currency (Lavigne, 1999:115).

In Bulgaria, a 'shock therapy' approach was introduced in early 1991 but implemented inadequately. In spite of a stringent monetary policy, fiscal policy lacked consistency. While many prices were liberalized in early 1991, the prices for energy and housing were still being controlled in 1993–94. Romania, on the other hand, adopted a more gradualist approach, possibly because further 'shock therapy', following the sufferings of the 1980s, would have been politically unacceptable. This approach, initiated in November 1990, resulted in ineffective credit and fiscal policies. While prices were liberalized in three stages between November 1990 and July 1991, price controls were re-imposed in 1993. Nevertheless, by 1995 all prices except those for energy had been liberalized.

With regard to the exchange rate, this remained to all intents and purposes regulated in Romania until 1997, while Bulgaria pursued a 'managed float' regime (Lavigne, 1999:131). Incomes policies in both countries, moreover, involved wage bill taxes complemented by tripartite negotiations (Romania) and collective bargaining (Bulgaria). In spite of the incomplete implementation of the adopted transformation strategy both in Bulgaria and Romania real interest rates were positive by 1994.

In Albania, the reform process did not begin in earnest until 1992 following the election victory of the Democratic Party. In a one-year programme between 1992–93 comprehensive price and exchange system reforms were implemented, coupled with fiscal and monetary control This one-year programme was followed by a three-year programme (1993–96) of further reforms.

The impact of the system change and stabilization packages manifested itself in a range of economic indicators. In all three countries GDP and industrial output fell, while consumer prices and the rate of unemployment rose. By 1995, GDP in Bulgaria and Romania was only 76 and 85 per cent, respectively, of its 1989 level. In both countries, gross industrial output had fallen to 57 per cent of its 1989 level. Moreover, consumer prices had undergone considerable annual increases in the early years of the system change, peaking at almost 340 per cent in 1991 in Bulgaria and 296 per cent in 1993 in Romania, subsequently falling to around 30 per cent in both countries by 1995. At the same time, unemployment had risen from zero to around 10 per cent of the total labour force.

The situation in Albania was somewhat different. Although Albania faced many of the problems experienced by Bulgaria and Romania, the collapse of industry drove many Albanians into unemployment or back into agriculture. By 1993, 40 per cent of the labour force was unemployed and 10 per cent of the population had emigrated (Goldman, 1997:72). However, the reform packages appeared to be working effectively and the country was regarded as one of the success stories of the East European transformation (Kume and Llaci, 2000:108). From 1993, GDP began to grow and inflation declined to 6 per cent in 1995. Nevertheless, Albania remained the poorest country in Europe.

The conditions in the three countries, however, became critical in 1996–97. Bulgaria experienced a two-year crisis with falling GDP and soaring inflation. Lavigne (1999:141–42) explains the Bulgarian crisis in terms of the impact of weaknesses insufficiently counterbalanced by assets which might have had a mitigating effect. Bulgaria's liabilities included the devastating impact of the dissolution of COMECON which resulted in Bulgaria losing most of its traditional markets; the enormity of its foreign debt burden estimated at \$12 billion (Crampton, 1997:217); the legacy of SOEs which were not privatized in order to safeguard employment and continued accordingly to be subsidized by the state-owned banks; inconsistent implementation of macro-economic policy, in particular regarding the base interest rate which resulted in a push to inflation, a loss in public confidence and a run on the Bulgarian currency.

The situation in Romania in 1997, while not as drastic as in Bulgaria, displayed many of the symptoms of the Bulgarian crisis, with declining GDP and rising inflation. Even more dramatic in some respects than the Bulgarian events was the collapse of the Albanian pyramid schemes in early 1997. While pyramid schemes were not a purely Albanian phenomenon, by 1996 they affected the whole country and accounted for 60 per cent of GDP (Kume and Llaci, 2000:116). The numerous pyramid schemes sucked in the population's savings, assets and remittances from abroad. The massive expansion of these schemes was fuelled amongst other factors by the general poverty of the population, lack of knowledge of the market system and insufficient measures by official bodies to counteract the influence of the schemes. The collapse of the pyramid schemes resulted in many Albanians losing all their savings and investments and the country came close to a state of complete social breakdown.

As a direct consequence of the events of 1996–97, the three countries re-intensified the transformation process. In Bulgaria and Romania, price liberalization was completed in 1997. Moreover, the currency was more closely aligned to international exchange rates, with Bulgaria linking the lev to the German mark and Romania letting the exchange rate float (Lavigne, 1999:131). In Albania, in order to strengthen control, the government tightened monetary and fiscal policies and proceeded with structural reforms. The GDP rose again in 1998 and inflation was brought under control, although unemployment remained high. The economy, moreover, continued to benefit extensively from the remittances of Albanians working abroad.

The first decade of transformation had proved extremely challenging for the three countries. The initial system shock had been followed by a brief period of recovery. The crises of 1996–97 served as reminders that trans-formation needed to be carried out profoundly and consistently and, since the crises, there is some evidence of improving economic performance. However, Bulgaria and Romania were still a long way off achieving the level of GDP registered in 1989 (in 2000 in Bulgaria GDP was 70 per cent of that of 1989, in Romania 77 per cent (EBRD, 2001a:167)). Albania, whilst having achieved the 1989 level of GDP, remained the poorest country in Europe. A further consequence of a decade of transformation was the massive shrinking of the industrial sector, accompanied by an expansion of services. The situation was particularly striking in Albania where agriculture overtook the industrial sector and in 2001 accounted for 49 per cent of GDP (World Bank, 2002).

The implementation of new economic policies following the system change also involved a range of structural reforms in order to create the framework and conditions for a market economy. Of particular significance were previously mentioned policies on prices, wages, interest and exchange rates as well as competition policy and laws on foreign direct investment. A further significant aspect of the reforms was the restructuring of the banking system to create a two-tier system. In Bulgaria and Romania, banking reform was undertaken in the early 1990s. Further developments in the financial sector included the establishment of stock exchanges in Sofia (1992), Bucharest (1995) and Tirana (1996), although the volume of their activity remained discrete.

The issue of monetary policy and banking reform were in many respects pivotal to the transformation process. The maintenance of traditional relationships between enterprises, banks and government generally resulted in the continuing subsidization of inefficient SOEs by state-owned banks drawing on the resources of public finance. The failure to eliminate 'soft budgets' (Kornai, 1992) was a primary cause of the Bulgarian and Romanian crises. The need to contain public spending and use it efficiently and effectively has, moreover, had to be balanced against other requirements such as the provision of social welfare, even if only at a relatively low level. Strict monetary policies were clearly difficult to implement in conditions of a shrinking, or only slowly growing, economic base and substantial external debt. Even though Bulgaria is an extreme case, in 2000 the total national debt was equivalent to 86.5 per cent of GDP (World Bank, 2002).

## *Privatization*

The privatization of state-owned assets has been considered the primary mechanism for achieving the transformation from a command to a market economy (Lavigne, 1999:162). In Albania, Bulgaria and Romania the process of privatization has been slow, influenced in part by the legacy of large and inefficient SOEs. Whilst some legislation was passed in the early 1990s in all countries, even the privatization of small enterprises proceeded at a slow pace in Bulgaria and Romania (Lavigne, 1999:123). In Albania, while privatization in agriculture, housing and the SME sector made rapid progress, this was not the case with the SOEs (Hashi and Xhillari, 1997).

Nevertheless, the private sector soon out-performed the state-owned sector in terms of contribution to GDP. By 1997, 75 per cent of Albania's GDP, 60 per cent of Romania's and 50 per cent of Bulgaria's originated from the private sector. However, these figures are as much a reflection of the decline in output of SOEs as of the growth of the private sector. Certainly, by 1997 small-scale privatization had been virtually completed in all three countries (in Albania the process was actually completed). However, the privatization of large-scale enterprises remained problematic. Albania was still very much at the beginning of the process, while in Bulgaria and Romania less than 50 per cent of state assets had been privatized. Where privatizations had occurred there was substantial insider ownership and ineffective corporate governance mechanisms (EBRD, 1998). Large-scale privatization was also impeded by the limited interest on the part of potential foreign investors.

In all three countries, the process of large-scale privatization was revived and intensified after the 1996–97 crises. In 1998 the Albanian government initiated a large-scale privatization programme in the telecommunications, electricity, petroleum, gas, transport, banking and insurance sectors. Some successes have been registered with a Greek–Norwegian consortium acquiring Albanian Mobile Communications and Vodafone obtaining a second licence. Moreover, a Turkish bank acquired a majority shareholding in the National Commercial Bank (Studio Legale Tonucci e Economisti Associati, 2002). In spite of these acquisitions large-scale privatization remains problematic.

Similar difficulties face Bulgaria where the relative smallness of the market as well as the kind of industrial assets available for privatization had not tended to be particularly attractive for potential investors. As the Bulgarian general manager of a Bulgarian-foreign joint venture commented: 'The atmosphere is difficult, you must be very brave and tough to invest in Bulgaria' (Koparanova, 1998:38).

In Romania, the privatization process, even after 1997, has been beset by lack of clarity between coalition partners. Even though the process was speeded up and some significant privatizations occurred in the telecommunications and banking sectors, little progress was made in privatizing the large state monopolies, the *regies autonomes*.

## New firm development

The development and, in particular, the creation of small businesses have been considered as central elements of the transformation process (Bateman, 1997:222). The development of small businesses was seen as a means of counteracting the preponderance of the large SOEs, fostering more flexible markets and creating employment opportunities.

As mentioned in the previous section, small-scale privatization was to all intents and purposes completed by 1997 in Albania, Bulgaria and Romania. However, continuing high levels of unemployment indicate that the growth of small businesses has been insufficient to absorb employees shed by large enterprises. Small firm development appears driven, nevertheless, more by the decline of established companies and the consequent rise in unemployment (the so-called Birmingham model) than by entrepreneurs responding to opportunities created by the system change (the Budapest model) (Bartlett and Prašnikar, 1995). Certainly, small businesses and entrepreneurs have not been encouraged by bureaucratic inflexibility, lack of finance, difficulties with property acquisition and limited government support.

The European Commission (Commission of the European Communities, 2001a, 2001b) has noted the ongoing difficulties experienced by SMEs in Bulgaria and Romania, whilst acknowledging that the situation has improved. Nevertheless it reports that there are still significant administrative barriers in Bulgaria to SME creation and management. Moreover, the business environment in Romania is described as hostile and unfavourable to SMEs (Nicolescu, 2001). Not surprisingly, considerable business activity is conducted in the informal sector.

As Kume and Llaci (2000) have noted with regard to Albania, greater state intervention is required to support new firm creation and development, including financial support; organizational support in the form of training and consultancy; and institutional support through establishing a positive legal framework and infrastructure.

## Capital and labour

The relationship between capital and labour evolved as a consequence of the system change. Under the communist regimes the trades unions, as representatives of the labour force, had been closely linked to the ruling communist parties and involved in the development of policies and enterprise management. Proposed reforms in Bulgaria in the 1980s had included workers' self-management and the election of enterprise directors. Ideologically at least, labour, the working class, was considered the pre-eminent social grouping in the communist regimes.

Privatization, obviously, saw the re-emergence of capital as a significant economic and social force, even though the outcomes of privatization included widespread examples of insider buy-outs involving both managers and employees. In Romania, for example, management and employee buy-outs were in the initial years of transformation the most common form of privatization. Consequently, labour issues are not always necessarily clearly polarized between capital and labour as both parties had a common interest in extracting as much financial and other support as possible from governmental sources. In addition the representatives of the employer associations often failed to establish a united approach. In Romania incomes policy allowed for tripartite negotiations on nominal wage levels and in Bulgaria collective bargaining (Lavigne, 1999:131). Nevertheless, there have still been substantial company closures and job losses. In Bulgaria, for example, these have been particularly high (Edwards and Lawrence, 2000:97).

The system change in the respective countries witnessed the establishment of independent trade unions. In Albania trade union activity has been limited historically and was subservient politically to the communist regime. There are now approximately 50 trade unions. Around half of the unions are members of three trade union confederations, of which the Union of Independent Trade Unions of Albania (UITUA) and the Albanian Trade Union Confederation (ATUC) are the largest (Llaci and Kume, 2002). In Bulgaria most trade union members belong to CITUB (Confederation of Independent Trade Unions of Bulgaria), the former communist trade union. The CITUB claims to have around 3 million members (*The Europa World Year Book 2002*, 2002).

There has been a greater fragmentation of trade union membership in Romania. The largest union is the National Trade Union Bloc, established in 1991 with *ca* 3.4 million members (*The Europa World Year Book 2001*, 2001). Other unions with sizeable membership include Alpha Cartel, established in 1990 and with 1.1 million members and the Confederation of Democratic Trade Unions of Romania, established in 1994 and with 640,000 members.

Although the trade unions, particularly in Bulgaria and Romania, have been able to exert a certain political pressure and mitigate somewhat the impact of the system change on their members and the population in general, the unions have not been able to resist the pressures of the system change, including increasing unemployment and declining real wages. According to Martin (1999:130) the relationship between capital and labour has been characterized to a large degree by 'labour quiescence'.

### Regional and global links

The system change and collapse of COMECON have resulted in the development of new global and regional relationships. Romania's independent foreign policy had caused it to join the WTO in 1971 and the IMF in 1972. Bulgaria, because of its acquiescence to Soviet dominance, joined the IMF only in 1990 and subsequently became a full member of the WTO. Albania meanwhile joined the IMF, World Bank and the European Bank for Reconstruction and Development (EBRD) in 1991.

The main aspiration of Bulgaria and Romania, however, is to join the European Union. Both countries signed association agreements with the European Union in 1993 but are not among the first group of former communist states to gain accession. Nevertheless, both countries are working towards meeting the comprehensive conditions considered necessary for EU membership. The significance of EU membership for these two countries is indicated by the extent of trading relations between the respective countries and the 15 member states of the European Union. By 1997 trade with the European Union accounted for 56 per cent of Romania's exports and 52 per cent of its imports (Commission of the European Communities, 1999b). In the case of Bulgaria the figures were 43 and 37 per cent, respectively (Commission of the European Communities, 1999a).

As both countries are unlikely to be granted accession in the near future, other closer relationships are of significance. Romania joined CEFTA in 1997 and Bulgaria in 1998. Membership of CEFTA liberalized trade between the two countries and former members of COMECON in Central Europe (CEFTA was founded in 1991 by Poland, Hungary and Czechoslovakia).

Bulgaria, moreover, has entered into bi-lateral trading agreements with neighbouring countries such as Turkey and Macedonia and has been, with Romania, a keen promoter of a Black Sea trading area, of which Albania was also a founder member. Although the countries have not found it easy to establish new regional and global links since the system change, the reorientation of trade provides substantial evidence of changing relationships. To take the case of Bulgaria, in 1990 trade with the former USSR accounted for 50 per cent of trading turnover (Kolev and Pencheva, 2001:379). By 1999, 50 per cent of Bulgaria's trade was with the European Union (Kolev and Pencheva, 2001:386).

In comparison to Bulgaria and Romania, Albania's economic position has been extremely precarious and the country has depended considerably on financial support from the IMF, the European Union and the United States. Since the mid-1990s imports have been far in excess of exports and the balance of payments situation would have been far worse had it not been for the substantial remittances of Albanians working abroad. These remittances annually exceeded the value of Albanian exports over the period 1995–2001. Albania's main trading partners are Italy and Greece which accounted respectively for 72 and 12 per cent of exports and 33 and 29 per cent of imports in the first nine months of 2001 (Studio Legale Tonucci e Economisti Associati, 2002:5).

### Foreign direct investment

Foreign direct investment has been regarded as one of the key drivers of post-communist transformation as it brings in capital, a wide range of expertise, skills and manpower into former command economies. In all three countries, the levels of FDI have been very low when compared with the average for Central and Eastern Europe and the Baltic states (Table 3.1).

A long catalogue of reasons has been adduced to explain the low attractiveness of the three economies with regard to FDI. In general companies have identified more attractive investment opportunities elsewhere in the region and globally. More specifically, the three countries have been slow to develop an environment conducive to foreign investors because of political ambivalence towards transformation and foreign investment and, particularly in the case of Albania, considerable social upheaval and unrest. What appears to have developed is a vicious cycle of mutually reinforcing insufficient transformation and limited foreign investment.

In spite of a favourable legislative and fiscal framework, incidences of FDI in Bulgaria have been few and at a relatively low level, with 65 per cent of investments in the early 1990s below $2000. Although Germany and Belgium have been leading investors in volume terms, a significant proportion of investment has come from neighbouring Greece and Turkey (Bobeva and Bozhkov, 1996: Koźmiński and Yip, 2000). According to the results of a survey of managers in Bulgaria, Hungary, Poland and Slovenia (Marinov and Marinova, 2001), only a small percentage of Bulgarian managers admitted to the significance of FDI in the transformation of the economy, although the impact at company level appeared to be greater. In Romania too, FDI has been attracted in relatively small amounts and from a variety of countries. Up to 1997 the largest single investor by far had been the South Korean company Daewoo (Koźmiński and Yip, 2000).

However, Albania has attracted the lowest FDI per capita since 1989 than any other CEE country except Bosnia and Herzegovina and Yugoslavia. There has been some foreign investment in banking and telecommunications. One of the principal sources of FDI has been Italy, with involvement in about 500 firms in the fashion industry, construction, food and beverages and other light industries as well as in the Italo-Albanian Bank, established in 1994 as a joint venture between the Bank of Rome and the local National Commercial Bank. The employment impact of Italian involvement is, however, modest as

*Table 3.1* Foreign direct investment in Albania, Bulgaria and Romania (US$ m)

|  | *Cumulative FDI – inflows per capita 1989–2000* | *Cumulative FDI – inflows per capita 2000* |
|---|---|---|
| Albania | 161 | 27 |
| Bulgaria | 388 | 101 |
| Romania | 303 | 45 |
| Central and Eastern Europe and the Baltic states | 782 | 143 |

Source: EBRD, 2001a:18.

the 500 firms have only around 20,000 employees (Studio Legale Tonucci e Economisti Associati, 2002:15).

## Internal/micro issues/factors

### *Organizational restructuring*

The process of corporate restructuring, which is crucial for the development of efficient enterprises capable of competing under market conditions, has been held back by the slow pace of privatization and indecisiveness on the part of the political elite as well as by a range of other negative factors. On the one hand, vested interests, including sections of the political elite, enterprise managers and employees were opposed to measures which would reduce their influence over and access to economic resources. Furthermore, there was concern that a rigorous approach to corporate restructuring would result, as a large proportion of enterprises were barely viable, in economic collapse, massive unemployment and social unrest. On the other hand, in all three countries expectations were unsustainably high after the fall of communism and politicians were often reluctant to face the reality of the situation and even less so to communicate it to their electorates. The situation was compounded in Romania by the fact that the population had already suffered considerably in the 1980s under Ceausescu's own 'shock therapy' (Shen, 1997). Consequently, there was an even greater reluctance in Romania to impose harsh, even if necessary, measures in terms of corporate restructuring.

If we apply Pučko's (2001) stages model of corporate recovery to former and still state-owned enterprises in the three countries, the overwhelming majority are still experiencing latent or acute crisis or at best are undergoing some form of revitalization. In Bulgaria, the process of corporate restructuring proceeded at a fitful pace throughout the 1990s, at the end of which decade official sources were still pronouncing on accelerating the privatization process. In fact, the first SOE was not privatized until 1993. Even though SOEs were being decentralized and broken up into smaller entities, thus creating a larger number of firms and potentially a more competitive business environment, privatization itself was carried out only very slowly. The rising private sector share of GDP, which had reached 50 per cent by the middle of 1997 (EBRD, 1998:12), reflected as much the decline of overall economic activity as the expansion of the private sector comprising former SOEs and new private companies.

Corporate restructuring in Bulgaria was also held back by the limited number of acquisitions by and joint ventures with leading international companies which could act as exemplars of corporate restructuring. In fact, as mentioned previously, during the early 1990s the amounts invested by foreign investors tended to be extremely low.

In Romania, the process of corporate restructuring was similarly held back by a range of inherited factors. The continuity of the political elite and its indecisiveness were contributory factors. Moreover, the highly centralized nature of the Romanian economy and the existence of the large state monopolies acted as further barriers to a rapid privatization and restructuring. Even when privatizations were carried out, there was frequently evidence of abuse of privilege, the granting of political favours and of managers exploiting their positions and knowledge as insiders to acquire the shares of enterprises which were deemed to have a good probability of success in the post-communist environment (Shen, 1997:133). As in the case of Bulgaria, the limited volume of foreign investment left corporate restructuring largely in the hands of domestic players. Enterprise managers were thus able to continue using practices which had been deployed under the former regime. Such an approach was feasible, at least in the short term, because of the continuity of the political elite. Managers who had survived the system change continued to seek support from their former ministries either to gain tangible benefits such as critical inputs, subsidies and credits or to devise means to survive on the market, for example, job-reduction schemes and the general resurrection of old enterprise networks (Stan, 1997).

A considerable further barrier to corporate restructuring were managers themselves, although they were only one of a range of internal barriers to change (Vlachoutsicos, 1999). Moreover, the larger the size of the company and the greater its significance to the national economy, the greater the resistance to change (Catana *et al.*, 1999). In general, although company restructuring has taken a number of forms (Kelemen and Hristov, 1998), it has been largely motivated by the necessity to survive (that is, the early stages of Pučko's (2001) model). Furthermore, Kelemen (1999:202) has argued that no more than 10 per cent of Romanian companies have embarked on any significant form of economic restructuring.

While data on Albania are limited, there is no evidence to indicate that corporate restructuring there has proceeded at a faster pace than in Bulgaria and Romania. It is indeed probable that the corporate restructuring process has been held back by the small size of the economy, its history of isolation, limited interest on the part of foreign investors and the political difficulties and civil unrest experienced in the 1990s. However, there is some indication that the privatization process is being accelerated and foreign investment is finding its way into some of the larger Albanian enterprises, even though 80 per cent of foreign-invested and joint-venture enterprises involve either Italian or Greek capital (Slaveski and Nedanovski, 2002). Much of the overall foreign investment, however, is provided by national governments or international organizations rather than from the private sector.

Regular updatings on the situation in Bulgaria and Romania are provided by the respective European Commision Regular Reports on Progress Towards Accession (Commission of the European Communities, 2001a, 2001b). In the case of Bulgaria, according to the 2001 Report, progress has been made with respect to privatization, although the slow development of the banking sector has not contributed to a rapid restructuring of industries and services.

Moreover, continuing control by the Bulgarian authorities of privatized companies, by imposing company-specific obligations, has continued to slow down enterprise restructuring.

With regard to Romania, the European Commission's assessment is even more gloomy. State involvement in the economy remains strong, particularly in the banking sector, and the approach to privatization continues to fluctuate. All in all, privatization and restructuring are considered as remaining areas in which much work still needs to be done.


### Corporate strategies and alliances

In spite of the system change, numerous factors have hindered the development of corporate strategies in the three countries of this chapter, including continuing government involvement, the inadequate creation of market economies and the slow process of privatization. Such impediments are further compounded by facets of the national culture. Catana and Catana (1999), for example, have identified within Romanian culture a time-horizon focused predominantly on the present which clearly inhibits the development of corporate strategies. With a temporal horizon focused largely on the present, Romanian managers have only a limited preoccupation with future events and it is consequently difficult for managers to take a longer term view of situations.

One strategy adopted by still state-owned companies, as mentioned previously, was to exploit or revive networks of cooperation from the former system. Such a strategy assisted short-term survival but was not likely to remain effective as privatization progressed and governments withdrew from exerting direct control on the operation of companies. However, such an approach remained viable for longer in the three countries than in the Central European countries.

Companies, furthermore, adopted most of Pučko's Stage I strategies, including workforce and output reduction, reorientation to new markets (because of the collapse of COMECON), cost reduction, management buy-outs, joint ventures and other forms of cooperation with foreign partners – albeit limited – and some organizational changes.

There is also some evidence of Stage II changes aimed at revitalizing the enterprise. In Bulgaria, Peev (1999) found that enterprises were undertaking product and marketing improvements, including identifying new customers and markets. These strategies were found among all four types of firms in his study, that is, non-transformed SOEs, corporatized enterprises (i.e. enterprises awaiting privatization), privatized enterprises with so-called perverse behaviour and privatized enterprises with market-oriented behaviour.

In Albania, moreover, many small businessed are acting as sub-contractors for Italian companies, providing semi-finished goods for completion in Italy. Such activity is particularly evident in the fashion sector (Studio Legale Tonucci e Economisti Associati, 2002). Other Stage II strategies implemented include divestment of peripheral areas and focus on core business areas, divestment of assets, preparation for and implementation of privatization itself and productivity improvement.

There is evidence, moreover, that in spite of some reluctance to adopt effective corporate strategies, external circumstances may be sufficiently strong as to force strategy development. Vatamanu (1998) and Gavril and Vatamanu (1998) have investigated the transformation of Romania's Galati steel complex, the country's largest steel producer with over 36,000 employees in the mid-1990s. The transformation of the complex was primarily driven by external factors such as the tariff relationship with the European Union and Romania's aspiration to join the European Union. Priorities of the transformation were the improvement of the enterprise's financial structure and an upgrading of the technology used to produce steel. The respective authors note in particular the modernization of technology and the establishment of a number of joint ventures with foreign companies in the areas of production and sales.

The Galati steel complex was eventually sold to a foreign investor in 2001. By then, employment at the complex had dropped below 30,000 and further job losses were forecast. The significance of the privatization was that the steel complex was responsible for 80 per cent of the losses generated by Romania's SOEs and was a major local employer. Sixty per cent of the population of Galati and its surrounding area were directly or indirectly dependent on the complex for employment (Privatization Authority and State Participation Administration, 2001; Connolly, 2002).

## Functional strategies

### *Human resource management*

The HRM concept is only gradually being absorbed and implemented and the management of human resources is still strongly influenced by traditional personnel management practices, although foreign companies are bringing with them new approaches. Key issues in the HRM area are over-staffing and training (Koźmiński and Yip, 2000). Reduction of the workforce has to be undertaken cautiously to overcome trade union concerns and forestall strikes and even civil unrest. Romanian managers may also feel reluctant to dismiss employees for social reasons (Edwards and Lawrence, 2000). Even when Romanian managers have sought to implement Western HRM, the use of HRM has been fragmentary and *ad hoc* and has often conflicted with employees' cultural values (Heintz, 2002). Some larger companies soften the impact of redundancy by providing retraining and outplacement facilities. Training, moreover, is regarded as necessary to overcome the continuing influences of attitudes and practices inherited from the former system and develop a more market-oriented mentality. Many employees also lack broader management skills. Not surprisingly, Michailova and Hollinshead (1998) found that HRM practices in a Bulgarian enterprise they investigated were 'a mosaic of policies, some of which were established in the previous era, sometimes masqueraded in a more modern guise, and others representing pragmatic adjustment to the new situation'. Moreover, Vatchkova (2002) found that the adoption of HRM practices has not been consistent and there has even been a regression in some areas.

## Marketing

The development of marketing has not proved an easy process. In Romania, for example, marketing and sales have been regarded by managers as low-status activities (Lascu *et al.*, 1997:188) while in Bulgaria there is evidence of a certain resistance to marketing (Koźmiński and Yip, 2000). Nevertheless, a more modern approach to marketing has been driven by the presence of foreign companies on the respective national markets.

## Operations

Production was regarded as the major function under the former system and continues to play a significant role. Many managers have a technical background and are regarded as possessing good technical skills. Bulgaria, moreover, inherited a strong base in information technology as a result of the division of labour within COMECON. This foundation in technical skills is, however, undermined by the widespread incidence of obsolete technology, although many companies have attained various ISO certifications, while those companies undertaking sub-contracting work for multinational companies have had to meet even more stringent requirements.

## Finance

The development of financial strategies has been held back by the slow pace of transformation. In all countries, soft-budget constraints persisted throughout the 1990s. As a consequence of poorly developed financial and equity markets, lax bankruptcy legislation and the persistence of practices such as inter-enterprise debt, financial discipline has in many instances been weak and has hindered the development of what might be considered real financial strategies.

## Research and development

General conditions have not encouraged development of R&D except in cases of considerable external pressure such as the need to meet sub-contracting obligations and raise product quality.

### Organizational structures and cultures

There have been some general trends in the development of organizational structures. First, there has been increasing decentralization and fragmentation as central planning authorities relinquished their grip and large SOEs were 'unbundled', normally prior to privatization. As has already been discussed, this process has been relatively slow. Second, enterprises have amended their traditional, predominantly functional structures to incorporate new marketing and sales departments.

The development of organizational cultures has to a large extent paralleled the privatization and corporate restructuring process. Where companies have continued to be shielded from the impact of market forces, with state subsidies and other forms of governmental interference, the corporate culture has changed little since the system change. In companies exposed to market conditions and competition, a more dynamic, market-oriented culture has emerged. According to Kelemen and Hristov (1998) only a small number of Romanian companies had enacted some form of cultural change, while Dumitrescu's (1997) study indicated that pressures for culture change were more likely to be present in companies run by foreign managers. In Bulgaria, Todeva (1996) found that privatized companies and new entrepreneurial companies were increasingly driven by the profit motive, whilst the cultures of SOEs were influenced more by the security-seeking behaviour of managers and employees.

### Management styles

In all three countries, management styles are predominantly authoritarian and autocratic. These styles reflect both the legacy of communism but also aspects of the respective national cultures. Michailova (1996) refers to a traditional Bulgarian characteristic of an inflexible attitude to power. Several authors (Michailova, 1996; Todeva, 1996; Koparanova, 1998) have exemplified this inflexibility by reference to managers' views and use of information. Information had been a key source of power for communist officials and remained so for managers in all types of enterprise after the system change. Moreover, managers both retained and manipulated information resulting in a management style which was authoritarian and, at least to a degree, manipulative (Aaby *et al.*, 1997). However, while the autocratic style of management is generally accepted by older employees, younger employees expressed a preference for a more consultative and consensual style (Reeves-Ellington, 1998).

There is, however, evidence that management styles are becoming more differentiated according to company type (Todeva, 2000). Managers in state-owned companies have remained generally passive and reserved, even if more adaptable. In contrast, managers in privatized companies have frequently developed more entrepreneurial attitudes and patterns of behaviour and, compared to their counterparts in the state sector, are likely to be more dynamic, proactive and risk-taking (Aaby *et al.*, 1997).

In Romania too, management style tends to be autocratic, with superiors expecting obedience from their subordinates and stifling individual initiative. This approach is particularly pronounced in private companies where owners, who are often also the managing director, exert their personal power and authority (Catana and Catana, 1996). Kelemen (1999), moreover, paints a picture of Romanian managers needing to know and control everything. Not surprisingly, Romanian managers are perceived more as leaders than professionals and consequently are expected to meet their employees' expectations in areas such as providing job security for employees and employment for family and friends (Gehmann, 1996).

There is some evidence, however, that the management style is beginning to change. Olaru (1998) has identified a group of managers who are more conciliatory in their approach, even though they could be tough and inflexible if the need arose. Change was also noted among Romanian managers working for foreign companies as they responded to the expectations of their employers (Dumitrescu, 1997).

Few data are available on management in Albania. Nevertheless, there are grounds for assuming that the management style is, as in Bulgaria and Romania, predominantly autocratic because of the experience of communism and the influence of the traditional hierarchical and strongly patriarchal structure of Albanian society (Doja, 2000), although managers in the old SOE investigated by Lee and Luthans (2000) expressed a preference for a democratic style.

*Management development*

All three countries faced a manifest managerial deficit as a consequence of the system change. Managers tended under the former system to be well educated, but largely from a technical viewpoint. In Romania, for example, 68 per cent of managers were qualified in engineering and a further 21 per cent in economics. Moreover, as noted by Dumitrescu (1997), managers attached a greater importance to knowledge than to skills.

There was a substantial need for managerial training and retraining in the 1990s, especially in areas related to the new market environment. Part of the 'knowledge gap' was filled by individual initiative but much was provided and supported from outside the countries themselves, for example, by the European Union and other international bodies as well as by foreign universities. In Bulgaria, for instance, new private universities were founded such as the American University and the New Bulgarian University, providing franchized courses from the United States and Western Europe (Koźmiński and Yip, 2000). Similar developments have taken place in Romania, where around 20 private universities, such as the Romanian American University in Bucharest and the Danubius University in Galati, are in operation. In

Albania, where there are as yet no private universities, management development has been spearheaded by foreign providers such as the University of Nebraska-Lincoln (Lee and Luthans, 2000; Lee and Trimi, 2001).

The process of developing a sufficient cadre of well trained managers is likely to require substantial investment and time. Many managers in these countries were educated and trained under the former system and the general experience since the system change has been characterized by a widespread persistence of traditional attitudes and behaviours in the political, economic and social spheres. Catana and Catana (2002) have indicated that there has been little progress in management development in Romania since the system change and that Romanian managers pay little more than lip-service to the concept of market orientation. Such factors, irrespective of the volume of advanced Western management education provided, slow down the development of what may be regarded as a modern managerial group.

## Outcome and performance: empirical evidence

As the previous sections have argued, the transformation of the economy and of management has been relatively slow, especially when compared with that of the countries of Central Europe and the Baltic states. Nevertheless, there has been development with regard to privatization and corporate restructuring, the establishment of new firms, FDI and integration into the regional and global economy and management styles. The internal drive to achieve such changes has, however, been relatively limited.

The evidence in fact suggests that change is more likely to result from external pressures, such as foreign ownership of companies, and the aspiration to join the European Union, with countries responding to externally set targets.

## Evaluation and conclusion

Albania, Bulgaria and Romania are representative of a group of countries which have experienced severe problems in the process of transition to a market economy (Kraft, 1999). Developments since the collapse of communism have been uneven, although there has been evidence of an increased urgency to undertake and implement reforms since the 1997 crises. One contributory factor for the severity of the problems has been the initial conditions prevailing in the countries concerned, supporting Stark's (1992) concept of 'path dependence'. A combination of rigid economic structures and limited exposure to reform created a legacy of national economies with considerable distortions from an economic point of view. These unfavourable initial conditions were not assisted by a general policy direction of protection and discouragement (World Bank, 2002) which held back the privatization of SOEs and the imposition of overall financial discipline. At the same time, insufficient encouragement was given to new and privatized enterprises to operate effectively under competitive market conditions.

The development of the economies of the three countries was further hampered by events outside their control such as the conflicts engendered by the collapse of Yugoslavia which deprived the countries of trading opportunities with part of their natural hinterland. In Bulgaria's case, the situation was further exacerbated by the Gulf War, as a result of which Bulgaria sustained considerable financial losses as Iraq had been a significant trading partner.

Furthermore, economic policy has not always been appropriately defined or implemented and necessary structural reforms have evolved only slowly. Privatization of SOEs has still to be completed and has detracted attention from supporting new and privatized companies which represent the more productive sectors of the respective economies.

Conditions in the three countries have consequently been generally unattractive for foreign investors. Voinea (2002) has argued that FDI has had only a limited impact on the Romanian economy and, as a result, the Romanian economy is insufficiently globalized (Postelnicu and Postelnicu, 2002). Mocearov (2001) and Bodea *et al.* (2002) have also commented that Romania and Bulgaria are no more than members of a peripheral 'club' of the European Union. The above comments apply more or less equally to the countries studied in this chapter, with the further observation that Albania is overwhelmingly dependent on economic links with Italy and Greece and on the remittances of Albanian emigrants often working illegally in these two countries. The degree of extroversion of the respective economies, already high in the case of Albania, is likely to increase if domestic opportunities fail to materialize. Emigration, however, is just one facet of the social problems – to which unemployment and poverty must be added – affecting these countries. Even though the European Commission has mooted 2007 as a possible date for Bulgaria's and Romania's entry into the European Union, this appears optimistic in view of the economic situation in these countries (*The Economist*, 22.11.2003). For example, GDP per head is considerably lower – at below $2000 – than that of other prospective entrants and way below the EU average of $21,675 (Evans-Pritchard, 2002).

At the enterprise level, moreover, much still needs to be done to establish efficient and competitive companies. Until competitive markets are brought about, companies will be able to continue resorting to uncompetitive and, in some cases, corrupt behaviours in order to survive. Within companies, too, numerous issues still need to be addressed, including that of corporate governance and transparency of conduct and operations. Referring to Bulgaria, Peev (2002) has described the situation as '"crony capitalism" characterized by a lack of appropriate capital market institutions and ownership objectives and behaviours inappropriate to a market economy'. More generally, mentality barriers to change need to be overcome (Muço, 1997).

Will the combination of initial conditions and subsequent inappropriate and ineffective policies condemn the respective countries to remain in the so-called 'Valley of Tears' (Peng, 2000) noted in Chapter 1, that is, in a situation which, according to the statistical evidence, has not yet recovered to the position of 1989–90? Is it possible to conceive of failure within the transformation process? A more optimistic view would be that, in spite of the relatively slow pace of transformation in the three countries, progress has, nevertheless, been made but that the process of transformation needs to be accelerated. There is some evidence that this has been happening following the 1997 crises, for example in the area of macroeconomic stabilization, even though developments have still been slow. It could be argued furthermore that the initial conditions were so unfavourable that the transformation achieved so far, albeit limited, has been considerable.

A further positive sign has been the moves to increase regional cooperation through organizations such as the Black Sea trading area and the cessation of hostilities in the former Yugoslavia could give greater impetus to such a development. Regional cooperation could stimulate not only the respective economies but also counterbalance over-reliance on the European Union.

All in all, however, after a decade of transformation, the evaluation of developments so far is hardly glowing. Considerable reforms are still required to develop competitive markets and, more generally, social infrastructures and mental attitudes to support such markets. With the collapse of communism, high expectations were raised which, unfortunately, have not yet been fulfilled for the vast majority of inhabitants. This does not mean that they wish to return to the former system but that the experience of post-communism has been a difficult experience. There is little indication, moreover, that future developments, at least in the medium term, will result in the general fulfilment of the expectations which emerged with the system change.

# 4 Russia

## The hard road from *perestroika*

## Introduction

Russia, measuring just over 17 million square kilometres, stretches from the Arctic in the north to the Kazakh, Mongolian and Chinese borders in the south, from the Baltic enclave around Kaliningrad in the west to around 100 kilometres from both Alaska and the northern Japanese island of *Hokkaido* in the east. Russia thus covers extensive areas of both Europe and Asia.

Transformation of the Russian economy turned out to be a much more difficult and painful process as compared to other Eastern European countries. Russia has had to go through not just one transformation but three: the country physically has changed with the collapse of the USSR, with the other 14 republics leaving the common economic and political space; the country's economic system had to be changed from a centrally planned to a market economy; and the political system had also to be changed from an authoritarian communist system to a democratic one.

It looks now that the easiest part of this complicated three-dimensional process was to change the political system. The belief that the communist system could deliver the prosperity that had been promised for more than 70 years, died some time under Brezhnev's rule. Even though there is still a strong communist party, the general feeling in society is that there is no real alternative but to follow the path of market reforms.

The collapse of COMECON and disintegration of the Soviet Union had a more profound and long-lasting impact on the Russian economy. Divided between different countries, mostly monopolistic producers found themselves without their traditional markets and suppliers. The reorientation of industries to the western markets was impossible due to the low competitiveness of the Russian products and the total absence of a system of credits. The situation has not changed much since the early 1990s and the Russian Federation's main exports now, as always in the past, are raw materials.

Another factor which made the Russian transition more difficult than in other East European countries was that the Russian economy was structured in much more complicated ways than the economy of other countries in transition (Poletaev, 1998:19). This difference is most obvious in industry, where three sectors could be identified: civil manufacturing of industrial products, export of raw materials and the military industrial complex, including scientific research. These sectors entered transformation with different markets, different sources of finance, and different ideas about the way a liberal economy should look. The civilian industries were hit hardest by the opening of the Russian economy, as they were the least competitive. Production by the military industrial complex also shrank six-fold.

## Historical background

The origins of a Russian state date back to the latter part of the ninth century, with its capital in Kiev, and had been preceded by a process of conversion to Byzantine Christianity (Obolensky, 1971:180–4). By the early thirteenth century, the state had declined and succumbed to the Golden Horde of Genghis Khan. The Mongols ruled Russia for around 150 years before Ivan I was able to free the country from Mongol rule. In the fifteenth and sixteenth centuries the centre of power moved to Moscow.

Under Ivan II in the sixteenth century Russia expanded eastwards, taking Kazan and Astrakhan, and into Siberia. The founding dynasty of the Ruriks was extinguished at the end of the sixteenth century and from 1613 Russia was rules by the Romanovs. Under Peter the Great (1689–1725) and Catherine the Great (1762–96) Russia continued to expand and experienced a process of modernization. Peter the Great gained access to the Baltic coast and built the new city of St Petersburg, using European expertise and skills and moving Russia's centre of power away from Moscow. Catherine the Great promoted education, agriculture and commerce and brought the Crimea and parts of Poland under Russian control The Napoleonic Wars and their aftermath confirmed Russia as a leading European power.

Russia in the nineteenth century was a vast empire characterized by extensive poverty and inequality. Serfdom was not abolished until 1863 and the nineteenth century saw the rise of various movements aimed at overthrowing the tsar. Although large, Russia also had fundamental weaknesses which were made manifest by Russia's defeat in the Russo-Japanese War of 1904–5.

Continuing domestic unrest, limited reforms and participation in the First World War created circumstances seized by the communists under Lenin to depose the tsar in 1917 and set the foundations for a communist state. In 1922, the Union of Soviet Socialist Republics was formally established.

The Soviet Union (as its predecessor the Russian Empire) was a multi-ethnic, multi-religious state although Orthodox Russians represented the overwhelming majority of the population. However, nationality itself was not a significant issue (Stalin and numerous other leading figures of the Soviet Union were not ethnic Russians).

The communists, first under Lenin, then under Stalin, transformed the Soviet Union with great brutality into a politically and economically highly centralized state. This included the abolition of private property, collectivization of agriculture, central planning and a one-party system. Massive projects were also undertaken to industrialize and modernize the country.

The outbreak of the Second World War found the Soviet Union unprepared for large-scale hostilities and it signed a non-aggression pact with Hitler's Germany. However, Germany's invasion in 1941 was vigorously resisted and the Soviet Union made a major – if not the major – contribution to the defeat of the Third Reich.

The Soviet Union emerged from the Second World War as a superpower and a major challenger to the United States, particularly in the military and political spheres. Its sphere of direct influence spread into Central and Eastern Europe as a consequence of the war and subsequently spread beyond Europe.

Following Stalin's death in 1953, the Soviet regime became less overtly brutal, but there was always a fine line between liberalization and retrenchment. Spectacular successes, such as in the space race, were later followed by widely publicized defeats in Afghanistan (1979–89). A succession of aged leaders in the 1970s and early 1980s seemed unable to deal with the political and economic problems facing the Soviet Union.

The election in 1985 of Mikhail Gorbachev to General Secretary of the Communist Part of the Soviet Union was intended to bring to an end a period of stagnation and uncertainty. A policy of *uskorenie* (acceleration) of the Soviet Union's socio-economic development was declared. Acceleration, however, did not progress far beyond *glasnost* (openness) and *perestroika* (restructuring). *Glasnost* revealed the shortcomings of Soviet developments and strengthened criticism of the system, while *perestroika* was intended to introduce structural and organizational changes.

Gorbachev's election set in train a series of fundamental reforms which included economic reforms such as the sanctioning of private entrepreneurship, the creation of a state based on legal principles and the emasculation of the Communist Party, proposals which ultimately led to the collapse of the communist regimes in Central and Eastern Europe and the demise of the Soviet Union itself at the end of 1991, even though over 70 per cent of Soviet citizens had voted for preserving the Union earlier in the year (Edwards *et al.*, 2000:41–4).

Since the sixteenth century at least, Russia had acted as a great imperial power, spanning both Europe and Asia. Furthermore, following the Second World War, it had acted as the leader of the not inconsiderable group of communist states. The period between 1945–90 was very much characterized by the ideological and military competition between the superpowers of the Soviet Union and the United States.

The Russian state, in its various guises, has also always been governed by autocratic rulers, from tsars to leaders of the communist party. It could be argued that this autocratic tradition has persisted with the presidents of post-communist Russia. It could also be argued that the conditions of the state, for example, its geographical scale and diversity, call for a strong hand.

The history of Russia is also characterized by extremes, extremes of wealth and poverty, power and powerlessness, self-sacrifice and brutality, great scientific achievements and empty shelves in the shops.

The collapse of the Soviet Union was perceived by many Russians in a way which was different from that of the countries of Central and Eastern Europe. For many Russians the transformation signified a loss of status and prestige, a reduction in global standing. From being leaders in the political and economic spheres, many Russians regarded themselves as being diminished (and to a certain extent humiliated) through the collapse of the Soviet Union. For a chronology of the reforms implemented in the Soviet Union and later Russia (Figure 4.1).

## Cultural background

The culture of Russia has been strongly influenced by the Orthodox religion and the century-long tradition of autocratic rule, which have mutually reinforced each other. Politics and religion combined to create a context for the imposition and acceptance of strong rule (on the richness of Russian cultural identity, see Figes, 2003).

Russian society has historically displayed strong collective characteristics. Smith (1976:375) noted 'a kind of primeval sense of community'. Communism reinforced (and to a degree perverted) this sense of community by subordinating the individual (and individual desires and aspirations) to the needs of society and the Party. However, collectivism predates communism. The novelist Vladimir Makanin, referring to events of the mid-nineteenth century, records 'the moment when conscience was delegated to the collective, and divine retribution to a group of human beings' (Makanin, 1995:97). According to Maslow (1998:31) a community-based model of economic activity evolved in Russia in the nineteenth century. This model stressed the role of the community rather than the individual, with decisions being taken on a consensual basis. In Maslow's view, this community-based model displays a close similarity to economic organization in Asian countries such as Japan, South Korea and Taiwan. Hosking (1997:xxvi), however, distinguishes between the egalitarian, communal values of the peasantry and the hierarchical, cosmopolitan values of the nobility.

The rapid transition from communism to capitalism has created a situation in which the new economic relationships are neither sufficiently tried nor trusted. New institutions and new commercial practices have yet to establish themselves. There are numerous cases where trust and property have been abused. In such a general context of uncertainty and apprehension, it is not surprising that family members, friends and personal contacts, rather than institutional mechanisms, play a significant role.

Clearly such personal relationships have both positive and negative characteristics. On the positive side, they permit the conduct of economic transactions in a climate of relative uncertainty, providing reliable information and access

| 1985 | Mikhail Gorbachev elected General Secretary of the Communist Party of the Soviet Union (CPSU) |
| | Central Committee of the CPSU announces *uskoremie* (acceleration) policy including *glasnost* (openness) and *perestroika* (restructuring) |
| 1986 | Third Party Programme of CPSU comprising legislation on leasing, co-operatives and joint ventures |
| | Law on working collectives establishing self-sufficiency of enterprises |
| 1988 | Law on Private Activities sanctions private entrepreneurship in a range of economic activities |
| 1989 | XIX Communist Party Congress announces establishment of a state based on legal principles |
| 1990 | Third Congress of People's Deputies revokes clause of the constitution which declared the CPSU to be the core of the political system of the USSR |
| 1991 | Dissolution of the USSR |
| | Gorbachev retires and is replaced by Boris Yeltsin |
| 1992 | Launch of radical economic reform programme by Gaidar with aim of creating market economy |
| | Programme for the Deepening of Economic Reforms in Russia (privatization of almost all state-owned enterprises) |
| 1996 | Yeltsin re-elected President of Russia |
| 1998 | Economic crisis (financial crash of August) |
| 1999 | Vladimir Putin appointed Prime Minister |
| 2000 | Putin elected President |

*Figure 4.1* Chronology of reforms in the Soviet Union/Russia.

to trustworthy expertise as well as to other resources. On the negative side such relationships can create new forms of dependency and abuses of political and economic power, increasing corruption and undermining the development of an open market economy.

## General background

Russian managers' experience of the collapse of the communist system in the early 1990s has been particularly acute for a number of reasons. The Soviet system of economic management had since 1917 functioned as the model of organizing economic activity in the socialist states. By the end of the 1980s, when the communist regimes of Central and Eastern Europe began to collapse, the Soviet model had been in place in the Soviet Union for over 70 years. There were therefore few people still alive with any memory or experience of pre-1917 forms of economic organization. Russia, moreover, had changed substantially from a predominantly agricultural and in many respects despotic state to one which had developed a significant heavy industrial and military base.

By the mid-1980s, it was evident that only a radical transformation of Russia's political institutions could remedy the failings of the economic system. The growth rates of national income had been declining since the

1950s, with the decline accelerating from the mid-1970s. By the latter half of the 1980s, the Soviet economy seemed to be coming to a standstill (Lavigne, 1999:58). In an attempt to make the Soviet socialist system operate effectively, Gorbachev began a comprehensive process of reforms.

The beginning of the changes which brought the Russian economy on to the path of the so-called transformation process from the centrally planned economy to the market can be dated as beginning in 1987, when two fundamental pieces of legislation were passed. One was the Law on State Enterprises, another the Law on Co-operatives. The former expanded considerably the autonomy of enterprises, the latter the autonomy of individuals (Gaddy, 1996:63). However, traditional elements of the system, such as the soft budget constraint, state ownership of enterprise assets and state-controlled prices, remained intact. Enterprises continued to receive thousands of indicators and requests to fulfil hundreds of different monthly, quarterly and annual forms of bureaucratic inventiveness. In fact, the then new Five Year Plan for 1986–90 was still being prepared on the basis of old assumptions and using the same traditional indicators.

Enterprises accustomed to limited independence were naturally keen to exploit (and abuse) the new opportunities granted them by the law, that is, of setting their own salaries and wages, and of converting the balances of the enterprises into cash. This situation, where on the one hand there continued to be tight state control over prices and on the other hand there was an opportunity for enterprises and individuals to increase cash incomes, could have only one outcome – severe monetary overhang. The result of this situation was shortages in almost everything, but most striking of all, in foodstuffs. Queues became a common feature of everyday life throughout the Soviet Union and 'where there is no queue there is nothing on the shelves' (Dyker, 1992:172).

In 1991, the Soviet leaders officially admitted for the first time the existence of inflation in the economic system. In fact it was running at 140 per cent a year. The government moved to revitalize the economy by giving incentives to enterprises facing problems 'such as the inconsistency between the *de jure* state ownership of most productive assets and *de facto* management control of most enterprise activities' (Ernst *et al.*, 1996:214). However, the inertia of the old system, developed over more than 70 years of its existence, combined with the elements of the new, created substantial confusion about the best way forward. The real choice was in any case limited: either to go back through repression to the old-style Soviet system, which still represented in the eyes of millions of Russians the lost security, non-conflict and paternalistic state attitudes or to advance fully to the creation of a market economy with its complementary phenomena of unemployment, inflation and the long forgotten need to rely on one's own strengths and abilities.

After an initial push democratization and *glasnost* created their own logical development which, as events demonstrated, became uncontrollable, and which represented the death knell of not only the former communist system of politics and economy, but the country itself. By the early 1990s, the communists were speedily losing power. The failed coup of 1991 discredited the Communist Party completely. The loss of its coercive powers brought about the dissolution of the Soviet Union. Russia was now facing a situation where 'neither state bureaucracy nor market performed co-ordination functions in the economy' (Ernst *et al.*, 1996:214). By 1992, when the economic reform package was introduced, Russian industry was experiencing perhaps the most difficult period since the revolution of 1917.

## External/macro issues/factors

In spite of the difficult starting conditions, the first period of Russian reforms took a surprisingly short time, considering the magnitude of tasks faced by the country. According to the Bureau for Economic Analysis, the basis of the system existing in Russia today was laid during 1992–95 (Poletaev, 1998:17). Through the mechanism of shock therapy, prices were liberalized and the economy became much more open to the outside world. It took three years for the economic agents to adjust to prices.

Achieving macroeconomic stabilization was perceived as the best way to start building a market economy. After inflation of about 2,000 per cent in 1992 was brought down to two digits in 1994, macroeconomic stabilization seemed to be very close. However, poor tax collection, a growing budget deficit, and collapse of the state created a financial pyramid known as GKO which brought about the catastrophic financial crisis of 17 August 1998, when the country effectively declared a default on its internal and external financial obligations. The results of the crisis were mostly unexpected.

The speculative character of the Russian financial system had cushioned the impact on the real economy. Since the beginning of economic reform in 1992 and up to 1999 the Russian economy was going down-hill, with GDP regularly falling. Compared to 1991, it shrank in 1992 to 85.5 per cent, in 1993 to 78.1 per cent, 62.2 per cent in 1996, 59.1 per cent in 1997 and in 1998 it was just slightly more than 56 per cent, reaching its lowest point (Goskomstat, 1999:96).

However, during the years following the crisis of 1998 the Russian economy has been on the rise. From 1999 to 2001, Russian GDP grew by 21 per cent, which represented 68 per cent of the 1989 level. The main reasons for this growth were the following factors. The severe financial crisis of 1998 shook the economy with a four-fold ruble devaluation, which sheltered the Russian economy from imports. Consequently, domestic production to substitute imports has substantially increased. This triggered growth in the sectors primarily serving domestic markets. The rise in world oil prices also contributed substantially to the improvement of state finances.

One of the main trends is that the Russian economy is now at its most stable compared to all previous years. The state has consolidated its control functions, the economy is expanding, and political and macroeconomic risk factors have been significantly reduced. The Russian stock market was one of the fastest growing and most profitable markets in the world in 2001. The economy is displaying considerable resilience and is likely to continue expanding, despite the worldwide economic downturn and then fall in oil prices (American Chamber of Commerce and Expert Institute, 2001:2).

Macroeconomic stability went hand in hand with the creation of institutions of a developed market economy. Intensive institutional reform, backed by the Russian president and pushed energetically by German Gref, Minister of the Economy, created conditions for the sustained economic development that allowed Russia in November 2002 to achieve the status of a country with a market economy. In 2002, substantial progress was made in improving legislation governing economic, business and investment activity. The year 2002 also saw the entry into force of the Labour Code and Land Code, four chapters of the Tax Code, and a number of other fundamental laws governing economic activity. These new laws are creating the conditions needed to consolidate and develop market economy institutions and to improve the investment and business climate in Russia.

In 2000, under President Putin, the government published its Social and Economic Policy Programme 2000–2010 (the Gref Programme) that demonstrates an understanding of the threats currently facing the country and which offers a development strategy based on a series of social and economic reforms intended to create a liberal market economy, governed by a democratic political system. The Programme was widely endorsed by the business community in Russia and refers to the task of improving the investment climate as one of the most important issues facing Russia today (American Chamber of Commerce and Expert Institute, 2001:12).

However, there is still a long way to go to ensure long-term survival and economic prosperity. Among the problems of a strategic nature is the urgent necessity to modernize the economy. In fact, the most acute problem is the large difference between the achievements at the macroeconomic level and the situation at the enterprise level, as a majority of enterprises still have obsolete equipment, poor corporate governance, a duel system of finance (one real and another for tax collectors) and unclear property rights. It is a very common situation that 51 per cent of shares give total control over a company and the remaining 49 per cent are unable to influence company policy at all.

There is, moreover, the acute problem of obsolete equipment, which could create dangerous and even catastrophic consequences. The last mass scale replacement and modernization of equipment in many plants and factories took place under the former Soviet Union and there has been no new investment since then. In order to realize the country's huge investment potential, a new mechanism for transferring savings into investment is needed. The country also has to attract much more FDI than it does now. According to a survey conducted by the High School of Economics on 1,000 industrial companies, two-thirds of them had negative investment, which means that they are 'eating up' their main assets.

The Russian economy is still heavily dependent on the export of raw materials and especially gas and oil and, as a result, on the world prices for them. According to an assessment by a group of Russian experts working under the Ministry of Finance, changes in world prices for oil of 2–3 dollars affect Russian GDP by 1 per cent. For instance, the decline in oil prices at the end of 2001 and beginning of 2002 were immediately reflected in a slowdown of the Russian growth rates (Poletaev, 2002:17).

Globalization is another challenge faced by the Russian economy. In spite of some Russian industrialists lobbying against Russian entry into the WTO, the general political decision is that Russia has to become a full member even though negotiations have been protracted. When this happens, Russia will face even stronger competition from the outside world and will have to learn how to make effective use of its resources and increase the competitiveness of its industrial production.

Furthermore, the Russian financial system needs modernization and better legal regulation. The reform of the Russian banking system is a most urgent problems. Russian companies in search of investment go, in the majority of cases, abroad. This is due to poor capitalization and consolidation of the Russian banks, the under-developed deposit guarantee system and near absence of risk management tools.

The Russian public administration system in general is not supportive of the ongoing economic reform. The very bureaucrats, who are supposed to create a supportive business environment, are largely very inefficient, due either to their incompetence or corruption. This is even truer for regional public administrations, which often make the reforms made at the federal level unrecognizable and even ridiculous.

Low productivity is another worrying issue for the Russian economy. According to the State Statistics Committee (Goskomstat), labour productivity in 2000 increased by 3 per cent whereas salaries went up by 19 per cent (Goskomstat, 2001). This was not just the result of salary increases but also of the introduction of a flat rate of 13 per cent for income tax which induced people to declare previously undeclared income. This increase is a worrying factor, which can lead to inflation, which in 2000 stood at 20 per cent in 2000 and 15 per cent in 2002.

In spite of the years of price liberalization, the price structure of the Russian economy is still very distorted. Historically, the Russian economy had excessively low energy and transportation tariffs. The situation is not much different today which distorts the entire system of economic signals such as prices, tariffs, interests rates and ruble exchange. The energy sector now subsidizes the entire economy and often there are no incentives to save energy, modernize plant and equipment and enhance efficiency. According to EBRD (2001b:81) 18.5 per cent of Russian GDP goes on subsidizing the internal prices for gas and oil. The average difference between prices for gas in Europe and Russia is at the moment 6.7–fold. The artificially low charges for housing and utilities, electricity and rail transport are yet another form of subsidy inherited from the centrally planned system. Attempts to correct these distortions meet with strong public opposition and represent one of the challenges for the current government.

According to experts, until structural reform is instituted and these price distortions are resolved, the Russian economy will remain trapped within a series of vicious circles: a stronger ruble leading to a fall in the competitiveness of the manufacturing sectors and an increase in imports of consumer goods; increased revenues from raw material exports leading either to increased inflation in a context of growing foreign currency and gold reserves, or to an excessively strong ruble; and a dearth of investment opportunities within the economy resulting in capital flight. The overall result will be poor yields, low (or negative) growth rates, a fall in the quality of capital and labour resources, and an overall worsening of the economic situation (American Chamber of Commerce and Expert Institute, 2001:45).

### *Privatization*

To demolish central planning institutions turned out to be the easiest task, which was successfully accomplished during 1991–92. Motivated by fear of the restoration of the old system and a certain naiveté in the creative power of private ownership the Gaidar government used a voucher privatization scheme to change the ownership structure of the economy almost overnight. The non-state economic sector in Russia now accounts for approximately 75 per cent of gross domestic product, compared to about 5 per cent in 1991. Russia is the leader among its East European neighbours with regard to the speed of the privatization process.

The main declared goal of privatization was the establishment of an 'effective property owner' who would then undertake restructuring under the new market conditions. Large-scale privatization involves the privatization of medium and large enterprises (with a value over one million rubles and total personnel exceeding 200). Large-scale privatization is being executed mostly though the creation of JSCs of open type from the assets of state enterprises. There have been three main procedures for the sale of the shares of newborn JSCs.

*The first option*: a proportion of shares is sold for a nominal value (in some cases free of charge) to the enterprise employees. This process resulted in most of the privileges given to workers of enterprises being dictated not by economic expediency but by political compromises with the industrial lobbies.

*The second option*: the system of privatization vouchers was introduced in order to involve wide groups of people in the privatization process. These privatization vouchers were given to every citizen of Russia, free of charge, and had a nominal value of 10,000 rubles. A special guarantee certified the right of the voucher owner to a part of a previously state-owned company. Russians used their rights under the system of specialized voucher auctions to secure ownership in companies. Such a system allowed anyone to become a shareholder of any enterprise regardless of location. At the end of 1994, there were more than 40 million such shareholders in Russia.

*The third option*: obviously mass voucher privatization did not and could not solve the main financial problem of bringing real investment into enterprises. Collected privatization vouchers did not give anything of real value to the JSCs. Investment bidding was intended to perform that function. Investment bidding is a method of selling the shares of JSCs. The shares are offered in one package (15 per cent and more of charter capital) and are sold at the nominal value to the aspiring owner who proposes the best terms for the enterprise.

The results of privatization were much worse than expected. The main companies are still looking for strategic investors or effective owners. Shares are heavily concentrated within enterprises in the hands of senior managers and workers. Ownership and control are tightly united in hands, which are often unable to see different strategic options. The struggle is still to control profitable companies but it is conducted by a minute wealthy elite, effectively excluding the possibility of smaller or foreign investors entering the game. Asset striping is still a common Russian reality and personal profit maximization at the expense of company prosperity is a universal fact.

### New firm development

Opening up the entrepreneurial potential of Russians through establishing small businesses was seen as one of the major factors in the success of the transformation process. So-called 'schools of entrepreneurship' appeared mostly due to small-scale (municipal) privatization. This involved the transfer of enterprises that were targeted to be transferred into private hands (these were mostly enterprises with a balance-sheet value of up to 1 million rubles as of 1 July 1992 and with no more than 200 employees). Such enterprises included a range of stores and shops, enterprises in the service sphere, barbers' shops, cafés, etc.

Small-scale privatization has been executed in two ways: sale of the whole enterprise through an open auction; and sale of the whole enterprise through commercial bidding (there is only one difference from open auctions – the bid winner has to fulfil certain conditions, so as to safeguard the nature of the enterprise, the number of personnel, etc.).

In the 10-year period since the beginning of active municipal privatization, about 90 per cent of all the stores and more than half of the total number of enterprises in the country, were transferred into the hands of new owners. By any standards these results are impressive. It is really truly remarkable that small businesses have survived and developed. From 1 October 2001 to 1 October 2002 the number of registered small businesses increased by 5.1 per cent and by the beginning of 2003 numbered 380,600 companies, equivalent to 611 companies per 100,000 head of population. Faced by a hostile bureaucracy and huge administrative barriers, threatened and abused by corruption and racket, in the absence of a supportive tax system and lack of finance and credit lines, small businesses have been struggling to contribute to Russian economic development.

Understanding the problem, Putin's government has been working on the introduction of several measures, which could help small businesses. One of them is the well-publicized campaign known as 'one window', meaning that for opening and registering a new business an entrepreneur would have just one point of contact for submitting the requested documents and registering the business. Current practice though confirms that it still takes from two to five weeks to register a new business (*Finansovaja gazetta*, 2002:3) and costs the entrepreneur substantial amounts in bribes to the state bureaucrats. Corruption in small business is the most common form of illegal activity. Reforms and unclear legislation have blurred the difference between legal and illegal activity. Nowadays, bribes have reached proportions that the Soviet bureaucrats could never have imagined, even in their wildest dreams (Radaev, 1994:80). In trying to fight corruption, the state very often actually breeds it. Frequently, small businessmen do not have a clear idea who has the right to inspect their activities. There are so many controlling organs with unclear responsibilities and duties that they often duplicate each other, confusing entrepreneurs. The EU-funded TACIS programme of providing support to the Russian Ministry of Economic Development and Trade launched in 2001 a project aimed, among other things, at assisting the Ministry which leads the reform programme in its efforts to de-bureaucratize and deregulate the economy (www.tacis-medt.ru).

Among other problems faced by small business in Russia is obsolete equipment, which represents only 3 per cent of the value of the main factors of production belonging to small businesses (Polonsky, 1998:525). Absence of a system of private or state insurance for small business also makes development difficult. There is obvious need for greater state support in terms of credit and grants, legislation favourable to small business and revised organizational support.

### Capital and labour

The system change brought back the concept of capital and labour relations, which had been forgotten during the communist years. Even though trade unions had always existed under the old system, their role was limited to allocation of '*putevkas*' – free holidays – for workers and collection of money for birthday presents to employees. Being the left hand of the red director (the right hand was the head of the enterprise party committee) trade unions followed closely the directives of the company management and ruling communist party.

The system change changed their role dramatically. The re-emergence of capital on a large scale as a result of mass privatization put trade unions back in their traditional role of defenders of employees. The absence of a history of pursuing labour issues, together with negative attitudes on the workers' side, as in their eyes trade unions had discredited themselves during the socialist years, has resulted in trade unions being a not very effective force in counterbalancing the overnight appearance of capital. Only a few Russian industrial companies, mostly in traditionally strong trade union areas such as coal and metallurgy, have active and powerful trade unions, whereas most companies either do not have trade unions at all or have weak and powerless ones.

In cases where trade unions enjoy influence, they are not very helpful in helping the company restructure. In most cases, restructuring in Russia presumes the closure of inefficient production facilities. This economically rational measure meets furious resistance from the trade unions. The former socialist mentality still prevails. The trade union leaders cannot accept the logic according to which, if one wants to save most of the jobs and an enterprise itself, some of the employees must be made redundant. In order to preserve existing employment, trade unions use all kind of pressures, including intimidation and threats of force.

The data for trade union membership show that, in order to become a strong force in counterbalancing the interests of capital, trade unions have to find a constructive role and attract new members who would feel that their organization is protecting their interests. At the moment, with a membership of less then 5 per cent of the labour force, this does not seem to be the case.

Weak trade unions could not initiate the organization of capital. However, different forms of organization of capital can be found in Russia. These forms evolved during the years of transformation, from alliances, which sprang to life, and which were at the beginning of the 1990s often based on common involvement in criminal or semi-criminal activities, to large and influential associations of leaders of large businesses in Russia at the beginning of the new century. The organization of capital was influenced by economic as well as political factors. During the first years of privatization, newly born capitalists grouped together in order to increase their strength in bidding and fighting for attractive pieces of state property.

The second stage of the organization of capital occurred between 1995–96 and during Yeltsin's second term which was critical for the future of Russian democracy. Often deep divisions among industrialists were forgotten for the sake of uniting and strengthening Yeltsin's position against Gennady Zuganov, the communist leader who was neck-and-neck with the first Russian president in the 1996 election. They understood very well that victory for Zuganov would mean that the results of privatization would be questioned and in fact the entire privatization and transformation could be stopped and reversed.

The third period in the organization of capital started with Putin's ascent to power. The government campaign to start a dialogue with big business in order to prevent capital flight and start 'working relations' with owners of the largest businesses in Russia brought into new light and strengthened the largest big business association, the Russian Union of Industrialists and Entrepreneurs headed by Arkady Volsky. The Union's meetings with President Putin are now regularly covered in the national press. As Russian capitalism develops, so called oligarchs, leaders of the largest businesses, start to play a more positive role in the country's economic development. However, Putin has also acted against the enormous power held by the oligarchs. Media interests had been taken back into state control and from the summer of 2003 the oil giant Yukos attracted the increasing attention of the prosecutor general's office (*The Economist*, 9.8.2003 and 8.11.2003).

### Regional and global links

The collapse of the Soviet Union severely changed the pattern of relationships between Russia and the rest of the world. Almost overnight, removal of often-imposed friendship on COMECON countries as well as former Soviet republics created centrifugal tendencies. Sometimes even logical economic ties were abruptly broken and sacrificed for closer co-operation with the West.

Eastern European countries were convinced that diminishing trade and other economic relations with Russia would strengthen their co-operation with the West and secure their political and economic independence from an insecure and unpredictable Russia. For example, purchasing Uzbek cotton became easier via the British market than through the bureaucratic and corrupt direct links between Russia and Uzbekistan. Thus, Russian trade with former Soviet republics went down twelve-fold from 1991 to 2001. Similarly, trade with the Eastern European countries diminished substantially. The loss of Eastern European partners and the problematic relationship with the Commonwealth of Independent States (CIS) countries made Russians look to the West for closer economic relationships. European Union countries became Russia's main trading partners. A policy of strengthening ties with the European Union was declared by Yeltsin and materialized into practical steps under Putin. This approach contributed greatly to closer Russian integration with the European Union and world economy. In 2000, 36 per cent of Russian exports and 33 per cent of registered imports were traded with the European Union. However, the European Union and Russia are still very unequal partners, with a large degree of asymmetry. Russian GDP expressed in purchasing power parity (PPP) amounts to less than 13 per cent of that of the European Union. Moreover, Russia's real GDP per capita is just one third of the European Union average (Havlik, 2002:2).

The commodity structure of Russian exports and imports differs hugely. European Union exports to Russia consist only of manufactured goods, whereas around one half of Russian exports to the European Union consist of energy and raw materials. This situation is unlikely to change much in the future. In the light of the above, Russian accession to the European Union is very unlikely in the near future.

Russia's economic relationship with the world is progressing slowly. However, based on ongoing consultations with the European Union and the United States, Russia is lowering and streamlining its imports tariffs. Support of the US policy towards terrorism gained Russians American support for

WTO accession. In spite of the numerous US and EU import restrictions and anti-dumping procedures against some Russian exports such as textiles, steel and nuclear fuel, in May 2002 Russia was recognized as a country with a market economy. Furthermore, even if the prospect of full Russian integration into the European Union seems to be unlikely, the creation of a Common European Economic Space, which tops the agenda in the EU–Russian dialogue, seems very feasible. This could not only positively affect Russian economic growth but could also create conditions 'for acceleration of sustainable growth and higher productivity' (Samson, 2002:7). Russian integration into the Common European Economic Space, however, requires Russian WTO membership. However, according to Maxim Medvedkov, the Deputy Minister of the Economy, the major obstacle is the WTO's request to harmonize Russia's internal and world prices on energy, which is unacceptable to Russia. 'We are not going to buy a place in WTO at such a price', said Medvedkov in an interview. This leaves the question of Russian integration into WTO problematic as, according to WTO experts, Russian energy prices are much lower than world prices, giving Russia an unfair advantage (*Profit*, 14 July, 2003:32).

## *Foreign direct investment*

Until recently, FDI was perceived in Russia as a panacea for the current investment crisis. Foreign direct investment has been widely regarded as a vitally important source of new technology and managerial know-how. It was supposed to provide much needed access to Western capital markets, considered critical for the restructuring of obsolete Russian industries. There were strong beliefs that Russian companies would gain access to western markets via FDI. It was also widely believed that FDI would help in de-monopolization, boosting competitiveness, the development of the private sector and creation of the new economic and democratic system.

After more than 10 years of transition, the expectation of attracting a large share of the world's FDI is much more modest. This is quite obvious when we compare in relative terms the Russian share of FDI and some other post-communist countries (Table 4.1).

A structural overview of foreign investment in Russia, including portfolio investment, can be seen in Table 4.2.

According to official Russian estimates, the most attractive industries for foreign investors for the last six years have been petroleum, trade and catering, construction, wood and paper, machinery and fabricated metal products.

The flow of FDI into the Russian Federation differs considerably from region to region. The factors most affecting distribution of FDI are: diversity of political, cultural and climate conditions and development/underdevelopment of infrastructure. These factors created conditions in which investment risks vary significantly between different economic regions. The current Russian government policy of strengthening its vertical power and

*Table 4.1* Foreign direct investment, 2000

|                | $ billion | % GDP |
|----------------|-----------|-------|
| Russia         | 3.3       | 1.7   |
| Czech Republic | 5.1       | 9.6   |
| Poland         | 7.4       | 4.7   |
| Hungary        | 2.0       | 4.1   |
| Romania        | 1.0       | 2.8   |
| Bulgaria       | 0.8       | 6.5   |
| Latvia         | 0.35      | 6.7   |
| Lithuania      | 0.49      | 4.6   |
| Estonia        | 0.3       | 6.0   |
| Ukraine        | 0.5       | 1.6   |

Source: American Chamber of Commerce and Expert Institute (2001:14).

*Table 4.2* Structure of foreign investment in Russia

|       | Total ($ billion) | Direct (% of total) | Portfolio (% of total) | Other (% of total) |
|-------|-------------------|---------------------|------------------------|--------------------|
| 1997  | 12.3              | 43.4                | 5.5                    | 51.4               |
| 1998  | 11.8              | 28.6                | 1.6                    | 69.8               |
| 1999  | 9.6               | 44.6                | 0.3                    | 55.1               |
| 2000  | 10.96             | 40.4                | 1.3                    | 58.3               |
| 2001[a] | 9.7             | 30.0                | 3.0                    | 67.0               |

Source: Goskomstat.

Note
[a] January–September 2001.

increasing the role of the centre over the regions is gradually eliminating this difference. Northern Russia and Siberia in particular have attracted the largest share of FDI, mainly due to their relative stability, favourable attitudes of the local authorities and richness of oil and gas resources. Siberia has 70 per cent of Russia's oil resources, 90 per cent of its gas, almost all of its metals, diamonds and timber, plus a well-educated labour force.

The central regions, including Moscow and St Petersburg, have a well-developed industrial base with a relatively developed infrastructure. Together with their relative geographical proximity to Western Europe and better-known business climate and business culture, these regions are of great interest in terms of Western investment projects. Moscow and the Moscow region are natural leaders in attracting more than 70 per cent of the total number of foreign investment projects undertaken since 1991.

Forms of market entry have changed greatly over the years, moving from joint ventures, which represented more than 80 per cent of market entries in 1992, to wholly-owned companies, which accounted for 75 per cent of entries in 2001. This trend is quite natural. Western companies are now familiar with the Russian business and market environments and do not need the help of a local partner. Another factor which explains the large share of wholly-owned subsidiaries in Russia is that Russian legislation does not discriminate in favour of joint ventures as compared to wholly-owned companies, thus providing no incentives for the Western company to form a joint venture with Russian partners and renouncing a large element of control.

Overall, the investment climate is gradually improving. New legislation actively put forward with obvious help from Putin, tighter control over economic and political activities in the Russian provinces, a certain political stability and active steps undertaken by the Russian government in its fight against crime, corruption and money laundering make Russia more attractive to FDI than ever before. According to official statistics, foreign direct investment in Russia last year amounted to $19.7 billion. This includes loans and credits. Long-term loans and credits account for the largest portion of this figure. In comparison, capital flight reached $19.9 billion, mainly in direct investment, although slowing down (*AmCham* News, March–April 2003:8).

## Internal/micro factors/issues

### *Organizational restructuring*

Restructuring was identified as the central and necessary element of the general economic reform and a condition for economic growth (*Nekotorye primery uspeshnoj restruktualizacii predprijatij*, 1997:2). According to research conducted during 1996–99, the aims and methods of restructuring often conflicted with the interests of different groups who in fact prosper on enterprise inefficiency; these groups pay lip-service to the restructuring process but do everything possible to slow down and block the process when their interests are threatened (Polonsky and Iviozian, 2000:231).

Among these influential groups one can find enterprise owners, top management, regional authorities, banks and criminal groups. The general manager and the enterprise owner can be corrupted or incompetent or both. Often large amounts of unregistered cash flows drain with differing intensity from the enterprise into managerial pockets. The regional administration has its own interests in enterprises. On the one hand it wants to see an enterprise as a constant source of taxes for the regional budget. To achieve this, all other considerations, such as enterprise well-being and long-term considerations, are often ignored. Interestingly, the restructuring which results in a reduction of the taxes paid by enterprises conflicts with the interests of the administration and local tax authorities. On the other hand, the administration is very much concerned about the reduction of social tension in the region. One of the ways to achieve this can be by keeping jobs at any cost. In this respect the administration's interests coincide with the interests of trade unions. The third reason explaining why the local administration is extremely interested in preserving its control over enterprises situated on its territory is politically motivated. The controlled enterprise is sure to provide needed votes during election campaigns.

Banks, which are often owners of companies, use their enterprises as a source of additional income for their financial operations. As a rule, when conducted under bank supervision, restructuring results in the cash flow of the enterprise being centralized under the control of the bank or its representative at the enterprise. The latter often does not understand the sector in which the enterprise is active and the peculiarities of the production process.

Widespread criminality is a known fact of Russian life. Even according to the official figures criminal capital controls more than one third of enterprises, banks and financial and industrial groups. Often the criminals themselves become owners of the enterprises. The purpose of this ownership is not restructuring or long-term investment but to use the enterprise as a milk cow, pumping out the financial resources of the enterprise and using it as a convenient source for laundering its criminal capital. In fact, their activity often resembles bank behaviour. In controlling the company's outputs or inputs, they dictate prices of raw materials or the distribution of production, thus making the economic performance of the enterprise unprofitable.

Russian legislation is another factor, which makes corporate restructuring problematic. The Russian tax system, which unintentionally creates situations where the restructuring is optimal from the viewpoint of enterprise strategy, management and enterprise economics, actually increases the already heavy tax burden on the enterprise and turns out to be pointless and often harmful to the financial well-being of the company. Under the current Russian tax legislation a company is liable for VAT on all of its purchases and should charge VAT on all of its sales at the standard statutary rates, unless exempted. The VAT on purchases may be offset against the VAT payable on sales. However, once restructured, the separate business units will be liable for VAT on their purchases from the business entities and will be obliged to charge VAT on sales to other business entities. Although the additional VAT charges can be offset in the books of the business units, the payments of VAT will increase the cash flow deficit and will force the company to resort to loan finance at prohibitively high interest rates (20–30 per cent per annum in 2003).

Under the current accounting and tax framework, business units cannot offset their profit or loss against the profit or loss of another business unit within a group. The limited opportunities provided by current legislation for offsetting losses against profits of other units mean that the quick and efficient restructuring of enterprises is problematic. In order to avoid the problems imposed by the legislation, companies choose to retain the existing structure although it may be inefficient or resort to manipulation of figures, tax arbitrage, tolling schemes or simply do not register their turnover, increasing the extent of the shadow economy.

In spite of the above mentioned obstacles, the restructuring process is gradually gaining momentum. Substantial changes have taken place in enterprise structures. The role and activity of planning, production and R&D departments has declined, with increasing importance being attached to accounting, finance, marketing and logistics. The structure of enterprises has become simpler and more transparent. The implementation of new structures has, however, been hampered by a reliance on hierarchical flows of communication and the difficulty of finding employees to fill newly created roles in areas such as marketing. Nonetheless, more and more companies are finding real owners and managers who see their future in the future of their companies.

### Corporate strategies and alliances

Ten years of the Russian economic reform, with its ups and downs, shaped today's companies' corporate strategies and their ways of forming alliances. Companies' corporate strategy has gone through dramatic changes. If, at the beginning of the reform process, survival was the major task, now many companies have much more ambitious goals. According to a survey of 150 Russian enterprises during 1999–2002, the majority, about 45 per cent of all companies located in the central regions of Russia and Moscow, already have a strategy which has a time horizon of at least 3 to 5 years. More then half of the requests which came from Russian companies to the European Union's TACIS–TERF restructuring programme came from companies which wanted to improve and often to be helped to identify their marketing strategies. About 60 per cent of the companies involved in the TACIS project started a cost reduction process, 30 per cent undertook organizational restructuring, about 20 per cent downsizing and new product development (Polonsky, 2002).

If in the first years of the reform companies saw their survival in re-establishing old ties and chasing up 'old special relations', now they are more focused on positioning their products, developing an efficient market strategy and looking not for favours based on who knows whom, but rather on working business alliances. There are still thousands of companies though, which see their survival in their general manager being elected to the regional administration or Federal Duma or in the amount and value of presents delivered to a friendly bank manager somewhere in Moscow. But this is true mostly of the companies in the Russian provinces where market relations are still emerging and, even then, at much slower pace than in Moscow.

The turbulent time of the first years of reforms, when company alliances were more of a 'gangster' nature, is gradually disappearing. There are numerous mergers and acquisitions and property rights are at least formally respected. Alliances are most evident in the metallurgical, gas and oil sectors. It is almost impossible nowadays to find a company producing fastenings, which does not have a large metallurgical plant in the background, supplying steel. Diversification initiated by the general market instability is another reason for company alliances. The relative weakness of the Russian institutions in ensuring fairness in the market place allows numerous cases of vertical and horizontal integration, which would not be acceptable in the more developed markets in Europe.

The process of redistributing assets is becoming more intensive and civilized. More and more cases go through arbitration courts instead of showdowns, which were common during the first years of the reform. For instance, the number of petitions for bankruptcy filed with arbitration courts against debtors was greater in the first half of 2001 than for the whole of 1998.

## Functional strategies

### Human resource management

It is still very common to find the old ideas of personnel management mixed up with the HRM concept. It is a matter of curiosity but in the first years of reform HRM issues were in the hands of old companies' communist party bosses. The logic of this was: who knew more about company employees than the former party boss? In spite of the fact that this logic is becoming more and more obsolete, there are still many companies where the HRM function is performed by a former party leader. The major issues which are on the agenda of Russian companies are training and downsizing. The latter is often called socially responsible restructuring. Motivation of personnel is less of an issue as having a job, even if badly paid, is in many areas of Russia motivation in itself. This is especially true for 25 million people (one sixth of the total population) living in 1,500 single company towns all over Russia.

Overstaffing as a result of the necessity of cutting production volumes is the major issue for HR managers. Even in the absence of strong trade unions, it is almost impossible for managers in a small provincial town to make his workers redundant, partly due to the fear of being hated by one's neighbours and partly due to inherited social and paternalistic concerns. Training and learning new ways of managing the business are the major tasks for Russian managers. This is true not only for the staff but for the company owners themselves. Most of them feel that the knowledge to run a company under the new conditions of a more developed market is not the same as when they were acquiring state property through suspect privatization schemes. Many Russian businessmen believe that they possess incredible business skill, but in fact all their successes were due to the old boys' network or similar schemes.

To entrust management of the company to professional managers is a dangerous business in Russia, as the owner can find him/herself without a company. Thus, the only way to manage the company efficiently is through education and acquiring new skills oneself first. As a response to this demand there are many distance learning MBA programmes with weekend classes aimed at young and wealthy manager-owners. Education of the personnel is also an important issue. It is a known fact that the general level of education was very good in the former Soviet Union. However, the skills required in the market economy were obviously either non existent as in the case of marketing, organizational development, HRM, strategic planning or substantially underdeveloped as in case of operational planning and accounting (Polonsky and Clark, 1997). The understanding of this deficiency is widespread among Russian managers and this could be a good sign that, based on the good general education, these missing skills will be gradually acquired.

### Marketing

The development of marketing was fast and furious and very uneven. From almost total absence of knowledge of marketing in the past, one can nowadays find quite sophisticated marketeers. This is mostly true for new companies led by young and as a rule well-educated managers. At the same time there are still companies, mostly run by former Soviet directors, who do not really understand the marketing concept. Very strong marketing capacities can also be found in Russian consultancies. In fact in most of the donor-funded projects in which Polonsky (2002) took part, Russian marketing consultants demonstrated excellent professional knowledge and skills. International marketing is obviously more of a problem. However, the presence of Western companies and the extensive international exposure of Russian companies are gradually remedying this deficiency.

### Operations

'Gigantomania' inherited from the Soviet past is still a problem in Russian companies. The huge areas on which companies were built, complicate the production process. Many companies, especially those situated in expensive urban areas, are renting out their premises in order to improve their finances. There are numerous companies in Moscow which receive more revenue from this sort of activity than from their core business. The fashion of obtaining ISO certificates, which was widespread in the 1990s, bore fruit in terms of better logistics and quality, even in companies, which had not yet obtained the certificate. Plant and machinery are obsolete and major companies, as well as the general public and government officials, are worried about the afore-mentioned problem as due to the lack of investment in maintenance, equipment is becoming unreliable and even dangerous to use.

### Finance

The development of financial strategies was probably the most difficult process for Russian companies. An enormous volume of barter, due to inconsistent government monetary policy and a general lack of stability in the macroeconomic environment, was a distorting factor for the development of companies' financial strategies. The crisis of August 1998 bankrupted almost 90 per cent of Russian banks, which in their turn dragged down thousands of Russian companies. Emerging legislation on bankruptcy and taxation and development, albeit slow, of equity and financial markets stimulated the formulation of short, medium and, in some cases, long-term financial strategies in Russian companies. This process is heavily dependent on general economic and political stability in Russia.

Financial issues were therefore a priority area and the role of finance departments had become critical and had changed enormously. Previously such departments had merely produced reports of the current situation. Now finance departments are actively involved in accounting and financial management, seeking out sources of finance, pressurizing debtors and identifying new ways of clearing mutual debts and credits. One manager described the finance department as 'the heart of the enterprise' on which the company depended for its well-being (Edwards *et al.*, 2000:142).

### Research and development

The total collapse of the Soviet system of networking between industrial companies and R&D institutions, mostly because of the poor state of government finances, negatively affected company development. In spite of the fact that thousands of R&D institutions were not really productive and were serving as artificially created institutions in which people were pretending to work and the state was pretending to pay, there were some real theoretical and practical research results which were passed on to companies. Recently, research activity at the state level is almost non-existent, apart from some small funding going to the defence sector. Lack of capital and the necessity to struggle to meet market demand give Russian companies little chance to develop their own R&D capacities. The huge brain drain of the 1990s, when almost 100,000 well educated people left Russia in the first years of reforms, was another negative manifestation. However, large cash-rich companies, mostly working in the gas, oil and aluminum sectors of the economy, understand the necessity of having their own R&D department, if they want to stay competitive.

### Organizational structure and culture

More than ten years of fundamental system change could not but affect the organizational structures of companies. Understanding the necessity of having separate marketing and sales departments with independent heads, changed companies' structures. Many companies separated their often large, non-core business activity into special independent departments with their own marketing, sales and product development facilities. There is also a tendency to isolate in independent departments companies' social infrastructure with their own deputy directors.

The internal management of organizations is generally characterized by traditional autocratic and hierarchical relationships and by a general climate of paternalism. Organizations continue to be structured in a largely hierarchical fashion, with vertical lines of communication. Some of the managers interviewed in Volgograd commented that there was a clear need for more effective communication across functional areas as well as for greater informal interaction. One manager noted: 'We still do not communicate well with each other. We are good at receiving orders and passing them further down, but we do not know how to talk about our common tasks to our colleagues in the parallel structures' (Edwards *et al.*, 2000:139).

The problem of communication appeared to be exacerbated by the autocratic behaviour of managers and of owner-managers in particular. The traditional autocratic style of management, based on superiors issuing orders and subordinates carrying out instructions, had been reinforced by the unwillingness of individuals to assume personal responsibility and the weakness of employee organizations. These aspects are reinforced when senior managers are synonymous with company owners.

What seems to have developed in many enterprises is a kind of paternalism where employees look to the managing director to safeguard their interests and the senior management team continues to express a genuine responsibility towards the body of employees. This paternalism is exemplified by the experience of enterprise demanning where job cuts, even when massive, are proportionately less than might have been expected, taking into account the actual decline in sales volume. Any cuts that are made thus appear to have been 'forced' upon senior management.

Organizational culture can be positively affected by the introduction of the so-called corporate code, which sets the framework for corporate governance. By 2003, only two Russian companies have adopted corporate management codes. They are two giants: Sibneft and UCOS. The largest Russian oil company, LUKoil, is at the final stage of introducing the corporate code.

The code does not differ from the similar codes of corporate governance used by Western companies. The Russian code expects companies to do business openly: use of insider information is strictly forbidden. Real financial information should be available to all and the relationships between companies and shareholders, including the government and employees, have to be ethical and clean.

According to a survey conducted by the Russian Institute of Directors (RID), which regularly monitors and analyzes Russian corporate government practices since 1999, Russia has achieved significant progress in several areas but most visible is greater disclosure and transparency. In mid-2000, Tempex Consultants of the UK conducted a survey of the quality of investor relations policies in 27 emerging market countries. Russian oil companies like Sibneft, Surgutneftegaz, LUKoil and TNK, for example, ranked highly on 11 of 13 criteria, including depth and clarity of information provided to investors, quality of information provided at one-to-one meetings and quality of information provided through corporate websites. However, according to Igor Belikov, Director of RID, despite these achievements, the Russian corporate community still faces the need for dramatic improvements in a number of very important areas, such as disclosure of ownership structure, clear rules for mergers and acquisitions, reorganizations, dividend payments, board composition, independence and effective practices (*AmCham News*, March–April 2003:17).

Changes in organizational structure, due to the acceptance of the corporate governance code, are making Russian business more acceptable to Western partners. However, often the idea of making companies accept corporate governance enters the minds of the heads of corporations, only when the relationships between the company and a foreign investor become difficult, or as in the case of UCOS, the company wants to launch its shares on Western stock exchange markets.

There are cases when a professional and well-motivated group seizes the entrepreneurial function. When this is the case, the company is successful and business develops steadily. However, as reality shows, this happens quite rarely.

The search for the Russian type of corporate model is still ongoing. The recent failure of the Anglo-Saxon model, strongly suggested by Western consultants to ensure proper corporate control, makes this search even more important.

### Management styles

The traditional Soviet management style is still widespread. It is a style, which developed over more than 70 years under communism. The Soviet-type managers are authoritarian and assertive. He (they are overwhelmingly male) is expected to exercise his authority with firmness and frankness. It is expected that the manager not only tells you how to do certain things, even of a technical nature, but also is actually able to do them himself. The role of manager is still perceived as of a paternalistic nature and defender of his labour collective. In the majority of cases it is almost impossible to criticize the general manager without falling into the category of an enemy. Criticism of opinion is still considered as a criticism of the person.

The authoritarian management style is generally more accepted by older workers and much less so by younger employees. According to the main author's observations, one of the main reasons for leaving the company after young Russian managers have spent three months abroad working in EU companies in the framework of the TACIS education and training programme, MTP, was a rejection of the existing management style, which had been quite acceptable before going abroad. Following experience of a much more consensual management style, the present management style became unbearable. Moreover, form of ownership heavily influences the management style. As a rule, privately-owned companies are much more dynamic, entrepreneurial and more willing to adapt to the changing market environment and take necessary risks.

One also can find companies with the appearance of a Western organizational culture, however, the Western organizational culture which existed somewhere at the beginning of the twentieth century. Absence of trade unions, poor legislation aimed at protecting employees and the general manager's rather primitive perception, based on socialist books on the exploitation of workers, of how things should work under the conditions of a free market, create a situation in which employees are abused and really exploited. Use of vulgar language by senior managers (often with a criminal past) and sexism are typical and common features of many newly established companies.

Transformation of the Russian economy, however, brought about new phenomena and a new type of manager. To understand fully the behaviour and problems of the current Russian management one has to keep in mind that the percentage of newly established companies is quite large, much greater in relative terms than the percentage of young companies in Western countries.

One of the pathological features of Russian companies is that the managers who created the company also become involved in operational management. The intensity of this involvement does not decrease with company growth, as happens in western companies, where, after the company reaches a certain size, it turns into a JSC with operational management transferred to professional managers. In Russia this does not happen. There are two main reasons for this. One of them is that the Russian stock market is under-developed. But the most important is that there is a deep mistrust of the idea of giving voluntarily management of the company into the hands of outsiders. The whole concept of the company owner and appropriate behaviour are still unclear.

In fact, all previous Russian experience warns that delegating the decision-making process to someone else, even within the company, is a sure way of losing the business. Trapped between the danger of turning into ineffective and not well qualified operational managers on the one hand and the danger of handing business to professionals and thus, as a rule, losing it, Russian managers have developed their own model which is often called the entre-preneurial model of corporate management. The model is an attempt to find a solution to two extremes: one is when the respective functions and roles of owners and managers are well defined and well separated and another is when the owner is totally involved in the everyday functions of the company.

Polonsky (2002), when working in Russia, often came across situations where managers of large industrial companies were involved in decisions about what colour storerooms should be painted or in making decisions about the size of entrance gates. In the emerging Russian model the functions of owners and hired managers are not well defined. Parallel with the group of professional managers running the company there is a group of managers acting on behalf of the owner who supervise operational managers in order to ensure that they behave in accordance with the interests of the owner and do not have notions of taking the company away from the existing owner. A so-called 'strong gun' is created which blends owner, board of directors and senior management.

There are numerous problems related to this Russian hybrid. First of all, this created an institution that resembles a closed JSC where the formal mechanism of corporate governance is overruled. The interests of those who happen to be outside and not part of the group are completely ignored. Thus the whole process of corporate governance is a constant fight between those in power and those outside of it. It appears that owners are to blame for the existing situation. External factors, such as government or financial markets, which could play a positive role in unraveling the relationship and establishing efficient corporate governance, are very weak and so far inefficient. Government policy is, moreover, a subject of constant political pressure and is changing all the time, creating uncertainty at the company level.

### Management development

Over almost ten years since the beginning of reforms, Russian managers have come a long way from being inexperienced and extremely poorly qualified from the point of business disciplines to being sharp, well-educated managers with extremely diverse experience. Involvement in teaching on the Moscow State University MBA programme reveals the huge creative potential of the young businessmen, who in their late twenties and early thirties are often running large corporations, employing thousands of people. Interestingly enough, that absence of 'proper business experience in a proper business environment' created a situation where the Russian managers can easily deal with all sorts of non standard management problems, even though they may get confused when facing a standard Western textbook situation (Polonsky, 2002).

The influx of people without proper business education into managerial positions during recent years was beneficial when companies had to deal with different, unusual situations created by an under-developed market, which was often very confusing for their Western counterparts.

Another obvious tendency among Russian managers comes from the fact that all their experience was acquired during the period of 'wild capitalism' in the 1990s, when all sorts of unethical and often criminal behaviour was almost the norm. It is not clear if this background and its norms have yet been effaced in the early years of the new millennium.

### Outcome and performance: empirical evidence

Russia has recovered from the economic crisis of 1998 and the economy has continued to display real GDP and industrial production growth. However, the empirical evidence indicates a slow pace of transformation at national and corporate levels. The overall picture is moreover very mixed, with considerable regional and local disparities. Corporate restructuring, for example, is still constrained by concerns for its wider social impact. Corporate governance, moreover, appears often more concerned with personal enrichment than economic efficiency. As argued by Filatotchev *et al.* (2003), insider privatizations have led to managerial entrenchment and reduced levels of enterprise restructuring, whereas external ownership involvement and more intensive development of organizational capabilities may facilitate effective restructuring.

Furthermore, there appears to be widespread reluctance at the individual level to adopt Western management approaches and practices. As indicated by Gurkov (2002) in the HRM field, many Russian managers have rejected so-called modern methods of managing employees, arguing their inappropriateness to the Russian context.

### Evaluation and conclusions

Russia has always been a country that was difficult, if not impossible, to categorize and label. Still, in assessing the economic transition that has happened so far, we are rather optimistic. The country has gone a long way from being a leader of the communist world to a country with recognized market economy status. The swiftness of the privatization process was impressive. However, one can argue that there was no justice in the process and a small group of people became enormously rich, while great numbers of people found themselves in economic hardship. Nevertheless, the ownership structure of the country changed almost overnight, leaving little chance for the restoration of common ownership and thus a return to the old system. On the negative side is the fact that after more than ten years of economic reform, it is still unclear who is effectively controlling the privatized assets. The state and especially regional authorities still have a large influence over privatized companies.

The direct influence of the regional authority has increased. Feudalization of regional life and constant lobbying by regional interests often weaken the effectiveness of the reforms coming from the federal centre (Poletaev, 2000:39). Putin's attempts to have more control over the regions appear to many Russians as necessary if further reform is to be implemented.

The economic distortions, which were plaguing the economy during the first years of transition, are somehow becoming less of an issue. All governments since the beginning of the economic transformation have stuck to a liberal course. The current government goes even further. Since Putin came to power, many of the bases for structural reforms and improvement of the investment climate were drafted or implemented. They included laws on economic deregulation, laws aimed at alleviating administrative and other barriers to investment and business activity, laws aimed at enhancing the protection afforded to property rights, laws aimed at ensuring fair and equal competition, labour law reform, pension law reform and laws aimed at fostering the use of information and telecommunication technologies in different spheres.

The investment climate is also improving with the amendment of the existing legislation and adoption of new legislation favourable to foreign investors. However, until the country's investment infrastructure, such as the banking system, property rights mechanism, stock market, legislative reform with proper enforcement together with improvement of personal security, is developed, it would be unrealistic to expect a dramatic increase in the amount of FDI and portfolio investment.

Moreover, the speed of structural reform needs to be intensified, if Russia wants to sustain its growth rates. Direct and hidden subsidies have to be removed once and for all, especially in the Russian energy and transport sectors. This is also necessary in order to gain acceptance by WTO. In fact, WTO member states rightly believe that the existing pricing mechanism for gas and electricity effectively subsidizes Russian companies and provides unfair competition.

In order to become truly competitive in the world economy Russia has to change the structure of its economy so that the energy and raw materials sectors no longer dominate and stop being the country's major source of hard currency. Moving from this addiction to obtaining relatively easy hard currency could be difficult. The state must develop a comprehensive policy aimed at development of high-tech manufacturing industries; radically improving quality and competitiveness of industrial output should be a priority for the Russian government

Reform of the public administration system has started, but has not progressed very far. The transparency of bureaucratic actions is still poor, though improving, and their responsibilities and the limits of their power are often unclear. However, the most worrying fact is that the majority of bureaucrats are just not capable of coping with the new demands of democratic society and the market economy. Widespread corruption among the public administration is a known fact of Russian life and it seems that at the moment there is no immediate solution for dealing with this problem.

Small businesses are the most exposed to the unclear and confusing powers of the public administration. They suffer numerous and often conflicting regulations, are inspected by different rent-seeking institutions, are subject to underinvestment and limited access to lending resources and they often feel unprotected from racketeers and corrupt police. An indication that the situation for the small business sector is not improving, is the fact that during the last three years from 1999 to 2002 the number of registered small businesses has not increased and remains around 800,000.

At the enterprise level, the situation is very uneven. In Moscow, one can find effectively restructured and efficient companies having Western business attitudes, modern equipment, excellent competitive products and which are transparent or almost transparent about their financial situation. However, this is more of an exception than the rule.

On the positive side, one can argue that enterprises understand now that old 'special relations' which allowed them to survive often do not work anymore. This pushes them into investing considerable time and effort in evaluating their products, developing new ones and in identifying markets for their products. In the general context of economic uncertainty (and in some respects ignorance), enterprises have moved from a situation where they were fundamentally production units instructed to deliver a certain volume of outputs and with minimal concern for demand. Enterprises are now fully aware of the need to find customers for their products as without customers products accumulate at the plant! Managers have thus begun to develop a clear understanding of the relationship between supply and demand and of the impact this has on the functioning of the company. This is particularly evident in those companies supplying consumer products.

A further area of intense activity has been in restructuring the enterprise. On the one hand, enterprises have divested themselves of the political and also of many social functions and managers tend to focus clearly on the core areas of business activity. On the other hand, enterprises have also had to take on board a number of functions previously carried out by external bodies such as the relevant industrial ministry. A most obvious manifestation of this has been in the establishment of sales and marketing departments, which previously, where they existed, tended to be rudimentary. Other areas of development have been in accounting and finance, quality and public relations. Some managers explained the difference with reference to Western textbook descriptions of organizational structures. Certainly, the structure of enterprises now approximates more closely to practice in traditional capitalist economies, even though the content of the work undertaken in the 'new' departments may not necessarily have changed so substantially.

Managers, especially senior managers, have acquired substantial new knowledge and skills and have considerable opportunities to apply them. However, the application of this new learning can be problematical because of the relative inexperience of the learners and the context in which the new learning has to be transferred. However, there is no doubting the enormous willingness to learn among managers as well as a realization of the need to operate differently by employees (Edwards *et al.*, 2000:167)

One of the potentially worrying features of the Russian economic develop-ment is the formation of a specific business morality (Polonsky and Iviozian, 2000:231). Previous experience tells new Russian businessmen that there is a possibility of short cuts to enormous wealth, using fraud in business relation-ships. Capital flight and transfer of a company's assets abroad to personal companies or Western bank accounts are damaging for business morale as well as bad from the investment point of view. Managers and owners believe that there is nothing wrong in avoiding tax payments, bribing or usage of non-economic forms of persuasion, which often include physical violence and use of criminals. However, there is more understanding among the business elite that if one is to be profitable and successful in the long run one has to be ethical, but this belief is not widespread and the business environment is still far from ideal.

After more than 10 years of economic reform, Russia still stands on the threshold of major changes and a new crossroads. The tasks of modernizing the economy, of the way the economy is run, changes in attitudes at all levels from the company and general public to government, evolution of law and public attitude to law, development of democracy and civil society are of mammoth proportions. There are many indications, from the Russian attitude to NATO and terrorism, that Russia is making its choice and in spite of the enormity of the task will move forward to becoming a developed and prosperous democratic society.

# 5 China

## 'Crossing the river by feeling the stones'

### Introduction

Modelling the transition process requires both exogenous as well as endogenous variables. Pressures from outside often have an initial role in initiating the path from 'plan to market', as in the case of international market or trade influences; internal exigencies, such as the need for greater factor efficiency are also important, in terms of setting in motion the 'reform' process.

Since the People's Republic of China (hereafter to be referred to simply as China) embraced economic reform for both of the above reasons in the late 1970s, substantial changes have occurred not only at the national level in terms of social and economic development, but also at the individual enterprise level in terms of corporate governance and management systems. The economic system embarked on a 'transition' essentially from 'plan' to 'market' in a step-wise progression (Child, 1994). The transformation of Chinese management systems is thus closely related to the gradual adoption of wider market forces *vis-à-vis* both greater external globalization and internal market-orientation. However, China claims its transitional process has been 'special', indeed 'distinctive'. The notion of a 'socialist market economy with Chinese characteristics' is here seen as creating a new identity for itself, particularly if compared with the so-called 'transitional economies', namely economies that used to be under a socialist planning system (at least the cases in this book) such as those of the former Soviet Union (FSU) and Central and Eastern European (CEE) countries. This chapter provides a detailed analysis of the transition of Chinese economic and management systems in terms of the notion of such a distinctive 'socialist market economy with Chinese characteristics' (Zhu and Warner, 2000a).

In the transition process, economies will each have both general and particular characteristics that mark their evolution. It is often the case that there are general patterns that are often modified when applied to each case. The transformation of formerly communist economies and societies observes this rule but the Chinese experience has explicitly conformed to an attempt to apply transition 'with Chinese characteristics'. This latter factor may help to distinguish this specific case from the others covered in this study but we can initially ask if its importance is more likely to be a matter of degree, that is to say a relative rather than an absolute one.

We will now first examine the Chinese case in terms of the common headings we have used throughout this book. We start with the general and move on to look at the particular. To start, we briefly note the literature on transitional economies in so far as it relates to the themes we move on to consider in this chapter.

So far, there have been a fair number of comprehensive analyses of transitional economies, such as the state socialist model (Thompson and Smith, 1992), the 'democracy' model in the Bolshevik programme (Davies, 1990), state socialism (Nove, 1983; Rakovski, 1977; Kornai, 1980), institutional reforms (Stark and Nee, 1989), the organization of labour (Braverman, 1974) and labour process (Burawoy, 1985). However, there are only a few analyses identifying the socialist market economy in terms of comparing, say, China and Vietnam, with the others (with the exceptions of Sheldon, 1993; Chan and Norlund, 1995; Zhu and Fahey, 1999). Much of the empirical literature on the socialist countries in Eastern Europe and the USSR has been cyclical, shifting back and forth between decentralization and recentralization, markets and hierarchical planning, openness and retrenchment and so on. After the failure of such partial changes, there was a rapid disorganization in the reforming régimes (Thompson and Smith, 1992) as the old-style rigidities and uncertainties were supplemented by new crises produced by limited marketization. In particular, the end of the 'social contract' between workers and the régime began to produce new social tensions and conflicts. As a consequence, the socialist systems in the USSR and Eastern Europe collapsed and they moved closer to the capitalist market model. However, the problem does not stop there. From the economist's point of view, the collapse of the communist régimes had the result that, with rare exceptions, all goods produced in these countries were incompatible with international standards due to low quality and/or high prices (Papava, 2002:796). This type of economy was referred to as the 'dead' economy or 'necroeconomy' (see Papava, 2002). Now, the challenges are to identify and utilize a mechanism that would enable these countries to cope with the problem of 'dead' enterprises in an 'automatic régime' and to switch to a market economy in which a 'necroeconomy' can be transformed into a 'vitaeconomy' (Papava, 2002:803).

It is important at this point in this overview, to employ a distinctly historical context that will provide insights into the mechanisms of change and the economic and non-economic factors shaping the stages of transition (see Rosser, 2002). An 'evolutionary approach' dominates much of the current debate regarding 'transition' and this approach identifies the origins of causal processes and integrates cohesively endogenous and exogenous factors that influence what has been transforming these economies (Ruth, 1996). In fact, transition of the formerly socialist planning economies has created a massive destruction of the previously existing institutions and a disruption of overwhelming uncertainty in decision-making and asymmetry in information flows (Rosser, 2002:446). It seems obvious that notable divergences exist among the former socialist economies, even though they all face the need to adopt a strategy of economic growth and development, likely to promote their economic recovery and technological and social progress.

The literature on the process of economic transition, we may see, spans the debates on the speed of transformation and draws generalizations from empirical country studies. The most contentious issue regarding the methods of transition has been the division between 'shock therapy' (or the so-called 'big bang' approach) and 'gradualism' (in other words as 'reform sequencing') in terms of economic policy and institutional changes (Kumssa and Jones, 1999). Although people have different views on the rationale of the effective reform processes (Aslund *et al.*, 1996; Fischer *et al.*, 1996; Montes, 1997; Rosser and Rosser, 1996), the evidence shows that most post-socialist countries suffered major declines in their GDP and industrial output at the onset of the transformation by following 'shock therapy', but China and Vietnam being exceptions as following an alternative model of 'gradualism'. This latter model has also been interpreted by Lau *et al.* (2000) as a 'dual-track' approach to transition, based on the continued enforcement of the existing plan, while simultaneously liberalizing the market (see also Jin and Haynes, 1997). This specific method makes implicit lump-sum transfers to compensate potential losers of the reform (Lau *et al.*, 2000:120).

Such debates lead to a consideration of the changing role of state and the policy implications. Generally speaking, for transitional economies to succeed they need to adopt comprehensive, well-designed and executed reform policies that will enable them achieve higher economic growth with equity (Kumssa and Jones, 1999:198). Key reform policies have been highlighted by Kumssa and Jones (1999) such as price and trade liberalization, encouraging the private sector into the market, relaxation of state controls over the economy and microeconomic restructuring, stabilization of the economy and the enactment of liberal investment laws to encourage the inflow of foreign investment, and so on.

Another area of the economic transition debates focuses on the human factors that play a decisive role in any economic process. One writer, Papava (2002:801), claims that fundamental changes in the society rely on the behaviour of a human who undergoes the transformation from *homo sovieticus* (one who is totally oppressed by and totally depends on the state), formed under the conditions of the command economy, into *homo economicus* (one whose motivation is based on either getting maximum benefits (in one's household), or maximum profits (in one's company)), a type of human being that is allegedly characteristic of the market economy. Non-successful economic performers certainly do not have the social and economic environments that allow individual people and companies to fully transform themselves.

In contrast to these former socialist economies in Eastern Europe, China is still nominally a socialist régime, as noted earlier, but in its transition to a hybrid form that their planners denote 'the socialist market economy'. Furthermore, the transition has been relatively peaceful and politically stable (despite some worker-unrest), although at times fitful (for example, after the 1989 Tiananmen Square Incident). As the economy is still significantly agricultural and in some cases at subsistence level – unlike the industrialized Eastern European counterparts – the negative impact of structural reform on people's ability to support themselves has been muted. In other words, reform has offered a better standard of living for enough Chinese peasants and workers to keep the majority on board the reform bandwagon.

The theoretical and empirical developments consonant with transition provide both the justification of and the space for this chapter. The literature about transition is heavily weighted towards Europe and the former USSR (as have been the chapters thus far in this book) and with far less attention paid to Asian developments. The literature about the labour process and management is similarly weighted towards Europe. Therefore, it is crucial that this chapter tackles these issues by invoking the case of an important transitional economy in Asia, namely China. The central tasks of this chapter are thus, as follows:

1   identify the *evolutionary path* of reform in China from the respective historical, cultural, political and economic perspectives;
2   explore both the *role of the state* and the resultant policy implications, on the one hand, and the human factors in terms of individual human beings' and organizations' survival strategies, behaviour and the performance outcome, on the other;
3   evaluate the so-called *'uniqueness'* of the transition process *vis-à-vis* Chinese management systems and to respond to the theoretical debates in the area of economic transition.

In order to achieve the above tasks, we must look at the underlying historical foundations of the Chinese system, both in terms of its recent past and its much longer tradition. We feel that these factors play a particularly significant role in shaping the way the Chinese economy developed, how modernization occurred and why the transitional process differed from that of other economies. Although China experienced comparable Soviet-style institutional changes imposing a planned economy, as did the CEE countries, both sets of cases following the 'Soviet model' plus or minus, it did so in rather distinctive ways and it was able to shed these institutional features in its own way, as we shall shortly see.

## Historical background

We now turn to China's recent history in order to elucidate the nature of its reforms. The Chinese transition-path started in the late 1970s, after experiencing several decades of isolation and ten years of the 'Cultural Revolution' between 1966–76. After Mao Zedong died and the 'Gang of Four' fell in 1976, both the régime and people faced tremendous pressure both politically and economically (Riskin, 1988). The increase in population that had occurred during the Cultural Revolution, combined with a reduction in the production of consumer goods, resulted in shortages of food and clothing (Zhu and Warner, 2000a). The economic gap between China and other developed economies and Asian newly industrializing countries (NICs) became even wider, in spite of the most popular slogan under Mao's leadership being about 'catching-up' with the British and American economies (*ganying chaomei*).

Mao's successor, Hua Guofeng, announced new changes based on the initial model designed by former premier Zhou Enlai, and introduced the Four Modernizations – of industry, agriculture, defence and science and technology – which became the new national goal until the year 2000 (Zhu and Warner, 2000a). However, political and ideological struggles continued among the party leadership, between the extreme left wing led by Hua and the reformist one led by Deng Xiaoping after regaining his power in 1977. Hua insisted on the 'principle of two principles' – everything that Mao said was 'truth' and everything that Mao did was 'right'. This principle blocked any attempts to break away from the then existing systems. Deng, however, believed that Mao had made a tremendous contribution to the liberation of China but recognized he had made a great mistake in the Cultural Revolution. According to Deng, the ratio of Mao's mistakes to his contribution was 3:7. For the Party and the people, the principle was 'seeking truth from facts' (*shishi qiushi*) and 'liberation of thought' (*jiefang sixiang*). This new belief led to a search for a new direction in economic development. The outcome of the struggle was that Deng's ideology gained the support of the Party and the people (Zhu and Warner, 2000a:120). Eventually, his reform agenda and 'Open Door' policy were formally adopted at the Third Plenary Session of the Chinese Communist Party's (CCP) Eleventh Central Committee in December 1978 as the central Party policy (Korzec, 1992).

Reform of the economy initially started in rural areas, as the responsibility system replaced the People's Commune system (Hsu, 1991; Riskin, 1988). Then, the fiscal system was reformed from the earlier state controls on enterprise investment and profit taking, to adopt greater enterprise autonomy of decision-making on investment and after tax profits (Wong, 1995; Blejer, 1991; Li, 1991). A new banking and financial system was introduced with the goal of establishing a commercial banking system (including a central bank, commercial banks, investment banks, financial companies and new local money and share markets) (Yang, 1995; World Bank, 1988). Meanwhile, the economy was opened up in order to stimulate international trade and foreign investment in China by establishing Special Economic Zones (SEZs), Open Cities and Open Regions. This step led to all the east coast regions, and finally the entire country, being opened up to trade and foreign investment being encouraged (Lardy, 1994; World Bank, 1994; World Bank, 1997; Sheahan, 1986; Kleinberg, 1990).

The reform philosophy followed Deng's pragmatic approach described as 'crossing the river by feeling the stones' (Zhu and Warner, 2002). Hence, a market-determined price system was gradually introduced into the traditional central planning system through a period during which there existed 'dual-systems' of plan and market between the 1980s and the early 1990s.

Certainly, political events such as the 1989 Tiananmen Square incident blocked further reforms until 1992, when Deng went to visit the SEZs in the South and pushed for further change under the banner of the so-called 'socialist market economy' (Lin, 1996; Goodman and Segal, 1996). Given this ideological 'green-light', more drastic reform initiatives were set in motion, such as the reform of SOEs, developing stock markets, opening up the price system based on market-criteria, new legislation to allow mergers, corporatization/privatization, as well as bankruptcies, more favourable regulations and physical environments for foreign investment and trade, and eventually further opening up the entire country to the global economy by joining the WTO as finally occurred in 2002 (see Figure 5.1 for a chronology of events).

China had seen impressive economic growth since the mid-1990s under the leadership of now outgoing Prime Minister, Zhu Rongji and retiring President, Jiang Zemin. The growth rate had stayed high but a little weaker than in the previous decade (it grew at nearly 10 per cent per annum on average over the last two decades). Whilst the management of the economy has seen its ups and downs, with ongoing indebtedness, especially in the state

| | |
|---|---|
| 1976 | Death of Mao Zedong |
| 1976 | The Four Modernizations |
| 1978 | The Open Door Policy |
| 1979 | Joint-Venture Law enacted |
| 1980 | Responsibility system in agriculture |
| 1983 | Profit-retention scheme for enterprises |
| 1984 | Enterprise management reforms |
| 1985 | Open cities established in fourteen locations |
| 1985 | Dual-price system introduced |
| 1986 | Regulation on labour contracts |
| 1988 | Contact responsibility system in industry |
| 1989 | The Tiananmen Square Incident; displacement of Zhao Ziyang by Jaing Zemin as Party Secretary |
| 1992 | Deng Xiaoping's Southern Inspection Tour and speech |
| 1992 | Enterprise decision-making powers enhanced |
| 1992 | The Personnel Reforms |
| 1994 | The new Labour Law |
| 1997 | Impact of the Asian financial crisis ably managed by Premier Zhu Rongji |
| 1997 | Hong Kong handover |
| 1998 | State-owned enterprise reforms and lay-offs of employees |
| 2002 | China signs up to the WTO |
| 2003 | New leadership of President Hu Jintao/Premier Wen Jiabao |

*Figure 5.1* A chronology of Chinese political and economic changes.

sector and deflation in the marketplace, China has continued to grow faster than most of its Asian neighbours, many of which have not fully recovered from the 1997 economic and financial crisis.

China's economic record has been questioned by those sceptical of its official figures. However, in terms of the official statistics, GDP per capita is now much larger than half a decade ago, if we take the five years from 1998 onwards (Table 5.1). In this half-decade, the economy grew impressively. Between 1998 and the end of 2002, GDP per capita went up from just over US$750 to just under US$1,000. The spending power of its citizens was boosted impressively. In 2002, for example, in nominal terms, it was somewhat under US$1,000; it was much higher than this in *purchasing power*, possibly three to four times so, according to World Bank estimates (see World Bank, 2000). By the beginning of 2003, the US$1000 per capita goal was achieved.

These bold changes appear in the last decade or so to have been associated with both positive outcomes such as high economic growth, better economic and investment environments, firmer legal frameworks, larger foreign currency reserves and FDI, higher national and individual incomes and so on,

*Table 5.1* The major economic indices in China since 1998

| Items | | 1998 | 1999 | 2000 | 2001 | 2002 |
|---|---|---|---|---|---|---|
| GDP (RMB billion) | | 7835 | 8207 | 8940 | 9600 | 10240 |
| GDP growth (at comparable prices %) | | 7.8 | 7.1 | 8.0 | 7.3 | 8.0 |
| GDP per capita (RMB) | | 6307 | 6547 | 7078 | 7516 | 7972 |
| GDP by sector | | | | | | |
| *Primary* | Value (RMB billion) | 1455 | 1447 | 1463 | 1461 | 1488 |
| | Growth (%) | 3.5 | –0.55 | 1.1 | –0.14 | 1.0 |
| *Secondary* | Value (RMB billion) | 3862 | 4056 | 4494 | 4907 | 5298 |
| | Growth (%) | 9.2 | 5.0 | 10.8 | 9.2 | 8.0 |
| *Tertiary* | Value (RMB billion) | 2517 | 2704 | 2988 | 3225 | 3454 |
| | Growth (%) | 7.6 | 7.4 | 10.5 | 7.9 | 7.1 |
| Per capita disposable income | | | | | | |
| Urban residents (RMB) | | 5425 | 5854 | 6280 | 6860 | 7703 |
| Rural residents (RMB) | | 2162 | 2210 | 2253 | 2366 | 2476 |
| Total trade | Value (US$ billion) | 324.0 | 360.7 | 474.3 | 509.8 | 620.8 |
| | Growth (%) | –0.4 | 11.3 | 31.5 | 7.5 | 21.8 |
| *Export* | Value (US$ billion) | 183.8 | 194.9 | 249.2 | 266.2 | 325.6 |
| | Growth (%) | 0.5 | 6.1 | 27.8 | 6.8 | 22.3 |
| *Import* | Value (US$ billion) | 140.2 | 165.8 | 225.1 | 243.6 | 295.2 |
| | Growth (%) | –1.5 | 18.2 | 35.8 | 8.2 | 21.2 |
| Savings deposits | Value (RMB billion) | 9570 | 10878 | 12380 | 14362 | 18339 |
| | Growth (%) | 16.1 | 13.7 | 13.8 | 16.0 | 18.1 |
| Exchange rate | (US$1.00:RMB) | 8.2789 | 8.2793 | 8.2781 | 8.2766 | 8.2773 |

Source: *China Statistical Yearbook*, 2000, 2001, 2002 and National Bureau of Statistics, PRC, 2003.

as well as negative consequences such as increasing income inequality both at personal and at regional levels, rising unemployment and insecurity among both urban and rural citizens (Khan, 1996; Long, 1999). The official rate of unemployment is now above 4 per cent but in reality is probably more than double this figure in reality (see Zhu and Warner, 2004). There is a vast labour surplus in agriculture as well as many already displaced from the over-manned urban SOEs. The latter are known as laid-off (*xiagang*) and retain their furloughed status for three years before they become officially 'unemployed' (Lee and Warner, 2005, in press).

Those in urban areas have nonetheless done better than those in rural ones; most urban workers have benefited *vis-à-vis* most peasants. But 'relative deprivation' is now the operative concept in analyzing the uneven welfare outcome. A 'new middle class' of consumers, possibly over 150 million, those enjoying the fruits of the last two decades, is now visible in this scenario, particularly in *Beijing* and *Shanghai* as well as in many of the big Eastern coastal towns and cities. Even within the cities, there are more gains for some than others. Indeed, income inequality has been stretched and the 'Gini Coefficient' (defined as the ratio of poor incomes to rich ones) is now bigger (between 0.40 and 0.45, some say even higher) than it was under Mao (around 0.2) and apparently converging with that of other East Asian countries (see World Bank, 2000). This negative outcome may lead to potential social instability and the new leadership under President Hu Jintao and Premier Wen Jiabao now pays particular attention to these problems.

## Cultural background

Looking deeper in the past, we now turn to look at the source of many of the values that long underlay the mind-set of the Chinese nation and that now impinge on its ongoing reforms. Its cultural tradition is indisputably rooted in philosophical thinking that can be traced back to the ancient China of thousands of years ago. China is the state with allegedly the oldest continuous governance in the world, some say over five thousand years.

During the period of Spring Autumn Warring States (770–221 BC), a number of different philosophical schools made their imprint in an age when it has been suggested that long-standing social rules were collapsing (in the early Zhou dynasty eleventh century BC–771 BC) and the search was on for new ways of thinking to help to explain the apparently resulting chaos (McGreal, 1995:62). It was to be seen as a momentous point in China's long history. This mould-breaking era has been regarded as of great importance and was even tagged as the 'contention of a hundred schools of thought' (Chu, 1995).

Four major streams, we may suggest, have long dominated traditional thinking but are today highly relevant to management thinking in contemporary Chinese society, namely Confucianism, Daoism, *Yi Jing* and War Strategies.

Confucianism was developed by the 'master' Confucius (Kongzi, 551–479 BC) as a set of teachings based on several principles, such as three basic guides (that is, the ruler guides the subject, the father guides the son and the husband guides the wife), five constant virtues (that is, benevolence, righteousness, propriety, wisdom and fidelity), and the doctrine of harmony. Confucius believed that *Ren* or human heartedness/benevolence is the highest virtue an individual can attain and this is the ultimate goal of education (see McGreal, 1995). Putting it in its context, *Ren* may be perceived as a strictly natural and humanistic love, based upon spontaneous feelings, cultivated through education.

According to Confucius, the right method of governing is not by creating legislation or by law enforcement but through the moral education of the people (McGreal, 1995:6). The ideal government for this thinker was a government of *wuwei* (non-action) through the solid groundwork of moral education. This doctrine of appealing to the human heart is central to the belief-system proposed: self-realization towards world peace (harmony) and a peaceful world and orderly society are the ultimate goals of Confucianism (Zhu and Warner, 2004).

*Daoism* is another highly influential school of thinking that has shaped Chinese culture. The philosopher Lao Zi (sixth century BC-?) inaugurated the idea of yielding to the 'fundamental paths' of the universe (Whiteley et al., 2000). Everything in the universe, it is said, follows patterns and processes that escape precise definition and imprecisely this is called *Dao*, the 'Way' (McGreal, 1995:9). In his work entitled *'Daode Jing'* (Classic of the Way and Its Power), Lao Zi argued that *De* (virtue) cannot be striven for, but emerges naturally. The best 'Way' to act or think is *wuwei* (effortless activity), by following the natural course rather than human intervention.

However, the most important element of Daoism is the 'Oneness' and 'Yin–Yang'. In his work, Lao Zi indicated that *'Dao* produces one. One produces two. Two produces three. And three produces ten thousand things (i.e. everything). The ten thousand things carry *Yin* and embrace *Yang*. By combining these forces, harmony is created' (*Daode Jing*, verse 42). These can be understood as the fundamentals of the universe that contains polar complements of *Yin* and *Yang*. *Yin* represents the dark, recessive, soft, feminine, low, contractive, centripetal, short, hollow, empty and so forth, and *Yang* represents the light, dominant, hard, masculine, high, expansive, centrifugal, long, full and solid. Nothing is ever purely one or the other; rather all things are in flux between one pole and its opposite (McGreal, 1995:14).

For Lao Zi, balance between the poles does not mean static parity but a dynamic process that perpetually counterbalances all propensities towards one extreme or the other (Zhu and Warner, 2004). However, the world tends to privilege the *Yang* while ignoring or denigrating the *Yin*. Daoism aims to re-balance this by emphasising *Yin* over *Yang*. In *Daode Jig*, Lao Zi claimed:

> Human beings are born 'soft and flexible'; when they die, they are 'hard and stiff'. Plants arise 'soft and delicate', when they die they are 'withered

and dry'. Thus, the 'hard and stiff' may be seen as disciples of death; the 'soft and flexible' are disciples of life, later echoed in Goethe's phrase 'green is the tree of life'. An inflexible army cannot be seen as victorious; an unbending tree will break.

(*Daode Jing*, verse 76)

Thus, Daoism shows us the path of clear enlightenment and to understand and follow the fundamental cycle of the universe, in order to attain the balance between the poles.

*Yi Jing* (*Book of Changes*) is the 'ever-changingness' of that Oneness (Chu, 1995). According to tradition, the book was composed in several layers over many centuries and it was initially a manual of divination, but with the 'Ten Wings' appendices attached, the resultant *Yi Jing* may be considered a work of philosophy. As McGreal (1995:60) claims, the *Yi Jing* has provided the stimulus for some of the most creative and useful thinking by Chinese seers and scholars, and in both its naive and its sophisticated uses the book has intrigued the Chinese mind and definitively affected the Chinese conception of the 'cosmos' and of the relations of human beings to the continuing changes that are the foreseeable outcome of the universal interplay of opposing natural forces.

The major ideas of *Yi Jing* include the following issues (McGreal, 1995:60): hexagrams made up of *Yin* and *Yang* lines can be used as the basis of prognostications; the *Yang* line denotes strength and movement, the *Yin* line denotes pliancy and rest; there are eight basic tri-grams: earth, mountain, water, thunder, heaven, lake, fire and wood (or wind); change is of two different kinds: alternation (the reversal of polar opposites) and transformation (random change, or chance); the sequence of hexagrams is a model of the cosmos.

As these programmes of thought were debated in the intellectual centres of the various kingdoms, venerable texts such as the *Yi Jing* were reinterpreted. Confucian moralists concentrated on ethical issues reflected in the social content of the text. Daoists and *Yin–Yang* theorists were interested in cosmological issues suggested by the numerological and symbolic relations between the graphic matrices (McGreal, 1995:63). Certainly, military strategists were interested in combining those elements into the formation of military strategies – so called '*Bing Fa*'.

*Bing Fa* (*War Strategies*) is a form of strategic thinking that was first developed for military purposes and has since been applied to almost all human interactions. One of the famous *Bing Fa* works was *Sun-zi Bing Fa*, written by *Sun Zi* in the fourth century BC (Chu, 1995).

In his book *Sun-zi Bing Fa*, Sun Zi discussed the five elements that must be considered in formulating a strategy (Chu, 1995:25–30):

1   moral cause: the *Dao* addresses the morality and righteousness of a battle;
2   temporal conditions: heaven is signified by *Yin* and *Yang*, manifested as summer and winter and the changing of the four seasons;

3    geographical conditions: the earth contains far and near, danger and ease, open ground and narrow passes;

4    leadership: the commander must be wise, trustful, benevolent, courageous and strict;

5    organization and discipline: organization and discipline must be thoroughly understood. Delegation of authority and areas of responsibility within an organization must be absolutely clear (Zhu and Warner, 2004).

The harmony of the five elements is of great importance to success in any endeavour (Chu, 1995:32). These elements are intangible, spiritual, as well as psychological, and are more related to people's mindsets.

The implications for the Chinese management systems, both pre-transition and post-transition, of the above schools of thought can be identified in terms of the fundamental and relational values that help influence the formation of managerial knowledge in the society and are as follows (see also Figure 5.2):

1    The establishment of the fundamental virtue of good heartedness/ benevolence within the organization. Under such influence, the concept of 'workplace as family' is widespread among Chinese organizations.

2    Collectivism and interdependent relational value: it is a well-defined principle within Confucianism that an individual is not an isolated entity. Therefore, the concept of family life as the basic unit in society is emulated within the work setting and with it the broader societal values that ensure social harmony and behavioural ritual are preserved (Whiteley *et al.*, 2000).

3    The doctrine of harmony and the balance between *Yin* and *Yang*: the effort to achieve harmonization of the workplace and maintain a dynamic process that perpetually counterbalances all propensities towards one extreme or another puts the organization in a stable and sustained position.

4    *Bing Fa* and the philosophy of *Yi Jing* lead to strategic thinking and strategic management. The outcome of combining different philosophies such as *Bing Fa* provides the general guidance for strategic thinking that helps organizations to form business strategies.

The virtues and quality of leadership emphasised by Confucianism were later adopted by current management thinking in the area of leadership, it has been suggested: managerial leadership requires the qualities of wisdom, trust, sincerity, benevolence, courage and strictness to carry out policies (Chu, 1995:29).

These implications show that traditional philosophies have had a profound influence on the formation and practices of modern Chinese managerial theory and practice, both under the planned economy in perhaps a weaker form (see Zhu and Warner, 2000b) as well as *vis-à-vis* the market reform

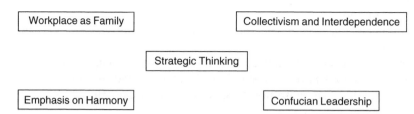

*Figure 5.2* Summary of Chinese management characteristics.

model in a stronger vein (reverting to older, pre-1949 practices, many of which are found abroad in the Chinese Diaspora, as in Taiwan for instance), if in different and distinctive ways (see Child, 1994; Douw *et al.*, 2001; Noronha, 2001; Tang and Ward, 2003; Schlevogt, 2002). However, modification of theory and practice does exist in different societies, in spite of their cultural affinities, in order to make their management more relevant to their social, political and economic environments.

## General background

Economic development in East Asia after 1945 was praised by many commentators and branded as the 'East Asian miracle' (World Bank, 1993). The rise of Japan and the four Asian little 'Tigers' or 'Dragons' (Hong Kong, Singapore, South Korea and Taiwan) constituted a tremendous challenge not only for the Western developed economies but also their own neighbouring countries, in particular China. In order to catch up with these economies and develop more robust domestic political and economic environments, within a two decade-period (that is, from 1978 to 1997, before the Asian crisis), China adopted economic reform and achieved remarkable progress, associated with a rise in real GDP per capita (Cheah, 2000:163). By 2002, its economic performance had achieved levels unimagined when the reforms were first envisaged (see Table 5.1). A significant shift occurred in economic structure from an agricultural to an industrial orientation, with a decline of the contribution of agriculture to GDP from over 33 per cent in 1976 to just under 20 per cent in 1997, while increasing manufacturing sector's contribution from just over 30 per cent to just under 40 per cent over the same period (Cheah, 2000:163). The SOEs contributed over 80 per cent of industrial production in 1978 but now this is down to less than 25 per cent.

   This step improved China's ability to export and generate foreign currency reserves, such that today they are so substantial that they underpin a strong, if over-valued currency. In fact, China has now a significant global competitiveness in the export of lower-skilled labour-intensive products and has become a 'world factory' producing manufacturing goods. This development may indicate that China has more than the potential to catch up with her neighbours in the short term, and other developed economies in the long term.

The major contributing factor for such changes can be traced to the pragmatic and entrepreneurial strategies undertaken by the state, domestic entrepreneurs and foreign investors. Policies and reform steps can be observed as the rationalization of SOEs, the growth of non-state sectors, including both domestic private enterprises (DPEs) and foreign-owned enterprises (FOEs) through product imitation, subcontracting, incremental and evolutionary innovations, spatial arbitrage and production and market diversification being claimed as an *adaptive entrepreneurship* (Cheah, 1993).

Therefore, China's development pattern has been seen by commentators as an 'entrepreneurial state', with the tendency of 'evolutionary innovation' towards hybrid economic systems (Cheah, 2000; Zhu and Fahey, 2000). Cheah (2000) claims that there are several significant features of this hybrid, namely:

1   Authorities in China will continue to retain partial or full control and ownership of a substantial number of state sectors with strategic influences, even after SOE restructuring.
2   This new environment will enable the development of 'governmental entrepreneurship' (or innovativeness) with a significant influence on corporate entrepreneurs, in both state and non-state sectors.
3   This 'adaptive entrepreneurship' allows useful models to be borrowed and modified (for example, the Singaporean development pattern being seen as a model for China) as well as accepting and implementing suggestions from civil servants, academia, professionals and business people.

### External/macro issues/factors

The environment of entrepreneurship that has been gradually established in China provides new opportunities for foreign multinational corporations (MNCs) to move into China and using China as one of their global business strategic locations as well as for Chinese companies to move out to be engaged in international trade and investment in other countries.

Under the 'Open Door' policy, a dramatic change has been the increasing value of FDI and the number of FOEs. In China, FDI comes in the following types: the equity joint venture (EJV), contractual joint venture (CJV), wholly-owned foreign enterprise (WOFE), JSC and co-operative development.

The growth of FDI in China over the past decade has been dramatic. By the late 1990s, for example, China was the second largest recipient of FDI in the world. Indeed it is currently estimated that foreign-owned firms now account for more than a third of China's total industrial growth (Tse, 2000). The rationale for FDI in China has been two-fold: first, to secure access to low-cost raw materials and labour and, second, to penetrate a large, and rapidly expanding, market.

In terms of the source country/region of foreign investors, Hong Kong, Taiwan, the United States and Japan are the top four. However, if we put the European Union as a group, the FDI from the European Union is also quite substantial. The major sectors in terms of amount of utilized FDI are: manufacturing; real estate; power, gas and water production and supply; and services (including hotels). The contribution of FOEs to the national economy is significant in terms of investment, industrial output, international trade and tax revenue. At the micro-economic level, FOEs bring advanced technology, management skills and higher standards of product quality into local production system.

Multinational corporations' involvement in China has gone through several stages over the past two decades. The first stage was between the 1980s and early 1990s when MNCs were tentative about China, making no major equity investments, but operating through licensing and product imports. Meanwhile, most of the 'foreign' investment came from overseas Chinese companies located in Hong Kong, Taiwan and Southeast Asia (Tse, 2000).

The second stage was after 1992 when Deng made his southern trip and speech. MNCs scrambled to enter China, as many of them feared that they would miss out on the big potential market.

After several years of feverish activity, MNCs started to grapple with the challenges of operating in China. Therefore, the third stage was characterized by difficulties and problems. The difficulties of doing business in China emerged due to the influence of factors such as changeable regulations, irregular business practices and competition from other local and foreign companies. These experiences did match the initial expectation of MNCs with regard to investing in China.

The fourth stage is the recent boom that came after China's WTO accession. Most MNCs have accumulated substantial experiences of both positive and negative aspects. The purpose of investing in China also shifts from a short-term orientation to a long-term plan with adjustments of their practices and expectations.

In contrast to the dramatic development of FDI and MNCs' operation under the 'Open Door' policy, reform of SOEs seems rather slow and cautious. It is partly due to the ideological barrier that emphasizes the socialist principle of public ownership and SOEs are the core economic players in the socialist economy, and any attempted change on SOEs' ownership might have a political risk. It is also partly due to the reform procedure of the 'dual-track' system between planning and market that dominated the reform agenda in the early years of reform. One of the key reform policies is giving SOEs sufficient autonomy to operate their business in a market-oriented economic environment. The management in SOEs obtained the decision-making power over material supply, capital investment, human resources, production process, output and marketing. However, SOEs still maintain a strong relationship with the government in terms of getting various kinds of favours. In fact, SOEs are dependent on the government for many forms of subsidies such as cheap credit, land, export permits, tax exemptions, permits to issue initial public offerings of company shares and so on (see Li, 2000). In return, the government also imposes its own objectives on SOEs in both economic and non-economic matters, such as maintaining employment, arranging re-employment centres and producing high growth. Hence, SOEs still have strong social and welfare roles to play.

Following the phasing out of the 'dual-track' system in 1992 after formal adoption of a 'socialist market economy', SOEs' problems became more obvious: profit losing, excessive employment and heavy debt burden. Further SOE reform became inevitable. In the middle and late 1990s, a series of reform policies came out, such as allowing loss-making SOEs to be merged with other profitable SOEs or claim bankruptcy, corporatizing SOEs into JSCs with shares sold in the stock market and selling SOEs to foreign or local private owners. The principle of the reform was based on the notion of 'holding the big one and letting the small go' (*zhuada fangxiao*). After this wave of reform, only large-sized SOEs with strategic influence were maintained as SOEs. The majority of small and medium sized SOEs were transformed into privately-owned companies or JSCs.

The key policies on encouraging the domestic private sector were gradually formed after several waves of ideological debate. Under Mao's ideology, everything in China was people-owned or, more concretely, state-owned. Private ownership was seen as the enemy of socialism. During the 1950s socialist consolidation period, many private enterprises were transformed into SOEs and collective-owned enterprises. However, after China adopted economic reform in the late 1970s, the private sector reappeared and performed an increasingly active role in the national economy. For instance, the growth rate of investment in fixed asets between 1981–96 for SOEs was only 18.6 per cent, but for the private sector it was 23.5 per cent (Wang and Zhang, 2000:35).

Among these privately-owned firms, the majority are SMEs. One of the advantages of these privately-owned SMEs is management autonomy. This allows flexibility in decision-making in response to changing market conditions. However, new problems such as imbalanced development and bottlenecks emerged as they grew rapidly to a bigger scale. The problems can be highlighted as: lack of strategic decision-making, poor quality of products, lack of modern human resource management and shortage of managerial and technical personnel, internal conflicts of interest among family members, and policy discrimination towards private enterprises such as the difficulty of raising funds (see Wang and Zhang, 2000:39–41).

The government policies on other areas can be summarized under the following key topics: monetary policy and development of financial markets, and labour market policy and regulations.

In fact, financial reform has become one of the two most urgent tasks (another one is the restructuring of SOEs) in the current stage of economic reform. The government expectation is two-fold: on the one hand, financial market reform will free economic activities from state control and help build a basis for civil society; on the other hand, recent events such as the Asian financial crisis have made Chinese policymakers especially cautious about the potential of financial crises to destabilize the national economy (see Chen and Feng, 2000:47).

Financial reform covers the following areas:

1   restructuring the banking system and maintaining stable monetary policy;
2   establishing government bond markets;
3   developing stock markets;
4   emerging insurance markets, non-banking institutions and credit cooperatives (Chen and Feng, 2000).

Before 1979, the People's Bank of China was the only bank in the country. Its functions were typical of a central bank, such as credit distribution, currency issuance and foreign exchange reserve management. In addition, it acted as a commercial bank by receiving deposits from households and firms, as well as making loans to and providing clearance services for business (Chen and Feng, 2000:49). In the beginning of 1984, the State Council allowed the transformation of the People's Bank of China into a central bank and allocated the commercial businesses to other newly developed state-owned commercial banks, namely the Bank of China, the Agriculture Bank of China, the Construction Bank and the Industrial and Commercial Bank. After two decades of development, the four state commercial banks are the major players in the structure of China's financial institutions.

Another important part of bank reform was the establishment of policy banks, namely the State Development Bank, the Export-Import Bank of China and the Agricultural Development Bank in 1994 (Chen and Feng, 2000:51). The function of providing preferential loans to projects deemed important in view of the government's industrial and agricultural policies was carried out by the four state-owned commercial banks. However, the government realized that it was necessary to separate the commercial function from the government administrative function. Therefore, the newly established policy banks took over such tasks to allocate resources to key industrial and agricultural sectors.

During the period of bank restructuring, the central bank played a key role in terms of maintaining price stability. Since the mid-1990s, the monetary policy has been focused on stability through stable exchange rates between the Chinese currency, the *Renminbi* or RMB and the US dollar (see Table 5.1, p. 113), no matter the pressures on devaluation of RMB during the 1997–98 Asian crisis or appreciation of RMB in the second half of 2003.

The second area of financial reform is the development of government bond markets. Since 1978 the government has run a budget surplus for three years only (Chen and Feng, 2000:52). In order to narrow the gap between government revenues and expenditures, the government started to issue bonds and more than 52 per cent of the central government expenditure was from bonds (Chen and Feng, 2000). In addition, the secondary bond market opened in 1988 in order to accommodate the exchange of bonds and bond-trading centres were set up in various localities.

The third area of financial reform is the establishment of stock exchanges. The Shanghai and Shenzhen Stock Exchanges were established in 1990 and 1991, respectively. In the 1990s, the government separated share markets between domestic and foreign investors: Share A, denominated in the Chinese currency RMB, was available to domestic Chinese investors only; while Share B, denominated in US dollars in Shanghai and Hong Kong dollars in Shenzhen, was open to foreign investors only. In addition, some companies were also listed overseas such as in Hong Kong (H-shares) and New York Stock Exchanges (N-shares) (Chen and Feng, 2000:52–3). However, in recent years, as part of efforts to join the WTO, the government removed the differentiation between Shares A and B.

The fourth area of financial reform is the emergence of insurance markets, non-banking institutions and credit cooperatives. The insurance categories in China's insurance markets include property, life, liability and agriculture. In the early years, only state-owned insurance companies were allowed to operate in the market. However, in recent years, more private insurance companies, in particular the foreign-owned companies, have been granted licences to operate in the Chinese market as part of agreement of WTO accession. In addition, non-banking institutions also developed rapidly, such as investment trust companies, security firms, finance firms and leasing companies. Two types of credit cooperatives exist in China: one is rural credit cooperatives and another is urban credit cooperatives. While the former have existed since 1949, the latter started in 1979 (Chen and Feng, 2000:55). Both have played important roles in savings and investments. They have made the loan process accessible to collectively- and privately-owned firms in both cities and the countryside.

The development of Chinese labour market policy and regulations can be distinguished into five phases: 1978–84, 1984–88, 1988–92, 1992–95 and 1995-present. In the first phase many reforms and regulations were introduced as experiments in carefully selected parts of the country, including in the SEZs, before being extended from around 1985 to the national level (Zhu and Campbell, 1996:34). A brief period of retreat from further reform occurred from 1988 until 1992, when Deng Xiaoping made his famous Southern Trip Speech on the goals of a 'socialist market economy' and an acceleration of the process of economic reform (Zhu and Campbell, 1996:34). Since then, the revised Trade Union Law was adopted in 1992 and the new Labour Law was introduced in 1994. Some of the previous temporary regulations were adopted as legal articles within those new laws (see Warner, 1995a, 1995b).

In 1986, 'Four Temporary Regulations' were introduced (Zhu and Warner, 2000a:120–26). The first of these – the Regulation on Labour Contracts – was directed at instituting a system of fixed-term contracts in place of the previous system orientated to permanent status among the SOEs and COEs. It provided detailed provisions on such matters as duration of labour contracts, job description, job secruity and working conditions, wages, labour discipline, termination of contracts and liability for breach of labour contracts.

The second temporary regulation – on the Employment of Staff and Workers – was aimed at reforming the recruitment system from one of administrative allocation and internal recruitment to open job-application and selection through objective standards. It provided enterprise management with the autonomy to recruit, select and allocate new employees based on the needs of the business and the quality of the potential employees.

The third regulation – on Discharging Employees – gave the enterprises the power to dismiss workers. Compared with the pre-reform 'iron rice bowl' (*tie wan fan*) system under which the enterprises were basically unable to dismiss any employee, the new regulation empowered the managers to exercise the right of dismissal in the case of employees who were not able to fulfil the requirement of production, or who severely damaged enterprise property or were involved in criminal activities.

The final regulation concerned the Insurance of Employees Scheme. It was directed at establishing a system of social insurance for unemployment, insurance for injury and illness and old age pensions for retired people. Generally speaking, it required the enterprises to pay up to an equivalent of 25 per cent of the employee's salary as a social insurance contribution (Zhu and Campbell, 1996:34–5).

During the immediate post-Tiananmen Square Incident (June 1989) period, both political and economic reforms stopped and there were no further labour market initiatives until 1992 when Deng Xiaoping made a tour of southern China. This further impetus to the process of economic reform resulted in further labour market developments, in particular, a speeding up in the process of drafting the new Labour Law and the encouragement of the tripartite system for regulating industrial relations and settling disputes between management and labour.

With the support of the ILO's Asian Pacific Project on Tripartism (APPOT), the Chinese government began to introduce the tripartite system in 1993 (Zhu and Fahey, 2000). It adopted the ILO's definition of tripartism as 'the interaction between government, employers and workers as equal and independent partners in active participation at efforts to seek solutions to issues of common concern' (Unger and Chan, 1995). Tripartism has since been promoted by both the ILO and Chinese government as a strong tool to develop industrial democracy, to improve industrial relations and productivity, to ensure safety and health and to contribute to stability in working life. Under the financial and professional support of ILO, regional and national workshops were conducted and the Labour Ministry and local Labour Bureaux played a crucial role in the formation of tripartite committees at both national and regional levels (Unger and Chan, 1995). At present, the tripartite committees comprise the government representatives from the labour administration, the workers' representatives from the trade unions and the employers' representatives from enterprise management associations (Zhu, 2000). The major functions of these committees so far have been restricted in practice to the mediation of labour disputes and collective agreements, and providing views on new labour laws. The new Labour Law had been approved by the National Congress on 5 July 1994. The establishment of this new law can be seen as a response to three factors: the government's concerns about ideological transformation and labour market stability, the needs of different interest groups in China and the pressure of external influences from international organizations (e.g. the ILO as noted above) and MNCs.

## Internal/micro issues/factors

Under the general direction of developing the *Four Modernizations*, the enterprise management agenda was based on introducing an advanced management system and new technology. The transformation of management systems was from the initial Contract Management Responsibility System (CMRS) to the later Modern Enterprise System (MES) (see Forrester and Porter, 1999).

The most important objective of the CMRS was related to performance – a desire to see industry achieve higher output targets through the inducement of retained profits (Forrester and Porter, 1999:50). Another objective was to increase the autonomy of SOEs with respect of operational decisions on a range of matters of concern to them, such as corporate strategy, organization, finance, procurement, marketing, technical innovation and human resource management. The third important objective was for government to maximize its revenue from SOEs, which led to fiscal measures (Forrester and Porter, 1999:50). These measures included the progressive application of a régime of income tax to all enterprises in place of the requirement to hand over all profits to the state under the planning system. It was assumed that the state would benefit from the new arrangements in the long term.

Under this guidance, experimentation with the CMRS commenced in the early 1980s (Nee, 1992). The change from profit transfers to taxation of enterprises began around 1984 but the widespread application of the CMRS around the whole country was in 1987 (Forrester and Porter, 1999:51). Apart from the introduction of the new 'income tax' system, two other important initiatives are worth mentioning here:

1  the growth of total wages and bonuses should be linked to any growth in profits and taxes paid;
2  targets should be agreed between the state and SOEs for technological upgrading and for investment in this (Forrester and Porter, 1999:51).

The CMRS led to certain positive outcomes, such as production being more efficient and profitable compared with the previous system. However, one fundamental problem was that managers began to adopt short term perspectives to improve profit figures in the near term rather than tackle the major problems requiring extensive restructuring and longer-term expenditure (Forrester and Porter, 1999:52).

With the intensive debates on the CMRS, the new modern enterprise system (MES) was introduced to replace the CMRS in 1993 (Forrester and Porter, 1999:61), though vestiges of the CMRS remained in some firms. The main rationale for introducing the new MES was based on the following criteria:

1   need to address the question of ownership of enterprises;
2   need to combat short-termism among managers;
3   the need to modify the very complex and fraught system of separate negotiations over contract terms with so many SOEs;
4   need to correct the negative impact of earlier tax reforms;
5   need to clarify the separate responsibilities of enterprise, state and party, and allow SOEs to be managed 'scientifically' (Forrester and Porter, 1999:61–2).

Since 1993, the MES was implemented and SOEs were reformed into three groups. The first group have been called 'state-owned limited liability corporations' which are exclusively funded and owned by the state directly with large size and strategic influence. These enterprises are intended to have a board of directors, a supervisory committee and a management committee, which monitor and control one another. They have an obligation to increase their asset value and respond to government policy (Forrester and Porter, 1999:62–3).

The second group have been labelled as 'shareholder corporations' which are owned by their shareholders who can be both internal shareholders such as managers and employees and external shareholders, namely, other companies or individuals who obtain the shares from stock exchanges in Shanghai and Shenzhen. Management consists of senior managers and a board of directors with greater autonomy with respect to government. These firms have been subject to a variety of regulations and forms of governance, and to overall supervision by the State Assets Administration Bureau (Forrester and Porter, 1999:63).

The third group are smaller enterprises designated 'shareholder partner companies', which allow individuals to purchase and manage them. Management may vary considerably in such enterprises, and the state plays little role in these firms (Forrester and Porter, 1999:63).

Except for the changes of SOEs, other non-state sector companies, in particular FOEs, have established non-state-owned limited liability corporations with the so-called 'modern enterprise system'. In fact, for most FOEs, transforming their international management system into Chinese operation is one of the significant contributions towards the development of the Chinese management system. For the domestic private enterprises, establishing MES is also one of the strategic approaches towards the development of a modern management system.

## Outcomes and performance – case studies

The emergence of multiple forms of ownership in China poses analytical channels for evaluating organizational performance. In the following section, we examine the outcomes and performance of three types of enterprises, namely SOEs, FOEs and DPEs, in the areas of organizational strategic planning; managerial cultures and styles; market orientation and sales; HRM and employee relations. The case studies were based on our recent field-work in China (see Zhu and Warner, 2004).

We illustrate these issues using the categories of the three enterprise groups noted above, namely SOEs, FOEs and DPEs, and each group contains four enterprises (Table 5.2). We now summarize the organizational character-istics in relations to the reform policy and recent WTO accession.

Among the four SOEs, Case E1 was one of the leading banks in China of over 30 years standing. WTO accession has built up competition in financial markets as well as in labour markets. Case E2 is a state-owned group corporation, formed after a merger in 1996 between two former state-owned machinery and clothing export–import companies, each with over 30 years' history. Its businesses had been diversified and the company shares were publicly sold on the Shanghai and Shenzhen Special Economic Zone (SEZ) Stock Market in recent years. Case E3 was a firm established in 1956 as a SOE, in charge of planning and distribution of electrical machinery and chemical products, under the leadership of the Jiangsu Provincial Bureau of Com-merce. It adopted the 'managerial responsibility system' with autonomy and self-reliance in 1990 and converted into a JSC in 1998 with 30 per cent of state shares, 20 per cent of other corporate shares and 50 per cent of staff shares. Similarly, Case E4 was also a firm established in the 1950s as a relatively small SOE located in the Western region (Chengdu). Under the government policy of 'holding the big ones and letting the small ones go' (*zhuada fangxiao*) in the mid-1990s, E4 became a JSC in 1996 with 20 per cent of staff shares and 80 per cent of other corporate shares. E4 experienced the difficulties of imple-menting the so-called 'modern management system' due to resistance based on its past practices.

The second group of enterprises comprised four FOEs. E5 is a Sino-Japanese joint venture with Chinese control of 60 per cent of shares and Japanese control of 40 per cent. It was an export-oriented enterprise, with an 80 per cent export rate. It had a mixed management system, involving Chinese and Japanese ways of managing. The labour force was very stable and its group-orientation in terms of rewards, performance evaluation and business operation in both production and trade sections was noteworthy. The challenge it faced was the competition from other FOEs in both domestic and overseas markets.

*Table 5.2* Case studies profile (2002)

| Firm | Ownership | Age (years) | Location | Size (no. of employees) | Business | Turnover (RMB ml) | Market |
|---|---|---|---|---|---|---|---|
| E1 | SOE | >30 | Beijing | 40,000 (in Beijing) | Bank | 50,000 | Domestic |
| E2 | SOEs/Group | >30/6 | Nanjing | 10,000 | Manufacturing and trading of machinery and clothing, and other businesses | 4,800 | Overseas (75%) Domestic (25%) |
| E3 | SOE/JSC | >30/4 | Nanjing | 800 | Wholesale and retail of electronic appliances | 2,600 | Domestic |
| E4 | SOE/JSC | >30/4 | Chengdu | 550 | Manufacturing of machinery | 300 | Domestic |
| E5 | JV (Sino-Japanese) | 9 | Shanghai | 800 | Manufacturing and trading of fax machines | 1,000 | EU and US (80%) Domestic (20%) |
| E6 | WOFE (US) | 9 | Shanghai | 1,600 | Manufacturing and trading of medicine and equipment | 5,800 | Domestic |
| E7 | WOFE (Dutch) | 9 | Shanghai | 7,000 | Manufacturing and trading of hi-definition TV and DVD | 3,000 | Domestic |
| E8 | WOFE (US) | 11 | Beijing | 700 | Software R&D and marketing | 5,000 | Domestic |
| E9 | DPE | 9 | Nanjing | 150 | Software R&D and marketing | 100 | Domestic |
| E10 | DPE | 12 | Nanjing | 1,000 (in Nanjing) 6,000 (nationwide) | Trade and production of electronic and electrical products, automobile, and real estate | 4,800 | Overseas (10%) Domestic (90%) |
| E11 | DPE | 5 | Nanjing | 1,900 | Manufacturing and trading of DVD, telecom and PC | 2,400 | Overseas (50%) Domestic (50%) |
| E12 | DPE | 9 | Chengdu | 850 | Manufacturing and trading of animal nutrition and agricultural goods | 500 | Domestic |

Source: authors' survey, October 2002.

Case E6 is one of the leading US-based MNCs operating in China as a WOFE. It had adopted an ambitious plan of production and marketing operations in China. In turn, Case E7 is a Dutch-investment MNC subsidiary with many branches in China, with its national HQ located in *Shanghai*. It had 'leading-edge' technology and appropriate management expertise in China and most of the employees were young and well educated. The management system, including HRM, was copied from its Singaporean regional headquarters and the HR manager was trained in Singapore. A combination of Western systems, with some East Asian modification (certainly the influence of Singaporean and Chinese management systems), was found in E7.

Case E8 is another leading US-based MNC operating in Beijing in the business of software R&D as well as in marketing. The management system and key managerial posts in the firm were in effect 'Americanized'.

The third group of enterprises includes four DPEs: two were large DPEs with 1,000s of employees, one was a medium one with over 850 employees and the other, a small one with over 150 employees. The management of E9 believed that both opportunities and challenges exist since China's WTO accession and their policy was to develop their products and the company with unique characteristics. The slogan of 'open thought' was in the company-booklets.

Case E10 is one of the leading DPEs in China with its headquarters located in Nanjing and over a hundred branches around the country. Its business had been enlarged from initially retailing electronic appliances to a wider range of businesses, including production of electronic and electrical products, automobiles and real estate development. However, due to its rapid business increase, HR was far behind the needs of business expansion.

In Case E11 we find a similar situation to E9 and E10. Its business had been increasing rapidly in the past five years but HRM was neglected during this rapid growth period. Now further competition, not purely based on price but on 'know-how' and human resources, intensified the need for improving HRM policies and practices.

Case E12 was an example of a DPE that was located in the inland region to the west (*Chengdu*) and was established by three brothers from one family to produce animal nutrition products for local farmers. E12 did not have a HR department and personnel issues were handled in a traditional Chinese family business manner, such that the boss (*laoban*) made all decisions.

From these empirical findings concerning the reactions of Chinese enterprises towards the challenges of reform and WTO entry, we find a division between enacting active responses through innovative strategies and new management practices on the one hand (described as '*proactive*') and being passive and less dynamic towards challenges on the other hand (described as '*reactive*') (Figure 5.3). The key variables that determine these different performance outcomes are ownership, location, history, experience and sectors, but the size of firm and market orientation become less significant.

**VARIABLES**

| | Ownership | Location | History | Experiences | Sectors | Size | Market |
|---|---|---|---|---|---|---|---|
| **Proactive** | FOEs/JSCs | Coastal | New | Modern management Internationalization | High-value/ New economy | N/A | N/A |
| **MANAGERIAL** | | | | | | | |
| **Reactive** | SOEs/DPEs | Inland | Traditional Family business | Planning system/ Labour intensive | Low-value | N/A | N/A |

*Figure 5.3* Enterprise managerial reaction.

Enterprises with foreign-ownership, or being transformed from SOEs to JSCs, are more likely to have *proactive* management performance than SOEs and DPEs; enterprises located in the coastal region are more likely to have *proactive* management performance than enterprises located in the inland regions; enterprises with weaker links with the traditional state planning system are more likely to have *proactive* management performance than enterprises under the shadow of the past; enterprises that have experienced the modern management system and internationalisation are more likely to have *proactive* management performance than enterprises with experience of the planning management system or the family business management system; enterprises in high value-added sectors and the new economy are more likely to have *proactive* management performance than enterprises in low value-added and labour-intensive industries; and finally size and market orientation become less significant.

The characteristics of enterprises with *proactive* management performance can be summarized as follows.

Organizational strategic planning focuses on both short-term gain and long-term sustainability, a sense of balance of duality. Enterprise autonomy and competitive advantages in the areas of organizational structure, investment capability, know-how and personnel are crucial factors for these enterprises to have the upper hand in the market competition.

Managerial culture and styles are consistent with international standardised practices, described in Chinese as 'connecting with the international track' (*yu guoji jiegui*). A modern corporate governance system is the foundation for implementing innovative management practices.

Human resource management and employee relations are part of their innovative management practices by adopting new HR dimensions which are distinguished from traditional personnel management (see Zhu and Warner, 2004). The major areas of HRM adoption thus appear to be in teamwork, quality control, new technology, adherence to rules, common values and norms, importance of line managers, harmonization of work conditions and in-house training (see Warner, 1995, 1999, 2003a).

In contrast to the *proactive* model, the *reactive* model has a very different outcome of management performance.

Organizational strategic planning mainly focuses on short-term survival rather than long-term development due to the accumulated financial burden (i.e. SOEs) or shortage of new capital funds (i.e. DPEs) and an unclear future direction. The constraints still maintain in SOEs and DPEs though with different perspectives: SOEs' constraints are more related to historical impact and government policy and control, while DPEs' constraints are more related to lack of financial support from state-owned institutions and shortage of new technology and experienced personnel.

Managerial culture and styles are under the shadow of either the planning system (i.e. SOEs) or the family business tradition (i.e. DPEs). A certain sense of egalitarianism still influences people's minds in most SOEs. The latter are supposed to carry out many social welfare functions even after decades of economic reform. The most important example is handling lay-offs and establishing re-employment centres. Organizational structure and management styles are changing but not so dramatically when compared with JSCs and FOEs. Personal and political connections are crucial for managerial survival rather than predominately relying on a performance merit-based system.

On the other hand, DPEs are carrying on the family business tradition. Family members control the strategic decision-making and organizational hierarchy is based on the Chinese boss (*laoban*) phenomenon. Because of the lack of prestige in society, most DPEs are less attractive in terms of obtaining capital funds and high-quality personnel, which may be the crucial bottleneck for their future development.

Human resource management and employee relations are predominately following the traditional personnel management pattern for the SOEs and irregular HR practices for the DPEs (see Warner, 1995a; Zhu and Warner, 2004). The major problem in SOEs is that personnel managers play a passive role in HR planning and coordination. Due to historical reasons and surplus labour, the function of HRM is limited to revitalizing employees' potential. On the other hand, most DPEs do not have a well-established HRM system. A common reason was given as a short organization history and HRM has not been seen as a crucial part of their business success. Another practical problem is the shortage of well-trained HR personnel available in the personnel market. Hence, newly-established DPEs normally do not have a well-established HR policy and practical system.

Certainly, we are aware that the generalization we offered above has its limitation. In reality, there are exceptions, such as some SOEs and DPEs do embrace the modern management system and are actively engaged in innovative management practices whereas some FOEs and JSCs have a relatively poor management performance. However, the distinction is made based on a judgement of the general trend in the majority of enterprises with a distinct ownership system.

## Discussion and conclusion

Since China started its economic reforms in the late 1970s, it has changed dramatically. Characterized by high economic growth over two or more decades, it has become a 'magnet' for international production and investment. However, rapid change has also brought uncertainties and anxieties for the average Chinese citizen, and this is no less the case *vis-à-vis* WTO accession, as joblessness and layoffs grow by the day.

The evolution of the transition process in China is based on the philosophy of Deng Xiaoping's idea of 'crossing the river by feeling the stones', a pragmatic and gradualist approach. Therefore, it is not unusual to observe that many reform agendas were initially of an experimental nature, from introducing foreign investment and the management responsibility system to 'dual-track' pricing systems and labour market regulations. When those policies were proved as useful and safe for the so-called 'Socialist Market Economy', then such polices might be transformed into permanent policies and regulations. However, if policies led to negative outcomes, modification and revision of policies became necessary. The pattern of Chinese transition shows that there is strong leadership at the top to drive the reform agenda, which may be different from other bottom-up models.

However, the top-down model does not mean that there is no initiative from below. In fact, the remarkable success story of Chinese reform is that individuals (human beings or organization) may benefit from the early reform and embrace the further reform process. Meanwhile, the transformation of the human mind from *homo sovieticus* to *homo economicus* claimed by Papava (2002) is significant among the Chinese. Travellers can see that even in a small mountain village in Yunnan province, villagers try their best to commercialize their products and maximize their income, for example, by selling fresh vegetables and flowers to the *Shanghai* market through air transportation. This entrepreneurship phenomenon sends a strong signal that, if individuals are involved in the transformation actively, the reform agenda can be continued and sustained.

Now the focus is on the notion of a 'Socialist Market Economy with Chinese Characteristics'. Is China indeed still a 'socialist country' and what is the meaning of 'socialism'? Our observation is based on the consideration of three major concepts, namely political, economic and cultural aspects. As for the political consideration, the party-State does not want to lose power. In fact, 'socialism' already lost its economic meaning such as a public ownership dominated economy and equal/planned distribution system, but the political meaning is still important for maintaining legitimacy for the Communist Party's political control as its main social/political identity. Without the epithet of 'socialist', the political system could be easily changed from a single-party system into a multi-party democracy.

As for the economic consideration, a market-oriented economic system had replaced the centrally planned system and all kinds of market mechanism are playing a crucial role in current Chinese economic life. The so-called 'adaptive entrepreneurship' is the fundamental dynamism pushing for further market reform and competition (both domestic and international).

As for the cultural consideration, the term 'Chinese characteristics' is used to reflect the national identity *vis-à-vis* the challenge of globalization. Both the régime and social elites (including scholars) call for new moral standards and social values to guide the citizens' behaviour, in particular in facing the attraction of materialism and desire-driven social phenomena labelled by the government as 'Westernization'. The ideological vacuum forces the elites to reintroduce traditional values and allow Confucianism to play an important role for maintaining morality. Meanwhile, management behaviour may fit well into such mixed systems by combining the advantages from both modern management practices and traditional thinking and values. Another convenience for the régime is that anything proved as useful and 'good', can then be claimed as a success with 'Chinese characteristics'. Otherwise, a 'bad' outcome certainly belongs to 'Western pollution'. This exercise has a significant political meaning that shows the leadership is on the right track towards future development and gains certain propaganda effects, given the fact that both régime and people are not sure about the future direction.

These considerations lead us to think about the future: is it inevitable that China be one of the 'capitalist brothers' sooner or later, or can China still continue as a different entity?

There is no explicit blueprint for the future reform however and nobody can clearly and adequately predict the Chinese future. So far, we have observed a pragmatic and step-by-step approach towards change and reform. Public debates on television and radio also focus on the future of China, in particular, in the wake of growing globalization. China has shown herself to be part of the global community by joining the WTO. Commentators show an increasing confidence (it also represents certain attitudes held by the leadership of the government and social elites) that China is big and strong enough to play the double-edged sword of globalization well. Historically, China had opportunities to open up the society to the international community. Openness and confidence were interrelated in Chinese history. 'Foreign cultures' came to China and influenced Chinese thinking and social systems. Meanwhile, Chinese culture is mature and strong enough to learn from others and modify other cultures into their own systems. History is a mirror here and the Chinese see hope for their future. So far, we have seen that both the Chinese leadership and her citizens are brave enough to embrace reform and eventually realize their dream that, as the most ancient of civilizations, she still can show an alternative way of social progress to the rest of the world.

# 6    Vietnam

## A pragmatic hybrid model

### Introduction

After China and Russia, Vietnam, with a population of around 80 million in 2002, is the world's third-largest transforming economy. Furthermore, the fifty or so years of the post-colonialist period have been strongly influenced by Vietnam's relationships with China, Russia and the United States. Vietnam's transformation – just as China's (see Chapter 5) – presents an alternative route to that undertaken by the former command economies of Central and Eastern Europe and the Former Soviet Union (especially Russia and the Baltic states), where economic reforms have gone hand in hand with the establishment of new, democratic political systems. In Vietnam, economic reform towards a socialist market-economy has taken place within the context of a communist political system. This alternative approach is thus of academic interest and may also be relevant for other former command economies where political transformation has not followed the democratic pattern (as, for example, in the Central-Asian republics of the former USSR).

Since the beginning of *doi moi* (economic renovation), Vietnam has experienced economic growth unlike that of the past (Fforde and Vylder, 1996). Real GDP growth rates peaked in 1995 with 9.5 per cent according to official statistics (ADUKI, 1997). However, the 1997/98 Asian financial crisis adversely affected the Vietnamese economy. Most economic sectors and regions in Vietnam reported declines in the rate of GDP growth, FDI, and international trade (Moreno *et al.*, 1999). For instance, GDP growth was only 4.8 per cent in 1999 compared to 8.1 per cent in 1997 (Table 6.1). The FDI inflow to Vietnam has continued a downward trend since 1998, with only US$0.6 billion of implemented investment, which was about 25 per cent of the FDI in 1997. The Asian financial crisis was the main cause of the sharply reduced FDI inflow (Freeman, 1998; Le, 2000). In recent years, FDI from Asian countries accounted for 70 per cent of total FDI inflow to Vietnam. In 1998, however, FDI from those countries decreased to only 45 per cent of total FDI (CIEM, 1999; Athukorala, 1999).

International trade was also adversely affected by the influence of the Asian crisis. In 1998, for instance, the growth in the value of exports was only 2.4 per

*Table 6.1*  GDP growth, inward foreign direct investment and unemployment in
         Vietnam since 1997

| Year | Nominal GDP(US$ bn) | Real GDP(%) | Inward FDI (actual, US$ bn) | Unemployment rate (%) |
|------|------|------|------|------|
| 1997 | 26.8 | 8.2 | 2.4 | 5.9 |
| 1998 | 27.2 | 5.8 | 0.6 | 6.9 |
| 1999 | 28.5 | 4.8 | 0.6 | 7.4 |
| 2000 | 30.6 | 6.0 | 0.5 | 6.4 |
| 2001 | 32.3 | 6.0 | 0.8 | 6.3 |
| 2002 | 34.9 | 7.0 | 1.8 | 6.0 |

Source: World Bank, 1998; Vietnam Ministry of Planning and Investment, 2003; Business Monitor International Ltd, 2003; *Vietnam Panorama – Vietnam Economy News*, 16 May, 2003.

cent, the lowest rate since 1991 (CIEM, 1999). Under this pressure, the government imposed administrative measures to control imports in order to reduce trade deficits. As a result, imports declined by 1 per cent in 1998 (CIEM, 1999). Although the current account deficit was reduced, in the long term this will have negative effects on domestic consumption and economic growth due to the increase of the prices of imported goods needed for production (Ariff and Khalid, 2000).

The liquidation of SOEs and other so-called 'production units' and less foreign investment have led to an increase in unemployment (Nguyen, 2000). In 1999, for instance, the official rate of unemployment in the urban areas was 7.4 per cent, compared to 5.9 per cent in 1997 (Table 6.1). There is a tendency towards higher unemployment in large cities and industrial centres. In addition, underemployment in the rural areas is serious. The internal migration from the rural areas to the urban industrial areas also increases the pressure on the labour market.

Hence, economic reform created both achievements as well as uncertainties. The chapter addresses the evolution of Vietnam's economic reforms and the extent to which they have improved the country's economic performance. It also deals with the dilemmas associated with the route to reform. For a chronology of the key events in Vietnam since 1945 see Figure 6.1.

## Historical background

Vietnamese national identity began to be formed in the period spanning the eleventh to thirteenth centuries AD in contradistinction to Chinese culture and involved resistance to incorporation in the Chinese Empire. Vietnamese independence ceased in the mid-nineteenth century with the establishment of French colonial power over Indo-China. Practically, French domination came to an end in 1954 with the defeat of the French forces at *Dien Bien Phu*. Key features of developments since this time have been the division of the country since the defeat of the French forces into North and South Vietnam, the former

| | |
|---|---|
| 1945 | Ho Chi Minh proclaims independent Democratic Republic of Vietnam |
| 1954 | French colonial forces defeated at Dien Bien Phu |
| 1956–75 | Republic of Vietnam founded in south |
| 1973 | US troops leave South Vietnam |
| 1976 | Reunification under Socialist Republic of Vietnam |
| 1970s | 'Bottom-up' reforms in north Vietnam |
| 1986 | Sixth Congress of the Vietnam Communist Party announces *doi moi* (renovation) policy |
| 1987 | New law on foreign investment; liberalization of internal trade |
| 1989 | Liberalization of foreign trade |
| 1990 | State-owned enterprise reforms launched |
| 1992 | Introduction of tight monetary policy |
| 1993 | New labour law |
| 1994 | Lifting of US trade embargo |
| 1997 | Asian economic crisis |
| 2002 | First stock exchange founded |

*Figure 6.1* Key events in Vietnam since 1945.

linked to China and the Soviet Union, the latter to the United States; the establishment of a communist state in North Vietnam; civil war with overt American involvement (1961–73); and the military victory of North Vietnam and its South Vietnamese supporters leading to the reunification of the country in 1976. Relationships with the United States subsequently remained understandably strained. Moreover, relations with China experienced a notable rupture in 1979 after Vietnam invaded Cambodia to suppress Pol Pot's Khmer Rouge regime. Vietnam consequently drew closer to the former Soviet Union.

Vietnam's history since the mid-1830s can be divided into overlapping periods, including French colonial rule, the struggle for national independence and unity and the relatively short recent period of national consolidation and development. The period since 1945 up to the early 1980s can moreover be described as a period of almost continuous warfare, so that in the early 1980s the Vietnamese economy bore many of the hallmarks of a socialist war economy. One of the features of this war economy was that, although it was based on the Soviet model of the command economy, the economy also displayed a considerable degree of decentralization as a means of responding to the consequences of war. In this respect, the Vietnamese economy, even under communism, had its own distinctive characteristics. The rationale of economic reform was based on the negative experience of economic development in the post-Vietnam War period. The attempt by the government after 1976 to unify the socialist northern economy and the hitherto capitalist southern economy in a national socialist economy proved economically catastrophic. The process was marked by economic crises and in 1985 there was widespread famine. One of the consequences of the poor economic performance was the increase in demands within the communist party itself for economic reform. Following considerable and intense debate the policy of *doi moi* (economic renovation) was officially announced in 1986.

*Doi moi* represented a recognition by the communist party of the need for economic change and was at the same time an assertion by the party of its claim to control economic reform. As, for example, Fahey (1997) and Griffin (1998b) have argued, economic reforms, especially in agriculture, predate the announcement of *doi moi*. Following the economic crisis of 1978–79, there had been grassroots initiatives involving 'fence-breaking', that is, introducing local reforms without official sanction (Fahey, 1997). These initiatives were particularly prevalent in the agricultural sector where the system of collectives was abolished and greater incentives were given for raising output and selling in the free market. Furthermore, even SOEs were permitted to sell on the free market any output that was additional to government-specified quotas (Griffin, 1998b). In fact, Fahey (1997) argues that the Vietnamese state was in a relatively weak position and was actually endorsing reforms that had already been implemented at the grassroots. In other words, the reform pattern can be described as 'bottom-up' reform initiatives.

Following official announcement of the *doi moi* policy, a series of reforms were rolled out, covering a range of areas (for a chronology of the reforms up to 1992, see Griffin (1998b)). In addition to reforms affecting the agricultural sector – the largest sector of the economy – and SOEs, internal trade was liberalized from 1987 and from 1989 foreign trade was also increasingly liberalized. By the end of the 1980s, many features of the command economy such as centrally administered prices, consumer and exporter subsidies and central planning itself had been largely discontinued. These actions were complemented by reform of the tax system and introduction of real interest rates (Griffin, 1998a). In the 1990s, moreover, a process of reform of the system of SOEs began. This mainly took the form of restructuring through merger, although a small number were privatized or allowed to go bankrupt. The SOEs became subject to tighter financial discipline and to the same tax regime as private companies. One consequence of the SOE reform was that the number of SOEs was reduced from 12,000 to 6,000 (Griffin, 1998a). However, as noted by Mallon (1993) with regard to the 1989 crisis, soft loans remained available for SOEs when circumstances became particularly difficult.

Reform of the agricultural sector and SOE reform were accompanied by a range of macroeconomic reforms. In addition to the introduction of real interest rates, in 1989 the foreign exchange rates were unified and the currency (*dong*) was closely aligned to the market rate. In 1992, in order to combat inflation, a tight monetary policy was introduced (Griffin, 1998a). The impact of the reforms manifested itself in a number of ways on the Vietnamese economy. Output, efficiency and wages rose. In fact, growth was rapid and widespread (Rondinelli and Litvack, 1999). Furthermore, macroeconomic stabilization was achieved by the mid-1990s (Griffin, 1998a). The state-owned sector was moreover subject to greater financial discipline.

A subsequent stage of reform included the establishment of independent commercial banks and a first stock exchange (*The Europa World Year Book 2002*, 2002).

Parallel to and an integral part of the reform process were the rise of small-scale private enterprise and the growth of a large informal economy (Williams, 1992). Following the reforms of the early 1990s, SOE employment fell from 12 to 10 per cent of the working population (Rondinelli and Litvack, 1999; Dollar, 1999). The non-state sector thus assisted the reform of the state-owned sector as well as contributing to output growth. The Vietnamese society has experienced a dynamic transformation from war economy, through a period of having a centrally planned economic system with obvious failure, to the current stage of economic reform. Compared with other transitional economies in Russia and Eastern Europe, the Vietnamese transition has its own distinguishing characteristics rooted in its cultural tradition and its political and social environments.

## Cultural background

Vietnamese society has experienced many changes, from the early years of Chinese political and cultural influence (111 BC–939 AD), French colonization, Japanese invasion, and American occupation, to later communist rule and independence, and more recently economic reform and engagement with the global economy. Therefore, there are traces in Vietnamese society of all those historical events. These influences have to some extent been mutually reinforcing. Traditional Confucian values of harmony and saving face and a general predisposition to collectivism have interacted with established socialist values such as egalitarianism. Vietnamese culture has been described as displaying high power distance, high collectivism, moderate uncertainty avoidance and high context (Quang and Vuong, 2000). Nevertheless, individualism is increasing, although this is not necessarily at the expense of broader social values.

Fundamentally, the traditional thinking in Vietnam was influenced by ancient Chinese philosophies (see Chapter 5), predominantly by Confucianism. Confucius (Kongzi, 551–479 BC) developed a set of teachings based on absolute respect for tradition (early Zhou Dynasty) on a carefully ranked hierarchy founded on primary relationships between members of families and between the people and their rulers (De Mente, 1994). It has been seen as a philosophy guiding people's daily life. The detailed description of Confucianism has been illustrated in the preceding chapter on China. Confucianism came to Vietnam after 111 BC when the Chinese emperor colonized Vietnam and brought important technology, including the water buffalo, plough, pig rearing, market gardening, printing, minting of coins, silkworm breeding, porcelain manufacture and international trade to Vietnam. In addition, a Chinese model of bureaucracy, judicial system and education system was implemented in Vietnamese society. Even the written language was based on the Chinese characters. These fundamental principles still influence current Vietnamese society (see Zhu, 2003).

However, another most profound influence in the modern history of Vietnam was communism. Several key issues are related to such influence. Politically, it emphasized Leninist democratic centralism and proletarian dictatorship that legitimize Communist Party control. Economically, it implemented for many years central planning in the economic system until the recent reform. The state had control over planning, material allocation, production, labour and distribution systems. In terms of social relations, it believed in egalitarian principles and mutual respect. Women's position was improved under communist rule, compared to the 'old society'. Wage differences were limited and collectivism was extremely important.

On the other hand, private ownership and entrepreneurship did exist in the South before unification in 1975. A large overseas Chinese business community was very active in *Saigon* (the current *Ho Chi Minh City*) until 1978 when the communist government wanted to take over the private sector in the South. These phenomena show that a mixed and diverse cultural element was rooted in Vietnamese society and a generalization of a homogenous cultural paradigm can be problematic. This is also the case for corporate culture due to the diversity of the ownership system in Vietnam now.

## General background

Following Vietnam's invasion of Cambodia in 1978 and China's negative response, the country became increasingly dependent on the USSR for aid and support. Vietnam had joined COMECON in 1978. However, the reforms in the Soviet Union from the mid-1980s ended in the collapse of not only the USSR but also its satellites in Central and Eastern Europe. With the demise of COMECON, Vietnam was in danger of becoming even more isolated. However, a process of integration into the global economy had begun from the mid-1980s, assisted by the reform of the trade regime (Khan, 1998). Vietnam after 1989 also sought out new trading partners (Griffin, 1998a) and the example of the 'Asian tigers' served as a model of how the Vietnamese economy might be developed. There was a substantial growth of exports and Vietnam became the world's second largest supplier of rice and the second largest producer of coffee.

The reform process, however, was driven by both external and internal causes (Fahey, 1997). External causes, for example, the collapse of the Soviet Union, forced the government to find an alternative way out. From the mid-1990s the relationships with China and the United States began to show some improvement and Vietnam became a full member of the Association of South-East Asian Nations (ASEAN) in 1995. Regionally at least, there was increasing signs that Vietnam was seeking greater integration with the international community, as reflected by its membership of the Asia Development Bank, Asia-Pacific Economic Co-operation and the ASEAN

Free Trade Area (AFTA). Furthermore, in 1993, Vietnam resumed financing agreements with the IMF and World Bank (*The Europa World Year Book 2002*, 2002). At the end of 2001 the US–Vietnam Bilateral Trade Agreement came into effect. The extent of Vietnam's regional integration is reflected in the flows of exports and imports. Over 40 per cent of exports go to Japan (18.1 per cent), the People's Republic of China (10.6 per cent), Australia (8.8 per cent) and Singapore (6.1 per cent). Over 60 per cent of imports originate in Singapore, Japan, Taiwan, South Korea and the People's Republic of China, with Singapore alone accounting for 17.7 per cent (*The Europa World Year Book 2002*, 2002).

## External/macro issues/factors

Following the reforms, there was increasing prosperity and per capita income rose by 60 per cent over the 1990s (Quang, 2001). The GDP increased at an annual rate of 7.6 per cent in the period 1990–2000. The GNP per head, low by international standards, reached $390 in 2000. In purchasing power parity terms, however, it was considerably higher at $2030 (*The Europa World Year Book 2002*, 2002). The increasing economic stability was also reflected in the reduction of inflation. Inflation peaked in 1986 at an annual rate of 487 per cent. By 1995, it had fallen to 12.7 per cent and remained below 20 per cent (Griffin, 1998a, 1998b).

In fact, the economic reforms were responsible for and accompanied a change in the structure of the Vietnamese economy. In a context of general overall growth, the relative composition of output changed, with agriculture, forestry and fishing decreasing, while the respective shares of industry and construction and services increased (Griffin, 1998a). By the year 2000, agriculture, forestry and fisheries accounted for 23.2 per cent of GDP and employed 62.6 per cent of the labour force. Industry accounted for 35.4 per cent of GDP and employed 13.1 per cent of the labour force. Within this, the non-state sector accounted for 22.4 per cent of industrial production. Finally, services amongst which tourism plays a salient role, accounted for 41.4 per cent of GDP and employed just under 25 per cent of the labour force (*The Europa World Year Book 2002*, 2002).

The process of privatization has been complicated by the tension existing between the urge to improve economic performance and a desire to retain state control over certain assets, especially SOEs, and the general operation of the national economy. Agriculture and retailing were effectively privatized by the end of the 1980s, partly as a consequence of the 1988 crisis (Williams, 1992). Privatization of SOEs has in many respects been more contentious as the SOEs remain the motors of the Vietnamese economy and the term equitization is generally used to describe the process of transforming SOEs into 'equitized' companies. The process of equitization is itself slow because SOEs see few benefits in equitization and by the end of 1998 only 116 SOEs had undergone the process. The obstacles to equitization have included lack of clarity in the guidelines, general inexperience with privatization, problems of asset valuation, the extent of inter-enterprise debt, the reluctance of potential 'owners' and resistance from SOE managers and employees. Not surprisingly, internal buyout is the most common form of equitization (Quang and Nhut, 2000).

At the same time, there has been instances of spontaneous privatization (Mallon, 1993; Rondinelli and Litvack, 1999) and cases of SOE directors establishing parallel private companies (Fahey, 1997) that then competing with the SOEs (Mallon, 1993). Interestingly, although equitized companies making a greater use of incentives than SOEs, wage differentials are actually lower in equitized companies than in SOEs where a culture of egalitarianism traditionally prevails (Quang and Truong, 2001).

The reforms of the 1990s placed increasing emphasis on commercialization and the regulation of economic relationships via market forces (Fahey, 1997). According to Khang and Doan (2000) the private sector was responsible for *ca* 60 per cent of GDP and 90 per cent of employment. New firms played a key role in absorbing labour released from the state sector and in creating further additional jobs. There was also a close link between privately-owned SMEs and the informal sector of the economy.

State support for the private sector and new firm development is evidenced by the Law of Enterprise which was implemented in 1999. In the following year, around 500,000 new SMEs were registered and created over 0.5 million new jobs which helped to alleviate unemployment (Quang, 2001). A key problem related to small firms is their relatively poor performance. For example, their contribution to employment is far greater than their contribution to GDP. The owners of SMEs, moreover, while driven by a personal drive for achievement as well as money, tend to be reactive and lack management skills and experience. These companies therefore tend not to be very competitive (Swierczek and Binh, 2001). In spite of these weaknesses, small businesses, including family and individual businesses, are a key component of the economy, especially in terms of employment and facilitate a wider distribution of the gains of economic growth made under *doi moi*.

The dynamic of reform is also related to the activities of FDI. Vietnam has had to compete with numerous other potential recipients of FDI and overall the volume of FDI has been described as disappointing (Griffin, 1998a) or modest (Khan, 1998). Following the 1987 Foreign Investment Law, FDI experienced a continuous increase up to and including 1996. In 1996 the FDI inflow amounted to US\$ 8,497 million, around US\$ 110 per head of population (Quang, 2000). With the Asian crisis of the latter part of the 1990s, FDI declined substantially and began to recover only in 2000 (Quang and Hanh, 2001). Although Vietnam is regarded as having a liberal foreign investment code (Williams, 1992), foreign investors find many causes for opting out of promised investments. To quote Quang (2000:4): 'In reality, most laws are still inactive due to lack of implementation as well as the limited competence and cooperation between the administrative levels. Many foreign

investors have complained about rampant corruption, harassment and inconsistency of regulations.'

Initially, FDI was directed predominantly at the oil sector, with Taiwan as
the leading foreign investor (Williams, 1992). Subsequently, there has been
increasing investment in the tourism industry (for example, hotels) as well as
in textiles and garments. There has also been a geographical concentration of
FDI. In the period 1988–95 54 per cent of FDI was located in the *Ho Chi Minh*
City (Saigon) area, with a further 28 per cent in the *Hanoi/Haiphong* area
(Khan, 1998). FDI has been activated mainly through joint ventures with
SOEs (Griffin, 1998a). One consequence of this approach was that SOEs
competed with each other to attract foreign investors and often reduced their
labour forces in order to appear a more attractive partner (Khan, 1998).

Thuy and Doan's (2000) study of joint ventures in Central Vietnam
highlights some of the difficulties joint ventures face, in particular regarding
the expectations of Vietnamese and foreign managers. Vietnamese managers
are reported as being more concerned with increasing export sales and
acquiring new technology, whereas foreign managers place greater emphasis
on risk sharing, market access, technology transfer and capitalizing on the
benefits offered by the government. Not surprisingly, these differences of
perspective have had a negative impact on the relationship between local and
foreign managers and both parties expressed dissatisfaction with the economic performance of the respective joint ventures.

## Internal/micro issues/factors

### Organizational restructuring

The transition of Vietnamese management systems at the micro-level is
represented by corporate restructuring and it was one of the key planks of the
economic reform policy. One of the aims of economic restructuring was to
improve the performance of SOEs that in 1997 accounted for 41 per cent of
GDP (Quang and Nhut, 2000). The sale of a limited number of SOEs was
announced in 1992, although this was initially limited to small or medium-
sized, viable enterprises. So-called strategic enterprises were, however, to
remain in state ownership. The process was termed equitization (*co phan hoa*)
and was intended to impose hard budget constraints on companies, at the
same time relieving some of the pressure on the state budget (Griffin, 1998a).
In this respect, Vietnamese SOEs were similar to SOEs in China, Central
and Eastern Europe and the Former Soviet Union. However, Vietnamese
SOEs differed in one significant aspect from their counterparts in other
socialist countries in that they did not provide a range of social services
(Griffin, 1998b).

Equitization involved selling enterprise shares to employees and outside
investors. It appears that the state was intended to retain around 20 per cent of
the shareholding while employees were expected to hold between 10–15 per

cent (Quang and Nhut, 2000). The impact of equitization has, however, been slow and limited. In the period 1992–96 only five SOEs were equitized and by the end of 1998 the number had risen to only 116 (Quang and Nhut, 2000). Numerous factors have contributed to the slow adoption of equitization, including incomplete and unclear guidelines, inexperience of the competent bodies, complex valuation problems, reluctance of managers to lose state privileges, employee concerns about job security, SOE links with the state bureaucracy and state-owned banks, etc. (Griffin, 1998c; Quang and Nhut, 2000).

The slow implementation of equitization is a reflection of the tension inherent in the overall process of economic reform. Whilst the state wishes to improve economic performance, it is less willing to relinquish political control. As SOEs are the key drivers of the economy, the state is understandably ambivalent about privatizing SOEs. This ambivalence is underpinned by a range of vested interests within and without the SOEs, including SOE managers and employees, governmental officials and institutions like the state-owned banks. This ambivalence to privatization can also be understood in terms of the economy's performance. Between 1990–95, the state-owned companies' share of total output rose from 32.5 to 42.2 per cent; their share of industrial output rose from 62.8 to 66.1 per cent; and their share of services rose from 44.2 to 51.0 per cent (Griffin, 1998c). The state sector was thus seen as making an over-proportionate contribution to economic growth. Whilst the private sector was also expanding, its performance tended to be low in comparison and its main contribution was in providing employment.

Equitization has nevertheless provided a precedent for the further development of SOEs. Equitized companies are expected to adhere to hard budget constraints and some have begun to shed labour, for example, in order to make themselves more attractive to potential foreign investors (Khan, 1998).

Another micro-level reform is in the area of corporate strategies and alliances that has taken a number of forms under the reform process. In the early 1990s the government actuated the merger of around 3,000 SOEs with other companies possessing related technology and operating in related markets. This concentration process was further developed by the establishment of so-called corporations (*tong cong ty*), often comprising a large number of individual enterprises (Quang and Nhut, 2000). At the same time around 2,000 enterprises were dissolved.

Zhu (2003) mentions a range of organizational strategies adopted by SOEs. These include restructuring in order to achieve equitization status, diversification, a stronger orientation to exports and, in general, achieving greater efficiencies and improving performance. In addition to the formation of conglomerates, the main form of alliance has been the establishment of joint ventures with foreign partners. However, this approach has proved problematical and Vietnamese companies do not find it easy to attract or to work with foreign partners.

*Employment relations and human resource management*

The most sensitive reform issue at the micro-level is the relationship between capital and labour. A mixture of modern employment relations and traditional family businesses practices is widespread and small businesses are generally run on paternalistic lines. A further determinant of the relationship is the extent of unemployment and the need for continuous job creation to counteract the possibility of social unrest.

Overall, unionization rates tend to be relatively low because of the predominance of the private sector and, in particular, agricultural employment and the corresponding relatively low level of employment in SOEs. The largest union, the Viet Nam General Confederation of Labour, has approximately 4 million members (out of a total workforce of over 36 million in 2000) and the Viet Nam Agriculture and Food Industry Trade Union just over 0.5 million members (*The Europa World Year Book 2002*, 2002). Most trade union members are found in the SOEs where participation rates exceed 80 per cent (Zhu, 1998). In SOEs the trade unions regard themselves as owners of the enterprise and are generally closely aligned with enterprise management. Under *doi moi*, with increased enterprise autonomy, the role of the trade unions has been enhanced and they often fulfil a mediating role between management and the workforce (Zhu, 1998).

*Doi moi* has also directly affected the role of trade unions. Whereas traditionally within the Soviet model they acted as transmission belts for communist party decisions and distributed various forms of welfare to their members, with economic reforms the unions are needing to consider more deeply the ways they represent the interests of their members and of workers in general (Zhu and Fahey, 1999, 2000). However, labour legislation is generally weak, although there is a Labour Code which includes a limited right to strike. Outside of SOEs the bargaining power of workers is on the whole very weak. More generally, the labour force is the key source of Vietnam's comparative advantage (Litvack and Rondinelli, 1999). As Griffin (1998b:13) has commented: 'Vietnam possessed at the outset of the reforms a skilled and healthy labour force that was able to respond quickly to economic opportunities'.

The management of human resources still takes the form on the whole of traditional personnel management in that it is largely administrative rather than strategic or developmental, although there is some evidence of change (Zhu, 2002). The relations between management and the workforce continue to be strongly influenced by the socialist system so that egalitarianism and collectivism are still prevalent values. These values are, moreover, consonant with traditional aspects of Vietnamese culture. The perception of companies as 'families' is still widespread and is particularly manifest in small and medium-sized companies. However, it is by no means inappropriate with regard to larger enterprises.

Recent research by Zhu (2003) illustrated the following characteristics of Vietnamese HRM systems. On the one hand, the influences of cultural tradition and the political environment (as a socialist state) are reflected in several dimensions, such as adherence to rules, common values and norms, less individual-oriented pay and harmony. Even the FOEs also adopt certain localized strategies in order to fit in the social/cultural environment. On the other hand, some international, standardized HRM dimensions have been introduced in some companies, such as the transformational managerial role, importance of line managers, freedom in personnel selection, in-house training and a strategic role of HR managers though the development is uneven among the sample companies. The strategic role for HR managers, in particular, is less developed among the case companies. This indicates that the traditional personnel management function is still playing a crucial role among most companies in Vietnam.

### Marketing

The economic reforms have expanded the need for and application of marketing knowledge and techniques. As markets become more competitive, companies have increasingly turned to marketing to consolidate and/or expand their market positions. Quang and Huyen (2000) give an illustration of the application of marketing knowledge and techniques in their case study of Bivina beer. The beer market in Vietnam has become very competitive, the industry being comprised of 320 state-owned, private and foreign-invested companies. The beer market is, moreover, becoming more segmented with premium, mainstream and low-cost segments.

Bivina beer was developed by Vietnam Brewery Ltd, a three-party joint venture involving Asia Pacific Brewery Co. (Singapore), Heineken (The Netherlands) and Hochiminh City Food Company No. 2, to compete in the lower-income segment. It also sought to capitalize on growing nationalistic sentiment in consumer purchasing. The launch of Bivina was not a success. However, it raised a number of issues related to marketing in Vietnam. First, the application of marketing knowledge and skills is neither easy nor does it guarantee success. Second, marketing is resource- and time-consuming if it is to be effective. Third, companies need to pay greater attention to consumer opinions and respond to them accordingly.

### Operational management

Raising operational efficiency and effectiveness is a key aspect of the economic reforms as SOEs still draw on government funds and many private companies are small with low levels of economic performance. There is thus considerable scope to improve company productivity. Quang and Hoa (2001) and Khang and Thuy (2001) give examples of actions taken to improve productivity in two companies. The former discusses the introduction of the JIT system in the Coats Phong Phu joint venture that manufactures threads. The introduction of JIT has helped to enhance the joint venture's competitive position. The second case deals with problems of late delivery at the Thanh Cong Textile & Garment Company that was facing more and more competition in its export markets. The cause of the problem was identified in obsolete labour standards and poor layout of the production line and new measures and layout were proposed to remedy the situation.

There is also an increasing concern with quality, both in manufacturing (see Khang and Thoai, 2001 for a case study of Floor Tiles and Slab Company No. 1) and services (see Khang and Nga, 2001 for a case study of supermarket retailing). More specifically, ISO 9000 is being implemented in Vietnamese companies, albeit very slowly. According to Quang and Hoc (2000:211), 'ISO 9000 registration is still at its initial steps in terms of awareness, understanding and implementation process' and only 78 companies were reported as claiming having implemented the international standard.

*Finance*

A key issue for SOEs has been the move from soft to hard budgets as part of the process of increasing enterprise autonomy. This has forced SOEs to consider more rigorously the issues of financial management. However, the pressure of hard budget constraints has been mitigated by SOEs' links with banks through which they can obtain credit. On occasions, the SOE actually owned a bank (Griffin, 1998c).

For private companies sources of external funds remain limited, even from foreign joint venture partners. The majority of funding in companies is therefore internally generated. Increasing competition in the domestic market has, moreover, highlighted the need for more effective cost accounting because competition often takes the form of price competition (see Ramachandran and Giang (2001) and Ramachandran and Duc (2001) for case studies on activity-based costing in the construction and hotel industries respectively).

*Organizational cultures*

The structures of SOEs are typically hierarchical, although the structures have been refined as a consequence of increased enterprise autonomy, the adoption of new business functions and increasing pressures for flexibility and efficiency. At the same time, the emergence of conglomerates may indicate the aim of retaining monopolistic powers in the face of increasing domestic and foreign competition. The SMEs tend to be paternalistic and organized on the family model. Irrespective of company size, moreover, interpersonal relations play an important role. Maintaining harmony and saving face are key cultural values which manifest themselves in all types of organization. Such values clearly impact on the resolution of conflicts between management and workforce and on the way redundancies are implemented. Overall commitment to the organization tends to be high.

Other values influencing organizational cultures include collectivism and egalitarianism. These values influence attitudes to group work and incentives and militate against highly individualized work and remuneration systems. These values are, however, evolving as a result of the economic reforms, for instance, the emergence of joint ventures and foreign-owned companies as well as the equitization process and redundancies. Zhu (2003) notes, for example, that especially younger employees are quite willing to change employer.

### Management styles

In line with the preceding discussion of organizational culture management styles are strongly influenced by Vietnamese cultural values. However, management styles also vary to some degree between organizational types. In their study of management styles and organizational effectiveness in state-owned, private and joint-venture companies Quang and Vuong (2000) found that SOEs were characterized by a mix of bureaucratic, familial, conservative and authoritarian styles, with an emphasis on clear reporting relationships, formal communication and strict control, even though such a style was not considered appropriate in Vietnam's increasingly competitive environment. Private enterprises, in contrast, were typified by a familial style while joint ventures often displayed a participative style which facilitated knowledge transfer. Both these approaches were considered congruent with achieving organizational effectiveness.

### Management development

The changes brought about and envisaged by the economic reforms have occasioned a considerable need and demand for management development. Already at the beginning of the 1990s, foreign expertise was being brought in to improve the delivery of management training (Mallon, 1993). Furthermore, management training and development needs are growing as the economy becomes more competitive. Managers need to acquire more people-oriented skills in addition to existing task-oriented skills. Moreover, industry-specific knowledge and skills are in need of updating (Swierczek and Anh, 2000). Even though private and foreign providers are helping to augment the provision of management development, Quang (2001) has argued for a total rebuilding of Vietnam's education and training system in order to create the foundations of a modern knowledge economy.

## Outcome and performance: empirical evidence

There is some evidence to indicate, as noted in the preceding sections, that enterprise and managerial behaviour is beginning to change. This change is linked to the economic reforms and the aim of improving enterprise performance, greater integration with the global economy and the influence, albeit limited, of joint-venture partners.

A recent survey by Zhu (2002) draws on fieldwork research, including interviews with managers, trade union leaders and workers' representatives in seven manufacturing companies in *Ho Chi Minh City*.[1] The city was chosen as the location because *Ho Chi Minh City* is at the forefront of economic reform. The old city of '*Sai Gon*' has been transformed into a new centre in terms of the development of industry, commerce, finance and tourism since economic reform was implemented in Vietnam. The transformation in *Ho Chi Minh City* can give an indication of development in Vietnam. These seven cases provide a representative mix in terms of ownership, size, culture and history (Table 6.2). Four of the companies (E1, E2, E3 and E4) are SOEs. Among them, one (E3) has completed the transformation into a joint stock company (JSC) and

*Table 6.2* Company profiles

|  | E1 | E2 | E3 | E4 | E5 | E6 | E7 |
|---|---|---|---|---|---|---|---|
| Ownership[a] | SOE | SOE | SOE/JSC[b] | SOE/JSC[c] | JV (Holland, Singapore and Vietnam) | WOFE (US) | WOFE (Japan) |
| Foundation year | 1975 | 1975 | 1975/1999 | 1978/2000 | 1991 | 1995 | 1995 |
| Size (employees) | 750 | 350 | 1,000 | 440 | 520 | 295 | 2,752 |
| Sales | 46 bn (Dong) | 7 m (US$)[e] | 2 bn (Dong) | 65 bn (Dong) | 1.5 m hl.[d] | 184 m (US$) | 450 m (US$) |
| Profit | 1.5 bn (Dong) | 70,000 (US$) | N/A | 5 bn (Dong) | N/A | N/A | N/A |
| Product competition | Medium | High | High | High | High | Medium | High |
| Main product and business | Wood furniture, garments and footwear | Processed seafood | Soft drinks and processed food | Fishing line and nets | Beer | Animal nutrition (AN) and trade of agricultural goods | PCBA and PWB computer components |
| Market | 60% overseas (EU, Asia and US) | 99% overseas (Japan, US, Australia and SE Asia) | 20% overseas (China, US and Australia) | 20% overseas (EU and Japan) | 100% domestic | 100% domestic of AN products | 100% overseas (EU, US, Japan and SE Asia) |

Notes:
[a] SOE: state-owned enterprise; JSC: joint-stock company; WOFE: wholly-owned foreign enterprise.
[b] SOE up to 1998, thereafter a JSC.
[c] Under restructuring into a JSC this year.
[d] Total volume of sale of beer.
[e] US$1 = Dong 14,500 (March 2000).

another (E4) is under restructuring to become a JSC. These cases represent the process of SOE reform. The other three companies are FOEs: one joint venture (E5, between The Netherlands, Singapore and Vietnam) and two wholly-owned foreign enterprises (WOFEs) (E6 with US investment and E7 with Japanese investment). Each case study involved meetings with a senior manager, the personnel manager and the union leader. Company documents were also collected.

With regard to managerial behaviour and management styles, Zhu's survey found that since enterprise management obtained greater autonomy, the quality of managers has become more important for the survival of the enterprise in market competition. In fact, the criteria for managerial selection have become more restrictive with an emphasis on educational background and experience. In addition, managers have become much younger than the managers of the pre-reform period, and nowadays most of them are in their forties (Zhu, 2002).

The survey also shows that the realization of flexibility and competitiveness in enterprises depends on the type of employment relations established and practised by the management (Zhu, 2002). There is a mixture of control and nurturing in the majority of the sample firms (Zhu, 2002). Most senior management did demonstrate a more transformational leadership, and the middle management and the HR manager demonstrated a more transactional approach. In addition, in all respondent firms the emphasis was placed on respect for rules. All of them emphasized personnel procedures and rules as the basis of good managerial practice. This indicates that compliance with rules is more important in the sample firms than the flexibility model, suggesting that the aim is employee commitment (Zhu, 2002).

In addition, the survey also tested three key variables which determine the outcome of management performance, namely ownership, size and market orientation of enterprises. With regard to ownership, the data suggest that there are varieties of management policies and practices between SOEs and FOEs, and also between joint ventures and WOFEs. However, it is not always the case that the greater the degree of foreign ownership, the more likely it was that formalized management practices would be adopted. In fact, there is a tendency to localization of FOEs' behaviour among the sampled companies. This is also related to the sectors in which FOEs are involved. On the other hand, the new JSCs which were transformed from old SOEs do adopt more formalized HR practices compared with other SOEs. With regard to size, the larger the number of workers employed in the firm, the more likely it was that formalized management practices would be adopted. The data suggest that large companies had more complex, formalized management policies and practices than small and medium companies. However, large companies may have higher transaction costs and would be less able to respond rapidly to market shifts. With regard to market orientation, the data suggest that the more oriented to the external market companies are, the more likely formalized management practices will be adopted. Several cases show that where companies are involved in overseas markets, international standards of quality control and management become important issues for their survival. Hence, market-orientation is a more important factor than ownership for an organization to adopt more formalized management practices among these manufacturing companies in Vietnam.

## Evaluation and conclusion

Vietnam has undergone a considerable transformation since the promulgation of the *doi moi* policy in 1986. The country has experienced substantial growth and achieved a relatively stable macroeconomic environment. The economy, moreover, has become more open and competitive and has achieved a degree of integration with the global economy. At the enterprise level reforms have been instituted and have contributed to a greater concern for economic performance. The private sector has also expanded and has been recognized as a key pillar of the Vietnamese economy. This situation is in marked contrast with the situation prevailing in the first decade of unification that was characterized by economic instability and crisis.

A key issue remains the goal and purpose of economic reforms and the relationship between the political and economic spheres. The goal of the reforms is not to create a market economy but a socialist market economy, with the communist party retaining overall control of the country. In this respect economic reforms have taken place in a context of only limited political reforms. Evaluations of the Vietnamese reforms, moreover, take different perspectives. On the one hand, it is argued that the reform process has still much to achieve and there is still a need to strengthen property rights, accelerate state enterprise reforms and establish a more robust policy environment for private firms (see Litvack and Rondinelli, 1999).

On the other hand, Fahey (1997:476) argues that 'evaluation or description of the workings of markets cannot be made independently of the social structure in which they operate'. As in China, the transformation began with microeconomic reforms and only limited, reactive political reform. Much of the initiative for and experimentation with economic reforms originated at the grassroots and was only subsequently ratified at the government level, which represents a different, 'bottom-up' pattern of reform from the Chinese version of 'top-down' reform. However, borrowing policies from China and then modifying them in order to fit the Vietnamese situation is part of its reform process, which can be observed during the transition period.

Vietnam has made considerable economic progress since the announcement of the *doi moi* policy in 1986. National prosperity has increased and has been distributed relatively widely. The government has also been successful in achieving a certain degree of macroeconomic stability. Exports have expanded as have a range of contacts with the international community and global economy. The overall structure of the economy has evolved, with a greater emphasis on the service sector, although agriculture remains very important, for example, for exports and especially for providing substantial employment opportunities. Furthermore, there is a flourishing private sector, comprised of small and medium-sized firms, which also makes a large contribution to job creation.

The areas, where progress has been much slower, have been in the equitization of SOEs and the development of the institutional context. The SOEs are important because of their over-proportional contribution to GDP and also politically. There has been some improvement in the productivity and efficiency of SOEs but the transformation of the SOEs is by no means complete. Nevertheless, management behaviours and attitudes are changing and there is evidence of knowledge transfer in joint ventures. On the other hand, the domestic private sector and foreign companies make an increasing contribution to the national economy and job creation. Localization of foreign management behaviour is also widespread due to the strong local culture and institutional factors. All these changes interact with each other and with the institutional context, which, in the absence of the kind of upheaval experienced in the former command economies of Central and Eastern Europe, is likely to remain resilient and hence evolve relatively slowly. However, whether Vietnam can continue pursuing its own path of reform, in the face of considerable global pressures, will remain a matter of considerable interest for academic researchers and policy-makers alike.

## Note

1   The fieldwork was conducted by the author in February 2000 with the assistance of the Vietnam National University and Ngan Collins.

# Part III
# Synthesis and conclusions

To get rich is glorious.

Deng Xiaoping (1902–97)

# 7  Conclusions

## Process and outcomes

## Introduction

The Berlin Wall is no more; economic planning has gone by the board; managerial autonomy is *de rigueur*. In this chapter, we try to sum up our findings on *management in transitional economies*. We have approached the topic by looking at not only the macro-dimensions but also the micro-economic ones, as well as the management-level equivalents, of the changes both economies and enterprises have experienced across the world during the transformation process, as they moved from a command economy to a market-led one.

As well as examining the broader features of the economies, polities and societies in Chapter 1, we have also focused on management institutions and practices in the dozen or more countries concerned over a period of two decades or so and dealt with them in some detail. Moving from west to east, we have looked at three sets of economies: first, those in the Central and Eastern Europe in Chapters 2 and 3, then that of the former Soviet Union in Chapter 4 – all these being formerly in COMECON – then turning to the People's Republic of China in Chapter 5 and the Socialist Republic of Vietnam in Chapter 6. This *tour d'horizon* spans a wider range of economies and their managements than previous studies in this genre have encompassed. We thus hope to have comprehensively covered the changes involved throughout the hierarchy of levels, moving from macro to micro levels.

Many books have been written regarding the one level, that is the macro-, or the other, micro-focussed one; we hope that our unique contribution has been to integrate both in this book. The links between the various economic levels and those of the management functions are both complex, as we have seen, and of course, highly interesting. In Chapter 1, for example, we attempted to set out appropriate models that would assist this. We now attempt to review our initial notions in the light of the weight of empirical evidence we have presented in the chapters subsequent to the Introduction.

In the light of the exploratory remarks, we will also attempt to explain not only the general phenomenon of transition but also the variations between the national experiences that characterized the demise of the command economies and end of the Cold War. As set out earlier, we will adopt an *institutionalist* focus throughout this comparative study (see Scott, 2001). This step will involve exploring how the institutional framework of planned economies, at both macro- as well as micro-levels, may have changed into those appropriate for market-led ones, over the period in question (see Peng, 2000). For each economy, it will be clear that there will be a point on a spectrum where a fully-fledged command-economy characterizes the case at one extreme, to the one at the other end where the market dominates, and a range of positions in between. How the specific national economies we have covered moved along this spectrum and why this has been the case, constitutes the main theme of this book.

As we noted in Chapter 1, the destruction of the formal institutions of the former system (de-institutionalization) may be carried out relatively quickly. Sometimes informal mechanisms may compensate for institutional rigidities and allow firms to bypass barriers to change. One writer, Peng (2000:277) defines de-institutionalization as 'the erosion or discontinuity of an insti-tutionalized practice'.

In a number of countries, many of the institutional edifices of the *ancien regime* were pulled down relatively quickly, Hungary being a case in point. However, the elimination, or reform of informal institutions (re-institutionalization) may prove particularly intractable. 'Institution-building' *grosso modo*, moreover, is not a quick process and may require more time than either 'Big Bang' or gradualist approaches to transformation predicated. In Russia, between the mid-1980s and the present day, there may have been at least four stages involved, *commercialization, privatization, nomenklatura* and *statization* (see Puffer and McCarthy, 2003). It still too early to see where this train of events is leading but it is unlikely that President Putin is leading the system back to the communist past.

We shall now sum up the main findings of the respective chapters that each deal with a major geographical unit, be it a country or set of countries.

## Sets of national economies

### Central and Eastern Europe

We have dealt with, in some detail, the changes in Central and Eastern Europe in two sub-sets. In the first one, we have included Croatia, the Czech Republic, Hungary, Poland, Slovakia and Slovenia; we have characterized their economies as having problems in the transition but these being less acute than in the previous sub-set. The former East Germany also belongs to this group of countries in spite of the fact that it is no longer a separate sovereign state but nowadays a constituent part of a lately unified Germany. In the second one, Albania, Bulgaria and Romania are representative of a group of countries we have characterized as having coped with very severe problems in the process of transition to a market economy (Kraft, 1999). The reformers in these countries and their more entrepreneurial managements faced the most difficult economic and political environments in the Eastern Bloc. The transition in these cases is still unfinished.

Developments since the demise of communism have thus clearly been *uneven* across a wide range of states and their economies, although there has been evidence of an increased urgency by several of them to undertake and put in place reforms since the 1997 economic crises. A number of the CEE states were ready to join the European Union proper in 2004, such as those in the second, above-mentioned group of countries (Croatia apart), a remarkable case of 'convergence'. Not only have they emerged from the planned economies of their past days but they now meet the criteria of the European Union, sometimes more so than some of the existing members.

One possible explanatory factor for the depth of the problems encountered in a number of cases had been the initial conditions prevailing in the nation states concerned, bringing to mind Stark's (1992) useful concept of 'path dependence'. There were initial conditions that existed in the form of institutions that had evolved over many years to channel economic activity in a particular direction. The conditions accordingly affect the subsequent evolution of change in the transitional process. The economies here, for example, had particular problems that needed to be confronted when they first emerged from their state-dominated inheritance, such as underdeveloped financial institutions, weakly-protected property rights and so on. A combination of rigid economic structures and limited exposure to reform created a legacy of national economies with considerable distortions, at least from an economist's perspective. These basically unhelpful conditions were not assisted by policies of 'protection' and 'discouragement' (World Bank, 2002) that delayed the privatization of SOEs and the tightening of financial discipline. In other words, the public authorities were not able or willing to 'bite the bullet' and move on to appropriate transitional policies.

The seeds of globalization and possible convergence, as we noted earlier, may even have been planted when economies were in COMECON via their international trade links and where the first international joint ventures (IJVs) between state enterprises and foreign corporations, in what were to become transitional economies, were started. Although the members of the socialist bloc might have been regarded, and possibly regarded themselves, as a discrete entity and distinct from the capitalist economies, there was, by the 1980s, considerable and increasing links, both commercial and financial, between socialist and capitalist economies.

Taking those parts of the economies that had been 'transformed', insufficient encouragement was given to newly privatized firms to respond to market signals and to operate effectively under competitive market conditions. They were, to put it in plain language, at a half-way stage that was neither moving them sufficiently closer to market signals nor at a fast enough speed. Ambivalent attitudes to entrepreneurship and, at times, bureaucratic hostility hampered the formation of new business and held back the development of those that had been established.

The first sub-set of CEE transitional countries plus the former East Germany had progressed along the path towards the market in various positive ways but only after the transformation of their national economic, political and social systems. Apart from Croatia, they have all achieved relatively comparable, if not optimal, transitional results. Moreover, they had all experienced one transitional crisis or another, the result of which was an initially significant fall in production, consumption, wages and salaries and the standard of living of the population. They have all already compensated for this and moved beyond – with the exception of Croatia – the GDP level that they had had before the transition. Here, Croatia and the Czech Republic were the only two examples that had seen negative real growth-rates at the end of the 1990s, mainly because of macroeconomic policy misjudgements.

Looking at CEE transitional countries entering the European Union in 2004 as a sub-set, we find that they have been among the most successful in implementing 'system-change' with as few painful effects for their inhabitants as possible, although the details may vary from country to country. The former East Germany entered the European Union, in effect, with the advent of German unification in October 1990. Others from the second CEE set, with the exception of Croatia, joined the European Union in the first wave of enlargement. Many of them have already arrived at a point where they will try to tell you that their transition is now over.

The privatization of the state(or socially)-owned enterprises in Central Europe has indeed been basically completed. It has enabled a new type of corporate governance system to be put into place but one that has not been without its drawbacks due to an insufficient change in institutional framework and value norms. These changes, however, do potentially mean that a new system of economic motivation is now present and that possibilities for higher economic efficiency are available. Private ownership of the means of production is still quite dispersed, but the ownership concentration process has already been evident for a few years. There is no doubt about the intense need to develop and strengthen further legal and regulatory institutions to oversee the transfer of private ownership and corporate governance rights.

Management reforms across CEE states vary in their nature. In many cases, due to the role of joint ventures and WOFEs, Western-style state-of-the-art managerial practices have been introduced. *VW* soon took over *Skoda,* now a world-class brand. Business schools too have become *de rigueur* in a number of capitals and major cities. The new generation of managers is likely to be well versed in Western business knowledge and skills and may have studied and worked abroad. Many will have a MBA degree.

## Russia

The Soviet Union, as it appeared after 1917, was clearly unique as the first 'workers' state', so-called, and provided the template for later communist entities and command/planned economies. Although economic autarky had been seen in the running of the economies of the main adversaries in the First World War, the new Soviet system created novel economic practices, although the role of the State had been long-standing in Russian historical experience and the new regime, a 'logical development' (see Buck, 2003:303). According to Pipes (1995), it was merely an extension of the older 'patrimonial' tradition.

But the former Soviet Union, as we have seen in Chapter 4, fell less neatly into the pattern set by the others in other respects. It had been the *initiator* rather than the *initiated*; the Soviet Union had built up and consolidated a newly industrialized colossus. This apparent achievement seemed to admiring outsiders 'a success story', especially in the context of the depressed capitalist economies of the 1930s. The Russian 'bear', in turn, militarily 'beat' the Nazi German 'beast'. Its armies had then carried 'system change' to its neighbours' lands and imposed such changes in the wake of military and political hegemony.

Russia had had a distinct and well-documented statist history, as well as the first Soviet-style institutions and planned economy. It may be characterized as '*sui generis*', as we have pointed out, but that may also be similarly true of China and Vietnam. But Russia has in fact always been a country, that was difficult, if not impossible, to categorize and label. Still, in assessing the economic transition that has happened so far, the prognosis may be relatively optimistic. The country has gone a long way from being the 'leading light' of the communist world, to a country with an internationally recognized market economy status, albeit with a tarnished reputation.

Yet Russia moved along the spectrum of transitional change better than most observers would have imagined, given its past. The swiftness of the privatization process has been surprising, according to those economists who praise the 'big bang'; many Russian firms are now 'global players', particularly in the energy sector, like the oil giant *Yukos*. However, one can argue that there were many flaws in the process and a small group of oligarchs became enormously rich, while many of the majority of citizens found themselves facing hard times. Nevertheless, the ownership structure of the country did decidedly change by the early 1990s, leaving little chance for the restoration of the old Soviet-style 'common ownership' and thus a return to the *status quo ex ante*, although as Puffer and McCarthy (2003) imply, the process of change was not exactly linear. Even after the 1990 Russian new enterprise law, not enough encouragement was at hand until the later 1990s and even then the new *nomenklatura* of business oligarchs were set to abuse power and impair appropriate corporate governance (see Puffer and McCarthy, 2003). Also, on the negative side is the fact that after more than 10 years of economic reform, it is still unclear who effectively, as well as legally, controls these privatized assets; huge discrepancies exist in the distribution of wealth and income; large sums of tax remain uncollected or unpaid. The state and especially regional authorities still have a great deal of patronage and influence over the newly privatized corporations.

### China and Vietnam

As we have seen, the People's Republic of China two decades or so ago set out on its reform path in the late 1970s in a highly 'pragmatic' fashion. It had even been claimed that there was no clear strategy behind its transition, for instance by Naughton (1995). But it had an original blue-print 50 years ago for its industrialization programme after Mao Zedong took power, even a template, in the form of its Soviet 'big brother's' achievements, whether or not the outcome was half-baked or otherwise (see Kaple, 1994). The slogan in the early 1950s was 'let's be Soviet, let's be modern' (see Warner, 1995a, 1995b).

Since China started Deng Xiaoping's economic reforms in the late 1970s, it has changed dramatically. Characterized by high economic growth over two or more decades, it had become a 'magnet' for international production and investment. It had the bulk of FDI in Asia going into its economy; in 2002 this was US$52.7 billion. Its foreign exchange reserves soared to US$356 billion, the next greatest in the world after Japan. However, it has relatively weak banks, many inefficient SOEs, inadequately developed financial markets and widening income inequalities. Rapid change has also brought uncertainties and anxieties for the average Chinese citizen, and this is no less the case than *vis-à-vis* WTO accession in late 2001.

The evolution of the transition process in China is based on the philosophy of Deng's idea of 'crossing the river by feeling the stones', a pragmatic and *gradualist* approach (see Naughton, 1995; Nolan, 1995). Therefore, it is not unusual to observe that many reform agendas had an initially *experimental* nature, from introducing foreign investment and the management responsibility system to 'dual-track' pricing systems and labour market regulations. Once those policies proved useful and safe for the so-called 'Socialist Market Economy', then such policies might be transformed into permanent policies and regulations. However, if policies led to negative outcomes, modification and revision of policies became necessary. The pattern of Chinese transition shows that there has been a strong 'top-down' leadership to drive the reform agenda, which may be different from other 'bottom-up' models, such as some have said is the case in Vietnam.

The degree to which Vietnam has evolved is a fascinating case study in transition. Although closer to the Chinese than the European and Russian experience of transformation, the Vietnamese process of transformation has had its own distinctive characteristics. A key feature has been the implementation and subsequent official acceptance of bottom-up reforms which preceded the launch of the *doi moi* policy in 1986. This sanctioning or toleration of ground-level reforms was due at least in part to the ongoing context of military conflict which lasted until the mid-1970s. The conditions of a war economy necessitated economic decentralization which was used at the local level to initiate reforms. The announcement of *doi moi* reform policy may thus be regarded as a move by the political elite to control and channel the reform process along a politically acceptable path (see Chapter 6).

A further distinguishing feature of the Vietnamese transformation is the continuing – and increasing – significance of SOEs for economic output. Whilst SOEs are undergoing reform involving job losses, mergers and liquidations, they still make the largest contribution to GDP among the various types of enterprise. In contrast, and differently from other trans-forming economies, the private sector's role has been primarily to provide employment.

## Factors shaping transition

We now look at a set of factors that have been instrumental in shaping the transition process, namely *economic*, *political* and *social.*

### *Economic*

While some regimes, as we noted earlier, experienced the 'big bang' in Eastern Europe, China by contrast explored a gradual, adaptive path, pro-ceeding by '*trial and error*'. There was, according to this interpretation, no 'shock therapy' as advocated for the Soviet economy, with the projected dismantling of the Soviet planned economy in the shortest time possible. However, Kazakevitch and Smyth (2005) have recently argued the contrary, that is, that the sequence happened the other way round. In the Former Soviet Union, the communist state, they argue, has mostly gone but in China for example with its strategy of 'reform from above' it still remains. This contestation of the received wisdom may have a ring of originality about it but may not be wholly convincing.

Nevertheless, one could also argue that a distinction could be drawn between the process and outcomes of transformation. In this respect, the reform process in China is likely to lead to changes of greater magnitude than have been experienced hitherto in Russia where the 'big bang' of the early 1990s had been followed by a decade of far slower reforms.

### *Political*

The political experiences of Eastern and Central Europe provided many of the clues that presaged the transition. The civic instability that appeared in East Germany, Hungary and Poland, in terms of workers' protest sets the scene for Hungarian open revolt in 1956, the Czechoslovak Spring of 1968 and the later Polish *Solidarity* campaigns of the 1980s. Unlike several parts of Central and Eastern Europe, the former Soviet Union had not for example seen large-scale, open street-level protests, at least as visibly, as far as we know. It did not develop an organized workers' protest movement, like the others, either.

*Social*

Social forces underlying the upsurge of market-driven change must now be mentioned here. Many of the Central and Eastern Europe economies, like the Czechoslovakian, the East German, the Hungarian, let alone the Soviet case, had by the early 1980s attained middle-income levels in terms of international comparisons. They had also developed a social structure and a set of social values that mirrored, or at least mimicked, Western models. In some countries, for instance Czechoslovakia and Poland, there were also strong memories of the pre-communist democratic régimes and societies. Whilst this was not 'convergence' *in strictu senso*, it was the beginnings of something that at least looked liked it. Pressures 'from below' were undermining the stereotypical communist *status quo*.

## Macro-analysis

*Why* the old order crumbled and the process of transformation was initiated is a major analytical question. A number of macro-themes come to mind here:

- marketization
- efficient and inefficient institutions
- private and domestic versus foreign ownership
- percentage of foreign trade with capitalist economies
- the 'Valley of Tears'.

### Marketization

Marketization appears gradually in a number of command economies prior to the 1980s. Attempts to introduce market mechanisms were particularly evident in Hungary and the former Yugoslavia. After 1990, moreover, marketization and privatization develop at varying paces in the respective transforming economies. Within CEE, countries experiencing relatively rapid marketization and privatization included the Czech and Slovak republics, Hungary and Poland (Figure 7.1), while Albania, Bulgaria and Romania represented a more dilatory approach to these processes. In between these two poles were Slovenia, Croatia and Russia.

### Efficient and inefficient institutions

The way the need for change became more obvious was the realization that the existing institutions in command economies were inefficient. This became increasingly obvious in CEE in the 1980s as the economies failed to keep pace with developments in the advanced western economies in areas such as innovation, computerization, and so on.

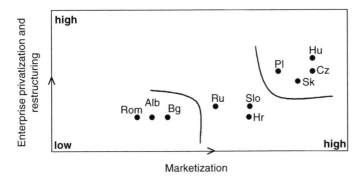

*Figure 7.1* Marketization and privatization in Central and Eastern Europe, 1997.

### *Private and domestic versus foreign ownership*

By the 1980s, injection of capital from the West became a realistic possibility and joint ventures began to appear in command economies. At the same time the view that the socialist economies could somehow avoid the impact of global economic changes became increasingly illusory.

### *Percentage of foreign trade with capitalist economies*

As the COMECON member states increased their trade with capitalist economies, two major consequences occurred. First, it became clear that the former were at a competitive disadvantage and, second, that they could learn a great deal from their Western trading partners, be they countries or companies.

### *The 'Valley of Tears'*

In the transition process, there are both winners and losers and the metaphor of the 'Valley of Tears' (as we pointed out in Chapter 1) helps to illustrate the position some transforming economies in Central and Eastern Europe and the Former Soviet Union found themselves in after the fall of the Berlin Wall (Figure 7.2). Following the system change and the introduction of economic reforms, all the former socialist economies in Central and Eastern Europe and the former Soviet Union (without exception) experienced a significant drop in output and GDP.

Some economies were better able to deal with this decline in output and GDP than others, as we have seen. The more successful economies were with the passage of time able to address the decline, bounce back and then surpass the output and GDP levels they had at the beginning of the transformation

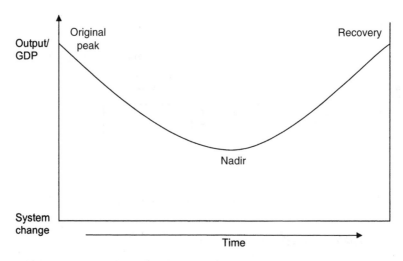

*Figure 7.2* The 'Valley of Tears' (revisited).

*Table 7.1* Real GDP in Central and Eastern Europe countries in transition, 1999
(1990 = 100)

| | |
|---|---|
| Czech Republic | 95 |
| Hungary | 99 |
| Poland | 122 |
| Slovakia | 100 |
| Slovenia | 109 |
| Bulgaria | 67 |
| Romania | 76 |
| Russia | 57 |

Source: *Annual Report 2000* (EBRD, 2001a).

process. In contrast, the less successful economies, even when arresting the decline, remained stuck at levels of output and GDP that were often considerably lower than those from before the system change (Table 7.1). But China and Vietnam did not seem to conform to this model.

## Micro-analysis

In this section, we emphasize micro-factors such as:

- actors, in particular enterprises
- enterprise managers
- external/internal factors
- functional areas
- enterprise management.

## Actors

Numerous actors have been involved, both positively and negatively, in the transformation process. These actors have come from the economic, political and social spheres, have been individuals and institutions, domestic and international. The transformation itself is the result of the interaction of all the various actors and the outcomes in particular countries are consequently the outcome of this interaction in each specific national context.

Key actors have been the old and new political elites, the emerging new economic elite and the workforce. These actors have not represented homogeneous and discrete entities and there has been considerable movement between particular categories, for example, from the former political to the new economic elite. Generally, at least in Europe, the old political elites have tended to be 'losers' in the transformation process as have members of the workforce amongst other social groups, for example, the elderly, women and academics. Against this, the 'new economic elite' have benefited considerably from transformation.

A prime actor (as well as object) of the transformation has been the enterprise or company and the privatization and restructuring of SOEs and the formation of new private companies have been at the core of the transformation process.

As indicated earlier (see Figure 7.1), privatization evolved in different ways and at different speeds in the respective countries as governments sought a balance between the benefits and disadvantages of privatization. In China and Vietnam the privatization process was complicated by the existence of continuing government and communist party interest in SOEs. Nevertheless, apart from Vietnam, the privatized and private companies now dominate the economic landscape.

In earlier Chapter 5, we examined the stages of the corporate recovery process in transitional economies, with companies moving from latent or acute crisis, through revitalization and strategic changes, to growth. While companies in many transforming economies are implementating strategic changes and seeking growth, there are still many companies – albeit diminishing – in the crisis and revitalization stages. Often such companies are concentrated in the less successful transforming economies.

Hand-in-hand with the transformation of SOEs has been the impressive growth of newly formed businesses in Central and Eastern Europe, Russia, China and Vietnam. Various factors, from entrepreneurial drive to unemployment, have stoked the upsurge of small businesses. In some countries, however, the growth of small businesses has been hampered by an unsupportive environment which has led to lower numbers of new businesses than might have been expected. This appears to be the case in the more slowly transforming economies of Central and Eastern Europe such as Bulgaria and Romania as well as Russia. In contrast, the rise of new private businesses has been one of the major developments in the economies of China and Vietnam.

Nevertheless, privatization, enterprise restructuring and the rise of new private businesses have been significant elements of the transformation process and the distribution and characteristics of firms have changed substantially since the transformation process began. If enterprises in the past have been instruments for achieving the ruling party's economic and, to a certain extent, its social and political goals, we find that companies are now functioning as primarily profit-seeking institutions.

### Enterprise managers

Enterprise managers too have been leading actors in the transformation process as they have to transform their enterprises from operating in a command economy to competing in a market economy. Many managers were unable to cope with the considerable scale of change and left their enterprises. It is difficult to generalize about those managers who remained. Many were young, although many older managers adapted. Many were from former political positions and now applied their knowledge and skills in the economic sphere. As discussed in Chapter 1, many of these managers suffered from role overload as they tackled the challenges of the transformation process.

Dobák (2003) has presented a four-stage evolution of managers in a transforming economy, based on the Hungarian experience. The first stage covers the period of the so-called 'guided market economy' up to the system change in 1989. In this period, managers need to be 'Janus-faced' as they strive to balance the demands of both bureaucratic and market mechanisms. The second stage is focused primarily on company survival and privatization as the economy becomes predominantly market oriented. At the same time there is an influx of foreign owners and managers. The third stage is largely a continuation of the previous stage. However, it is characterized by a rejuvenation of the managerial group and a heavy politicization of any remaining SOEs. The conclusion of the process of managerial transformation, the fourth stage, is characterized by the accomplishment of a fully fledged market economy.

In Hungary, the above four stages corresponded respectively to the period up to 1989, 1990–93, 1994–99 and 2000 onwards. Obviously the actual duration of the various stages and their conclusion vary from country to country. Dobák (2003) argues that Hungary has now reached the fourth stage and such a conclusion may also apply more or less to the first wave of entrants to the European Union. The situation in other countries of Central and Eastern Europe, Russia, China and Vietnam is, however, either not so clear-cut or different. In China, Vietnam and even Russia managers may need to retain a 'Janus-face' in order to deal simultaneously with bureaucratic and market issues, whilst at the same time operating in an increasingly market-oriented economy. Whatever the particularities of individual countries, managers in transforming economies are facing inherently different challenges from those they addressed 15 or even 20 years ago.

At this point it is appropriate to consider the issue of management development as managers have moved from operating under the conditions of a command economy to operating in a market or, in the cases of China and Vietnam, a socialist market economy. One impact of marketization and privatization has been to change the composition and characteristics of the management cadre. Inability to cope with the new pressures of the market system, in addition to natural attrition, reduced the numbers of managers with experience of the command economy. In some countries of Central and Eastern Europe, such as the former Czechoslovakia, this loss of command economy managers was increased by dismissals for political reasons. The quantitative managerial deficit was made good by an inflow of managers from the advanced western economies and a rejuvenation of the managerial group. Because of the system change in Central and Eastern Europe this management transformation occurred relatively rapidly, although unevenly, while in China and Vietnam change has been more gradual. In spite of these differences, the general picture has been one of command economy managers being replaced by managers with a market orientation.

Management development has played a significant role in facilitating this transformation. Former command economy managers needed to acquire new knowledge and skills as did the new generation of managers. There has thus been a proliferation of education courses and training targeted at providing the requisite knowledge and skills. In-company training has also changed to meet the requirements of the new operating environment. Foreign companies have also made a significant contribution to raising levels of knowledge and skills in transforming (often in the foreign companies' home country) and acting as role models for domestic firms.

## External/internal factors

This section focuses on the key external and internal factors which have had an impact on company and management change. Among external factors are included globalization, FDI, international institutions, regional integration, national governments and civil society. The main internal factors comprise the issue of ownership and control, corporate vision and strategy, the relationship of products to markets, capital and labour and general company goals.

The transformation in former command economies has been heavily influenced by globalization, that is, by the development of an increasingly global economy, rather than a world comprising discrete national entities. This general influence of globalization is exemplified by the mobility and transferability of capital, manifested by companies' investment and location decisions. All the transforming economies covered in this book have in varying degrees been affected, both positively and negatively, by the implications of globalization which also includes global communication, for instance, via satellite television and the Internet. A key impact of globalization has been to erode belief in the feasibility of closed economies and closed economic blocs.

Within globalization, FDI has been a major factor of change in transforming economies, both conceptually and practically. The FDI has been primarily regarded as a mechanism for raising economic standards in transforming economies, providing employment, knowledge and skills. However, FDI has also transferred the concept of FDI and transforming economies themselves are also beginning to invest abroad. The significant impact of FDI can be seen in the countries of Central Europe, China and Vietnam. In contrast, Russia and the countries of South-Eastern Europe have not been major beneficiaries of FDI and this has often been regarded as one of the causes of the relatively slow transformation in these countries, although it could also be argued that these countries for their part have been insufficiently attractive to foreign investors.

A further influence has been the role played by various international organizations such as the IMF and the World Bank, as well as more recently the WTO. These institutions have often provided blueprints for the transformation and loans to individual countries that have generally been dependent on accepting the respective donor's criteria. International institutions have thus strongly shaped the direction and shape of transformation in many countries. The early transformation in Russia and Poland was particularly influenced by the role of international institutions. This does not mean, however, that their influence was absolute as the protracted negotiations surrounding Russia's entry to the WTO indicate.

A major goal of the majority of transforming economies has been greater regional integration. In Central and Eastern Europe, this has signified accession to the European Union. EU membership has been regarded as significant evidence of the transformation and a political and economic re-orientation from the former Soviet Union. Those countries joining the European Union in 2004 can be considered as having to a considerable degree affected the transformation from planned to market economies and from one-party political systems to democracy. For those countries not yet admitted to the European Union, regional integration is still of importance as evidenced by the continuing aspiration to enter the European Union. This aspiration is in the interim being mitigated by less formal relationships with the European Union and membership of other regional groupings such as the Black Sea Economic Cooperation Organization (see Chapter 3).

The transformation in China and Vietnam was considerably influenced by the success of Japan and the Asian 'Tigers' that represented both an example to be emulated and a threat. Through FDI and resultant exports China is becoming increasingly integrated in the global and regional economies. This is similarly the case, albeit in smaller scale, with Vietnam that has become a member of various regional and international bodies, such as AFTA.

It would be wrong, however, to portray transforming economies as subject solely to the influence of foreign forces. National governments have played a considerable role in determining the direction and scope of transformation and in implementing related policies. The preceding Chapters 2–6 have given some indication of the roles played by national governments in the transformation. Governments have varied in the degree of commitment they have shown towards transformation and also in their overall approach, namely, the extent to which they have been concerned with the broad outline or the detail of transformation. The general situation in Central and Eastern Europe has been that governments have shown considerable commitment to the transformation and have created the general conditions for the establishment of market economies. Apart from privatization, companies have largely been left to fend for themselves. The Chinese and Vietnamese governments have also demonstrated considerable commitment to the reform process but have closely monitored the transformation, retaining a large degree of control over the detail of the changes. In contrast, the governments of South-Eastern Europe have tended to vacillate between commitment and ambivalence. Consequently, the transformation has been relatively slow and piece-meal, as governments failed to give the necessary direction and implement fundamental reforms. Finally, in Russia the position is characterized by the 'big bang' establishment of a market economy in 1992 which was, however, not supported by the appropriate implementation of further reforms.

The final factor to be considered in terms of country- and company-level transformation is the nature of the respective civil societies. The civil societies in the countries studied in the book have distinctive historical and cultural traditions, have particular experiences of pre-communist regimes, ranging from advanced democratic societies to less developed and authoritarian ones. The nature of civil society is thus one of the influences on the transformation process and is reflected in dimensions such as management style, attitudes to corporate governance, human resource policies and so on.

The transformation implemented the principle of private ownership of economic assets. Companies increasingly, in some countries overwhelmingly, belong to private owners. Owners now determine the overall purpose and scope of companies' activities. The process of creating private owners has varied between countries and has raised various issues relating to the open, ethical and legitimate privatization of assets. Cases of misappropriation are common in some countries. Privatization brought with it issues of ownership and control. In many countries employees became shareholders, generally in their own company, but control of company assets was frequently held by a restricted group of top managers. Insider ownership has generally not been regarded as conducive to the transformation process. In some countries, such as China and Vietnam, but not exclusively there, notwithstanding privatization, the state has retained a substantial interest in 'privatized' assets.

The transformation has also changed the relationship between companies and their markets. Whereas under the command economy planners determined products and their output, under the market system companies need to respond to customer demand with regard to products and product characteristics. This fundamental change of emphasis, namely marketization, has initiated a major change in the way in which managers view the activities and operations of these companies.

A further change has been the newly established relationship between capital and labour. Under the command economy the interests of labour were subsumed in the operation of the socialist system and trades unions were normally an element of enterprise management. In general, the influence of labour has diminished in Central and Eastern Europe and Russia, and trades unions have relatively little influence. In China and Vietnam, moreover, unions have had to rethink their roles as 'transmission belts' of government policy and seek to both represent workers' interests and act as mediators between capital and labour.

Finally, the essence of company goals has changed. Whilst primarily production units in the command economy, enterprises were an integral part of the socialist system, serving political and social as well as economic aims. With the transformation, and privatization and marketization, companies have become largely profit-seeking organizations. The extent to which this has actually been realized varies from country to country. However, this change is by no means absolute and in some countries the legacy of the former system and particular cultural values have resulted in companies which are not solely profit-seeking, economic organizations and in company managements that seek to maximize personal gain rather than company profit.

### Functional areas

As companies in the command economy were predominantly production plants, operations and, to a lesser extent, 'purchasing' were the key functional areas. For the first-mentioned reason the majority of managers in many countries had degrees in engineering. The change to a market system required managers to acquire not only new knowledge and skills but also a 'restructuring' of companies' functional areas. The significance of operations declined overall but acquired a new focus on quality issues (rather than output *per se*). Marketing and sales departments were set up or, where they already existed, enhanced. The finance function was also strengthened and expanded as cost and financial accounting and financial management became indispensable for company survival and growth.

The management of human resources now also became an area of major concern as under the command economy many enterprises had suffered from overmanning. Labour needed to be assessed, recruited, trained, developed and also made redundant when surplus to requirements. This change in the attitude to labour required a shift from administrative personnel management to HRM.

Finally, an area of considerable deficit was R&D. It had frequently been located outside the enterprise in state or industry institutes. In countries experiencing the system change funding for these research institutes was generally no longer available and many institutes closed. However, most companies lacked the resources to set up substantial R&D departments.

The extent to which the ideal changes delineated above were actually realized varied between countries and between companies. While there was widespread recognition of the need to change, implementing change was more difficult and time consuming as it required not only the acquisition of new knowledge and skills but also the acceptance of a new way of thinking, new behaviour models and exposure to a new *modus operandi*. In many cases the old ways had been rejected (and then not always) but the new ways of operating across the range of functions were not yet fully accepted or adopted. Company 'restructuring' was in this sense under way, but not yet achieved.

### Enterprise management

The development of enterprise management has been particularly influenced by the content in which managers operate as indicated by the characteristics noted in Figure 4 of Chapter 1. The degree of change has varied both between and within countries. Nevertheless, the overall trend has been for the context of enterprise management to display many of the characteristics of the market system. Economic criteria predominate whilst political and social criteria have on the whole diminished in significance. This trend is especially evident in the countries of Central and Eastern Europe where the transformation is virtually completed. In the other countries we have examined this conflict of underlying criteria is still evident and there is a manifest tension between economic, political and social criteria of transformation. However, privatization and marketization are without doubt driving forces of the transformation. Managers are now more and more accountable to private owners and shareholders, even though the owner may still be, at least temporarily, the state.

Enterprise management has also changed at the personal level as reflected by Dóbak's (2003) typology. Managers have had to respond to the changing context (or retire). On the positive side they have had to be proactive in acquiring new knowledge and skills, new attitudes and behaviour. Such a change has benefited enterprise transformation, although on the negative side there is considerable evidence of self-seeking behaviour such as in spontaneous privatization and personal enrichment to the detriment of the enterprise, its shareholders and employees. In general, enterprise management has been rejuvenated and revitalized by the transformation. Managers have also attained a new social status as key players in and beneficiaries of transforming and post-transformation societies.

### The propositions revisited

In Chapter 1 we derived the following eight empirical propositions: the greater the degree of transition:

1   the greater the degree of marketization;
2   the greater the diversification of ownership;
[as well as]
3   the greater the salience of accounting;
4   the greater the salience of business strategy;
5   the greater the salience of finance;
6   the greater the salience of HRM;
7   the greater the salience of management development;
8   the greater the salience of marketing.

Our study indicates that these propositions are generally valid and that, in the move from a command to a market economy, the issues expressed in the propositions have gained in significance. Transition has indeed been characterized by marketization and ownership diversification (even where the political system is still socialist), by the increasing significance of business strategy, other functional areas and management development. Furthermore, within the group of countries studied, the degree of transformation experienced by individual countries (as well as within individual countries) is reflected in the extent to which marketization and ownership diversification have been achieved. At the enterprise level, the particular role and significance ascribed to business strategy, the various functional areas and management development are clearly indicative of the extent of company-level transformation.

## Towards a model of transition

In this section, we will outline a model of transition we have inferred from the preceding. It basically sums up what we believe are the four phases of the transitional process (Figure 7.3).

These phases are common to all the cases we have examined in the book. We will now attempt to deal with each of these in turn.

### Reforming

In this 'reforming' phase, the first steps towards the transition to the market are initiated and the groundwork is laid for privatization. As Peng (2000:27) points out there were two paths to reform; one involved a 'rapid, all-out program', as in Central and Eastern Europe and the Former Soviet Union; the other was 'incremental' and 'partial' as in the case of China, and later, Vietnam.

### Storming

After the reforming phase, we move to the 'storming' phase, where conflicts occur regarding the reforms, as now there is a clash of interests among the

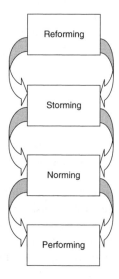

*Figure 7.3* Phases of the transitional process.

actors and parties involved. Here, there is 'institutional upheaval', where there is anxiety and uncertainty (Roth and Kostova, 2003:315).

### Norming

In the 'norming' phase, institutional norms start to form and the dust begins to settle. 'De-institutionalization', as discussed earlier, begins to take root, as old institutions collapse or decay and new institutions strive to become established. In this stage, the 'old' clashes with the 'new' and the outcome of this conflict determines to a large degree the nature of further transformation.

### Performing

In this last 'performing' phase, rule-based market governance systems are now in place. Roth and Kostova (2003:319) cite the cases of the Czech Republic, Hungary and Poland. Day-to-day operations regarding business transactions are safely legitimized. In this phase, the institutional transformation moves towards closure.

## Discussion

As noted above, the divergences among these transitional economies can be reflected in their economic performance and formed into different groups. Havlik (1996) and Rosser (2002) divide the Eastern European economies into three groups:

1   a *'Western'* group with quick economic recovery and better performance, such as the Czech Republic, Hungary, Poland, and Slovenia;
2   a *'Central'* group experiencing political instability and still lacking popular support for reforms, such as Bulgaria and Romania; and
3   a *'Depression'* group with political volatility, like many of the former Soviet republics.

To this we add:

4   a *'Sui Generis'* group, such as the Russian Republic, which does not fit into any of the above and perhaps even China and Vietnam (Table 7.2).

In contrast to these former socialist economies in Eastern Europe, China is still nominally a socialist regime, as noted earlier, but in its transition to a hybrid form that their planners denote 'the socialist market economy'. Furthermore, the transition has been relatively peaceful and politically stable (despite some worker-unrest) although at times fitful (for example, after the 1989 Tiananmen Square incident). As the economy is still significantly agricultural and in some cases at subsistence level – unlike the industrialized Eastern European counterparts – the negative impact of structural reform on people's ability to support themselves has been muted. In other words, reform has offered a better standard of living for enough Chinese peasants and workers to keep the majority on board the reform bandwagon (see Warner, 2003a).

*Table 7.2* A typology of transitional economies

| Country | Type | | | |
| --- | --- | --- | --- | --- |
| | Western | Central | Depression | Sui Generis |
| Baltic States | × | | | |
| Croatia | × | | | |
| Czech Republic | × | | | |
| Hungary | × | | | |
| Poland | × | | | |
| Slovakia | × | | | |
| Slovenia | × | | | |
| Albania | | | × | |
| Bulgaria | | × | | |
| Rumania | | × | | |
| Many FSU Republics | | | × | |
| Russia | | | | × |
| China | | | | × |
| Vietnam | | | | × |

# Concluding remarks

Finally, we may conclude that there has been a process of convergence occurring but with divergence in many cases. The mainstream theoretical position here hinges on the 'convergence' thesis, based on the writings of US-based academics as far back as the 1950s. The core theory-based arguments relating to how management systems may or may not be tending to look like each other, namely 'converging', with expanding globalization, have been summarized elsewhere (see Joynt and Warner, 2002). The concepts of *'convergence'* or even possibly *'cross-vergence'* (values overlapping between cultures (see Ralston *et al.*, 1997)) may be of interest here. However, both of these differ from the main streams of conventional debate, namely, the convergence approach based on globalization/universalism and institutional theory versus the divergence approach based on diversity (for the details of these two positions, see Braun and Warner, 2002). We can argue for a possibly increasing degree of *'relative convergence'*, which we might posit is based on a neo-Darwinian-like adaptation to changes in the external environment, as market forces assert themselves.

# Statistical appendix (derived from miscellaneous sources, for appropriate years, 1992–2002)

*A1* Population, total, 1998–2002

|  | 1998 | 1999 | 2000 | 2001 | 2002 |
|---|---|---|---|---|---|
| Albania | 3,109,690 | 3,114,420 | 3,134,000 | 3,164,400 | 3,195,100 |
| Bulgaria | 8,257,000 | 8,208,000 | 8,125,000 | 7,913,000 | 7,868,000 |
| China | 1,242,179,968 | 1,253,595,008 | 1,262,460,032 | 1,271,849,984 | 1,280,974,848 |
| Croatia | 4,396,570 | 4,374,510 | 4,380,000 | 4,380,780 | 4,376,860 |
| Czech Republic | 10,294,900 | 10,283,000 | 10,273,300 | 10,224,000 | 10,209,830 |
| Hungary | 10,114,000 | 10,068,000 | 10,122,000 | 10,187,000 | 10,166,000 |
| Poland | 38,666,152 | 38,658,000 | 38,648,000 | 38,641,000 | 38,626,192 |
| Romania | 22,503,000 | 22,457,990 | 22,435,000 | 22,408,000 | 22,354,650 |
| Russian Federation | 146,899,008 | 146,308,992 | 145,555,008 | 144,752,000 | 144,070,784 |
| Slovak Republic | 5,390,660 | 5,395,120 | 5,401,000 | 5,404,000 | 5,408,760 |
| Slovenia | 1,982,600 | 1,985,500 | 1,989,000 | 1,992,000 | 1,991,960 |
| United Kingdom | 58,531,768 | 58,625,840 | 58,720,000 | 58,800,000 | 58,857,872 |
| United States | 275,157,056 | 278,674,240 | 282,224,000 | 285,318,016 | 288,368,992 |
| Vietnam | 76,520,000 | 77,515,000 | 78,522,704 | 79,526,048 | 80,524,560 |

Source: World Development Indicators.

*A2* GDP (US$ billion), 1992–2002

|  | 1992 | 2001 | 2002 |
|---|---|---|---|
| Albania | – | 4.3 | 4.8 |
| Bulgaria | 10.4 | 13.6 | 15.5 |
| China | 454.6 | 1,167.1 | 1,232.7 |
| Croatia | 10.6 | 19.5 | 22.4 |
| Czech Republic | 30.0 | 57.2 | 69.6 |
| Hungary | 37.3 | 51.8 | 65.8 |
| Poland | 84.4 | 183.0 | 187.7 |
| Romania | 28.4 | 39.1 | 42.4 |
| Russian Federation | 442.1 | 309.9 | 346.5 |
| Slovak Republic | 11.8 | 20.5 | 23.7 |
| Slovenia | 12.5 | 18.8 | – |
| United Kingdom | 1,072.1 | 1,424.1 | 1.552.4 |
| United States | 6,261.8 | 10,065.3 | 10,416.8 |
| Vietnam | 9.9 | 32.7 | 35.1 |

Source: *World Bank.*

*A3* GDP (current US$), 1998–2002

| | 1998 | 1999 | 2000 | 2001 | 2002 |
|---|---|---|---|---|---|
| Albania | 3,058,029,568 | 3,676,410,112 | 3,752,070,912 | 4,113,723,392 | 4,695,412,224 |
| Bulgaria | 12,737,114,112 | 12,954,791,936 | 12,607,022,080 | 13,552,988,160 | 15,608,000,512 |
| China | 946,300,846,080 | 991,355,666,432 | 1,080,428,724,224 | 1,159,025,131,520 | 1,237,145,485,312 |
| Croatia | 21,628,010,000 | 19,905,840,000 | 18,427,800,000 | 19,533,510,000 | 22,420,760,000 |
| Czech Republic | 56,971,591,680 | 55,029,071,872 | 51,433,013,248 | 57,243,103,232 | 69,590,491,136 |
| Hungary | 47,049,158,656 | 48,044,236,800 | 46,680,461,312 | 51,832,954,880 | 65,843,048,448 |
| Poland | 158,445,223,936 | 155,038,515,200 | 163,882,745,856 | 183,028,400,128 | 187,680,309,248 |
| Romania | 42,115,497,984 | 35,592,339,456 | 36,865,777,664 | 39,714,115,584 | 44,427,829,248 |
| Russian Federation | 282,434,568,192 | 193,616,838,656 | 259,596,468,224 | 309,951,201,280 | 346,519,928,832 |
| Slovak Republic | 21,996,423,168 | 20,204,046,336 | 19,741,501,440 | 20,459,104,256 | 23,700,066,304 |
| Slovenia | 19,585,570,816 | 20,071,567,360 | 18,128,855,040 | 18,809,567,232 | 21,107,785,728 |
| United Kingdom | 1,423,934,095,360 | 1,458,230,132,736 | 1,429,670,068,224 | 1,424,094,003,200 | 1,552,437,346,304 |
| United States | 8,720,200,237,056 | 9,206,899,933,184 | 9,810,200,231,936 | 10,065,265,295,360 | 10,416,818,225,152 |
| Vietnam | 27,150,184,448 | 28,682,012,672 | 31,167,678,464 | 32,902,377,472 | 35,110,432,768 |

Source: World Development Indicators.

*A4* GDP growth (annual %), 1998–2002

|  | 1998 | 1999 | 2000 | 2001 | 2002 |
|---|---|---|---|---|---|
| Albania | 8 | 7 | 8 | 6 | 5 |
| Bulgaria | 4 | 2 | 5 | 4 | 4 |
| China | 8 | 7 | 8 | 7 | 8 |
| Croatia | 3 | −1 | 3 | 4 | 5 |
| Czech Republic | −1 | 0 | 3 | 3 | 2 |
| Hungary | 5 | 4 | 5 | 4 | 3 |
| Poland | 5 | 4 | 4 | 1 | 1 |
| Romania | −5 | −1 | 1 | 5 | 4 |
| Russian Federation | −5 | 5 | 9 | 5 | 4 |
| Slovak Republic | 4 | 1 | 2 | 3 | 4 |
| Slovenia | 4 | 5 | 5 | 3 | 3 |
| United Kingdom | 3 | 2 | 3 | 2 | 2 |
| United States | 4 | 4 | 4 | 0 | 2 |
| Vietnam | 6 | 5 | 7 | 7 | 7 |

Source: World Development Indicators.

*A5* GDP per capita (PPP US$), 2001

| | |
|---|---|
| Bulgaria | 6,890 |
| China | 4,020 |
| Croatia | 9,170 |
| Czech Republic | 14,720 |
| Hungary | 12,340 |
| Poland | 9,450 |
| Romania | 5,830 |
| Russia | 7,100 |
| Slovakia | 11,960 |
| Slovenia | 17,130 |
| United Kingdom | 24,160 |
| United States | 34,320 |
| Vietnam | 2,070 |

Source: UN Development Programme.

*A6* GNI per capita, Atlas method (current US$), 1998–2002

|  | 1998 | 1999 | 2000 | 2001 | 2002 |
|---|---|---|---|---|---|
| Albania | 870 | 1,010 | 1,220 | 1,340 | 1,380 |
| Bulgaria | 1,270 | 1,450 | 1,590 | 1,670 | 1,790 |
| China | 740 | 780 | 840 | 890 | 940 |
| Croatia | 4,730 | 4,560 | 4,500 | 4,410 | 4,640 |
| Czech Republic | 5,160 | 5,120 | 5,250 | 5,320 | 5,560 |
| Hungary | 4,480 | 4,620 | 4,710 | 4,830 | 5,280 |
| Poland | 3,860 | 4,060 | 4,230 | 4,340 | 4,570 |
| Romania | 1,520 | 1,580 | 1,680 | 1,710 | 1,850 |
| Russian Federation | 2,270 | 1,750 | 1,690 | 1,750 | 2,140 |

*A6* Continued

|  | 1998 | 1999 | 2000 | 2001 | 2002 |
|---|---|---|---|---|---|
| Slovak Republic | 4,000 | 3,860 | 3,800 | 3,760 | 3,950 |
| Slovenia | 9,720 | 9,980 | 10,060 | 9,760 | 9,810 |
| United Kingdom | 22,830 | 24,080 | 25,200 | 25,120 | 25,250 |
| United States | 30,700 | 32,260 | 34,370 | 34,400 | 35,060 |
| Vietnam | 350 | 360 | 390 | 410 | 430 |

Source: World Development Indicators.

*A7* Gross capital formation (% of GDP), 1998–2002

|  | 1998 | 1999 | 2000 | 2001 | 2002 |
|---|---|---|---|---|---|
| Albania | 16 | 17 | 19 | 19 | 19 |
| Bulgaria | 17 | 18 | 18 | 20 | 21 |
| China | 38 | 37 | 36 | 38 | 38 |
| Croatia | 24 | 24 | 23 | 25 | – |
| Czech Republic | 30 | 28 | 30 | 30 | – |
| Hungary | 30 | 29 | 31 | 27 | – |
| Poland | 26 | 26 | 25 | 21 | 22 |
| Romania | 18 | 16 | 20 | 22 | 22 |
| Russian Federation | 16 | 15 | 17 | 22 | 22 |
| Slovak Republic | 35 | 28 | 26 | 32 | 31 |
| Slovenia | 26 | 28 | 28 | 25 | – |
| United Kingdom | 18 | 18 | 18 | 17 | – |
| United States | 20 | 21 | 21 | – | – |
| Vietnam | 29 | 28 | 30 | 31 | – |

Source: World Development Indicators.

*A8* Inflation, GDP deflator (annual %), 1998–2002

|  | 1998 | 1999 | 2000 | 2001 | 2002 |
|---|---|---|---|---|---|
| Albania | 25 | 2 | –1 | 3 | 6 |
| Bulgaria | 24 | 4 | 7 | 6 | 5 |
| China | –2 | –2 | 1 | –0 | –1 |
| Croatia | 8 | 4 | 5 | 3 | 3 |
| Czech Republic | 11 | 3 | 1 | 6 | 3 |
| Hungary | 13 | 8 | 10 | 9 | 11 |
| Poland | 12 | 7 | 11 | 4 | 1 |
| Romania | 55 | 48 | 46 | 37 | 22 |
| Russian Federation | 16 | 65 | 41 | 18 | 15 |
| Slovak Republic | 5 | 6 | 6 | 5 | 4 |
| Slovenia | 8 | 7 | 6 | 10 | 8 |
| United Kingdom | 3 | 3 | 2 | 2 | 3 |
| United States | 1 | 1 | 2 | 2 | 1 |
| Vietnam | 9 | 6 | 3 | 3 | 3 |

Source: World Development Indicators.

180    *Statistical appendix*

*A9* Agriculture (% of GDP), 1992–2002

|  | *1992* | *2001* | *2002* |
|---|---|---|---|
| Albania | – | 34.2 | 33.3 |
| Bulgaria | 11.7 | 11.9 | 11.0 |
| China | 21.8 | 15.8 | 14.5 |
| Croatia | 14.9 | 9.7 | – |
| Czech Republic | 5.1 | 4.2 | – |
| Hungary | 7.5 | – | – |
| Poland | 6.6 | 3.6 | 3.4 |
| Romania | 19.4 | 14.8 | 13.1 |
| Russian Federation | 7.4 | 6.5 | 5.8 |
| Slovak Republic | – | 4.5 | – |
| Slovenia | 5.4 | 3.1 | – |
| United Kingdom | 1.8 | 1.0 | – |
| United States | 2.0 | – | – |
| Vietnam | 33.9 | 23.2 | 23.0 |

Source: World Bank.

*A10* Industry (% of GDP), 1992–2002

|  | *1992* | *2001* | *2002* |
|---|---|---|---|
| Albania | – | 23.5 | 23.5 |
| Bulgaria | 45.0 | 25.5 | 24.5 |
| China | 43.9 | 50.1 | 51.7 |
| Croatia | 33.1 | 34.2 | – |
| Czech Republic | 50.8 | 40.7 | – |
| Hungary | 34.5 | – | – |
| Poland | 41.4 | 37.3 | 33.8 |
| Romania | 44.0 | 37.0 | 38.1 |
| Russian Federation | 43.0 | 35.6 | 33.8 |
| Slovak Republic | – | 31.8 | – |
| Slovenia | 41.5 | 37.6 | – |
| United Kingdom | 31.9 | 27.4 | – |
| United States | 25.9 | – | – |
| Vietnam | 27.3 | 38.1 | 38.5 |

Source: World Bank.

*A11* Services (% of GDP), 1992–2002

|  | *1992* | *2001* | *2002* |
|---|---|---|---|
| Albania | – | 42.3 | 43.2 |
| Bulgaria | 43.3 | 62.7 | 64.5 |
| China | 34.3 | 34.1 | 33.7 |
| Croatia | 52.0 | 56.1 | – |
| Czech Republic | 44.1 | 55.1 | – |
| Hungary | 58.0 | – | – |
| Poland | 52.0 | 59.1 | 62.8 |
| Romania | 36.6 | 48.1 | 48.8 |

*A11* Continued

|  | 1992 | 2001 | 2002 |
|---|---|---|---|
| Russian Federation | 49.6 | 57.9 | 60.5 |
| Slovak Republic | – | 63.8 | – |
| Slovenia | 53.1 | 59.3 | – |
| United Kingdom | 66.3 | 71.6 | – |
| United States | 72.2 | – | – |
| Vietnam | 38.8 | 38.6 | 38.5 |

Source: World Bank.

*A12* Agriculture, value added (% of GDP), 1998–2002

|  | 1998 | 1999 | 2000 | 2001 | 2002 |
|---|---|---|---|---|---|
| Albania | 54 | 37 | 36 | 34 | 32 |
| Bulgaria | 19 | 17 | 14 | 14 | 13 |
| China | 19 | 18 | 16 | 15 | 15 |
| Croatia | 10 | 10 | 10 | 10 | – |
| Czech Republic | 5 | 4 | 4 | 4 | – |
| Hungary | 6 | – | – | – | – |
| Poland | 5 | 4 | 4 | 4 | 3 |
| Romania | 16 | 15 | 12 | 15 | 15 |
| Russian Federation | 5 | 7 | 6 | 7 | – |
| Slovak Republic | 4 | 4 | 4 | 4 | – |
| Slovenia | 4 | 4 | 3 | 3 | – |
| United Kingdom | 1 | 1 | 1 | 1 | – |
| United States | 2 | 2 | 2 | – | – |
| Vietnam | 26 | 25 | 25 | 24 | – |

Source: World Development Indicators.

*A13* Industry, value added (% of GDP), 1998–2002

|  | 1998 | 1999 | 2000 | 2001 | 2002 |
|---|---|---|---|---|---|
| Albania | 24 | 22 | 23 | 23 | 23 |
| Bulgaria | 31 | 29 | 30 | 29 | 29 |
| China | 49 | 49 | 51 | 51 | 51 |
| Croatia | 33 | 33 | 34 | 34 | – |
| Czech Republic | 41 | 41 | 41 | 41 | – |
| Hungary | 34 | – | – | – | – |
| Poland | 36 | 36 | 35 | 37 | 34 |
| Romania | 35 | 34 | 34 | 35 | 36 |
| Russian Federation | 36 | 35 | 39 | 37 | – |
| Slovak Republic | 31 | 31 | 30 | 29 | – |
| Slovenia | 38 | 38 | 38 | 38 | – |
| United Kingdom | 29 | 29 | 29 | 27 | – |
| United States | 25 | 25 | 25 | – | – |
| Vietnam | 32 | 34 | 37 | 38 | – |

Source: World Development Indicators.

*A14* Services, etc., value added (% of GDP), 1998–2002

|  | 1998 | 1999 | 2000 | 2001 | 2002 |
|---|---|---|---|---|---|
| Albania | 21 | 40 | 41 | 42 | 45 |
| Bulgaria | 50 | 55 | 56 | 57 | 58 |
| China | 32 | 33 | 33 | 34 | 34 |
| Croatia | 57 | 57 | 56 | 56 | – |
| Czech Republic | 54 | 55 | 55 | 55 | – |
| Hungary | 61 | – | – | – | – |
| Poland | 59 | 60 | 61 | 59 | 63 |
| Romania | 48 | 51 | 53 | 50 | 50 |
| Russian Federation | 58 | 57 | 55 | 57 | – |
| Slovak Republic | 65 | 65 | 66 | 67 | – |
| Slovenia | 57 | 58 | 58 | 59 | – |
| United Kingdom | 69 | 70 | 70 | 72 | – |
| United States | 73 | 73 | 73 | – | – |
| Vietnam | 42 | 40 | 39 | 39 | – |

Source: World Development Indicators.

*A15* Exports of goods and services (% of GDP), 1998–2002

|  | 1998 | 1999 | 2000 | 2001 | 2002 |
|---|---|---|---|---|---|
| Albania | 9 | 16 | 19 | 19 | 20 |
| Bulgaria | 47 | 45 | 56 | 56 | 51 |
| China | 22 | 22 | 26 | 26 | 27 |
| Croatia | 40 | 41 | 46 | 48 | – |
| Czech Republic | 59 | 60 | 70 | 70 | – |
| Hungary | 51 | 53 | 61 | 61 | – |
| Poland | 28 | 26 | 28 | 28 | 19 |
| Romania | 23 | 28 | 33 | 34 | 35 |
| Russian Federation | 31 | 44 | 45 | 36 | 31 |
| Slovak Republic | 59 | 61 | 72 | 74 | 73 |
| Slovenia | 57 | 53 | 59 | 60 | – |
| United Kingdom | 27 | 26 | 28 | 27 | – |
| United States | 11 | 11 | 11 | – | – |
| Vietnam | 45 | 49 | 55 | 55 | – |

Source: World Development Indicators.

*A16* High-technology exports (% of manufactured exports), 1998–2002

|  | *1998* | *1999* | *2000* | *2001* | *2002* |
|---|---|---|---|---|---|
| Albania | 1 | 2 | 1 | 1 | – |
| Bulgaria | 2 | 2 | 2 | – | – |
| China | 15 | 17 | 18 | 20 | – |
| Croatia | 8 | 8 | 8 | 10 | – |
| Czech Republic | 9 | 9 | 9 | 10 | – |
| Hungary | 20 | 22 | 26 | 23 | – |
| Poland | 3 | 3 | 3 | 3 | – |
| Romania | 2 | 3 | 5 | 6 | – |
| Russian Federation | 6 | 9 | 8 | – | – |
| Slovak Republic | 4 | 5 | 4 | 4 | – |
| Slovenia | 4 | 4 | 5 | 5 | – |
| United Kingdom | 28 | 29 | 31 | 31 | – |
| United States | 33 | 34 | 33 | 32 | – |
| Vietnam | – | – | – | – | – |

Source: World Development Indicators.

*A17* Imports of goods and services (% of GDP), 1998–2002

|  | *1998* | *1999* | *2000* | *2001* | *2002* |
|---|---|---|---|---|---|
| Albania | 32 | 39 | 40 | 42 | 44 |
| Bulgaria | 47 | 50 | 61 | 63 | 60 |
| China | 17 | 19 | 23 | 23 | 25 |
| Croatia | 49 | 49 | 52 | 55 | – |
| Czech Republic | 60 | 62 | 73 | 73 | – |
| Hungary | 53 | 55 | 65 | 63 | – |
| Poland | 33 | 32 | 35 | 32 | 26 |
| Romania | 31 | 33 | 39 | 42 | 42 |
| Russian Federation | 26 | 27 | 24 | 24 | 23 |
| Slovak Republic | 70 | 65 | 74 | 82 | 81 |
| Slovenia | 58 | 57 | 63 | 60 | – |
| United Kingdom | 28 | 28 | 30 | 29 | – |
| United States | 13 | 13 | 15 | – | – |
| Vietnam | 52 | 52 | 57 | 57 | – |

Source: World Development Indicators.

*A18* Foreign direct investment, net inflows (BoP, current US$), 1998–2002

| | 1998 | 1999 | 2000 | 2001 | 2002 |
|---|---|---|---|---|---|
| Albania | 45,000,000 | 41,200,000 | 143,000,000 | 207,300,000 | – |
| Bulgaria | 537,200,000 | 806,099,968 | 1,001,500,032 | 691,900,032 | – |
| China | 43,750,998,016 | 38,753,001,472 | 38,399,299,584 | 44,240,998,400 | – |
| Croatia | 932,300,000 | 1,458,200,000 | 1,076,900,000 | 1,511,800,000 | – |
| Czech Republic | 3,700,199,936 | 6,312,600,064 | 4,987,100,160 | 4,923,800,064 | – |
| Hungary | 2,037,100,032 | 1,976,499,968 | 1,646,300,032 | 2,439,800,064 | – |
| Poland | 6,365,000,192 | 7,270,000,128 | 9,340,999,680 | 5,712,999,936 | – |
| Romania | 2,031,000,064 | 1,041,000,000 | 1,025,000,000 | 1,156,999,936 | – |
| Russian Federation | 2,761,299,968 | 3,309,499,904 | 2,714,200,064 | 2,468,900,096 | – |
| Slovak Republic | 562,099,968 | 354,300,000 | 2,052,499,968 | 1,475,299,968 | – |
| Slovenia | 215,510,000 | 106,540,000 | 135,910,000 | 503,300,000 | – |
| United Kingdom | 74,651,623,424 | 89,534,799,872 | 119,932,600,320 | 63,109,480,448 | – |
| United States | 179,029,999,616 | 289,440,006,144 | 307,739,983,872 | 130,800,001,024 | – |
| Vietnam | 1,671,000,064 | 1,412,000,000 | 1,298,000,000 | 1,300,000,000 | – |

Source: World Development Indicators.

# References

Aaby, N.-E., Marinov, M. and Marinova, S. (1997) 'Managers' Characteristics: Results from an Exploratory Comparison of Young Managers in Bulgaria and USA and its Implications for Management Education in Bulgaria', *Journal for East European Management Studies*, 2, 1, 22–34.

ADUKI (1997) *Vietnam: Economic Commentary and Analysis*, Canberra: ADUKI Pty. Ltd.

*AmCham News*, Moscow: American Chamber of Commerce.

American Chamber of Commerce and Expert Institute (2001) *Ekonomicheskaja situacii i investicionnyj klimat v Rossii*, Moscow: American Chamber of Commerce and Expert Institute.

Ariff, M. and Khalid, A. M. (2000) *Liberalization, Growth and the Asian Financial Crisis: Lessons for Developing and Transitional Economies in Asia*, Cheltenham: Edward Elgar.

Aslund, A., Boone, P. and Johnson, S. (1996) 'How to Stabilize: Lessons from Post-Communist Countries', *Brookings Papers on Economic Activity*, 1, 217–313.

Athukorala, P. (1999) 'Developing with Foreign Investment', in Leung, S. (ed.) *Vietnam and the East Asian Crisis*, Cheltenham: Edward Elgar, 146–64.

Balaton, K. (2001) 'The Process Dynamics of Organizational Changes in Hungary During the 1990s', in Liuhto, K. (ed.) *Ten Years of Economic Transformation*, Studies in Industrial Engineering and Management No 16, Lappeenranta University of Technology (3 vols), vol. II, 2–21.

Bartlett, W. and Prašnikar, J. (1995) 'Small Firms in Slovenia', *Communist Economies and Economic Transformation*, 7, 1, 83–103.

Bateman, M. (1997) 'Comparative Analysis of Eastern European Business Cultures', in Bateman, M. (ed.) *Business Cultures in Central and Eastern Europe*, Oxford: Butterworth-Heinemann, 197–231.

Benaček, V. (2002) 'The Development of Authentic Private Sector in an Economy of Transition: Experience from the Czech Economy', in Sharma, S. and Galetić, L. (eds) *An Enterprise Odyssey: Economics and Business in the New Millennium*, International Conference, University of Zagreb, Graduate School of Economics and Business, Zagreb, 27–9 June, 61–75.

Benić, D. (2000) 'The Process of Restructuring in the Croatia Economy: Problems and Possible Solutions', in Edwards, V. (ed.) *Proceedings of the Sixth Annual Conference on Corporate and Organizational Restructuring*, Chalfont St Giles: CREEB, 29–54.

Blejer, M. (1991) *China: Economic Reform and Macroeconomic Management*, Washington DC: IMF.

Bobeva, D. and Bozhkov, A. (1996) 'Foreign Investments in the Bulgarian Economy', in Zloch-Christy, I. (ed.) *Bulgaria in a Time of Change: Economic and Political Dimensions*, Aldershot: Avebury, 119–31.

Bodea, G., Popescu, Gh. and Ciobanu, Gh. (2002) 'Dimensions of Romania's Transition to the Market Economy', in Sharma, S. and Galetić, L. (eds) ) *An Enterprise Odyssey: Economics and Business in the New Millennium*, International Conference, University of Zagreb, Graduate School of Economics and Business, Zagreb, 27–9 June, 84–98.

Bornstein, M. (1997) 'Non-standard Methods in the Privatization Strategies of the Czech Republic, Hungary and Poland', *The Economics of Transition*, 5, 2, 323–38.

Braun, W. H. and Warner, M. (2002) 'Strategic Human Resource Management in Western Multinationals in China: the Differentiation of Practices Across Different Ownership Forms', *Personnel Review*, 9, 4, 553–79.

Braverman, H. (1974) *Labour and Monopoly Capital*, London: Monthly Review Press.

Brezinski, H. (2001) '10 Years of German Unification – Success or Failure?', in Liuhto, K. (ed.) *Ten Years of Economic Transformation*, Studies in Industrial Engineering and Management No 16, Lappeenranta University of Technology (3 vols), vol. I, 2–19.

Bristow, A. (1996) *The Bulgarian Economy in Transition*, Cheltenham: Edward Elgar.

Brogan, P. (1990) *Eastern Europe 1939–1989*, London: Bloomsbury.

Buck, T. (2003) 'Modern Russian Corporate Governance: Convergent Forces or Product of Russia's History?', *Journal of World Business*, 38, 4, 299–313.

Buck, T., Filatotchev, I., Nolan, P. and Wright, M. (2000) 'Different Paths to Economic Reform in Russia and China: Causes and Consequences', *Journal of World Business*, 35, 4, 379–400.

Burawoy, M. (1985) *The Politics of Production*, London: Verso.

Carlin, W., Van Reenan, J. and Wolfe, T. (1995) 'Enterprise Restructuring in Early Transition: the Case Study Evidence from Central and Eastern Europe', *The Economics of Transition*, 3, 4, 427–58.

Catana, A. and Catana, D. (1999) 'Romanian Cultural Background and its Relevance for Cross-Cultural Management', *Journal for East European Management Studies*, 4, 3, 252–58.

Catana, D. and Catana, A. (1996) 'Aspects of Transformation of Corporate Cultures in Romania', in Lang, R. (ed.) *Wandel von Unternehmenskulturen in Ostdeutschland und Osteuropa*, Munich and Mering: Rainer Hampp Verlag, 195–208.

Catana, D. and Catana, Gh. A. (2002) 'A Framework for Management Development through Market-Oriented Learning', *Journal for East European Management Studies*, 7, 3, 298–315.

Catana, D., Catana, A. and Finlay, J. (1999) 'Managerial Resistance to Change: Romania's Quest for a Market Economy', *Journal for East European Management Studies*, 4, 2, 149–64.

Čater, T. (2003) 'Strategic Behaviour of Slovenian Firms at the End of Transition', *Enterprise in Transition*, Fourth International Conference on Enterprise in Transition (CD-Rom), Split – Hvar, 2260–75.

Chan, A. and Norlund, I. (1995) 'Vietnamese and Chinese Labor Régimes: On the Road to Divergence', paper presented at the workshop on 'Transforming Asian Socialisms: China and Vietnam Compared', RSPAS, ANU, 10–11/8/1995.

Cheah, H. B. (1993) 'Dual Modes of Entrepreneurship: Revolution and Evolution in the Entrepreneurial Process', *Creativity and Innovation Management*, 2, 4, 243–51.

Cheah, H. B. (2000) 'Raising the Dragon: Adaptive Entrepreneurship and Chinese Economic Development', in Richter, F.-J. (ed.) *The Dragon Millennium: Chinese Business in the Coming World Economy*, London: Quorum Books, 163–82.

Chen, B. Z. and Feng, Y. (2000) 'The Structure and Development of China's Financial Markets', in Richter, F.-J. (ed.) *The Dragon Millennium: Chinese Business in the Coming World Economy*, London: Quorum Books, 47–58.

Child, J. (1994) *Management in China During the Age of Reform*, Cambridge: Cambridge University Press.

Chu, C. N. (1995) *The Asian Mind Game: a Westerner's Survival Manual*, Crows Nest: Stealth Productions, Australia.

CIEM (1999) *Vietnam Economy in 1998*, Central Institute for Economic Management (CIEM), Hanoi: Education Publishing House.

Clark, E. (2000) 'Enterprise Restructuring in Local Czech Economies: Management Motive, Organizational Response and Emergent Economic Forms', in Edwards, V. (ed.) *Proceedings of the Sixth Annual Conference on Corporate and Organizational Restructuring*, Chalfont St Giles: CREEB, 162–192.

Clark, E. and Soulsby, A. (1999) *Organizational Change in Post-Communist Europe: Management and Transformation in the Czech Republic*, London: Routledge.

Collin, S.-O. and Cesljas, I. (2002) 'Corporate Governance in Transitional Economies: Business Groups in Croatia', *Journal of East European Management Studies*, 7, 2, 162–86.

Commission of the European Communities (1999a) *Regular Report 1998 from the Commission on Bulgaria's Progress Towards Accession*, Luxembourg: Office for Official Publications of the European Communities.

Commission of the European Communities (1999b) *Regular Report 1998 on Romania's Progress Towards Accession*, Luxembourg: Office for Official Publications of the European Communities.

Commission of the European Communities (2001a) *2001 Regular Report on Bulgaria's Progress Towards Accession*, Luxembourg: Office for Official Publications of the European Communities.

Commission of the European Communities (2001b) *2001 Regular Report on Romania's Progress Towards Accession*, Luxembourg: Office for Official Publications of the European Communities.

Connolly, K. (2002) 'Mittal's new staff worry about jobs – not UK fallout', *Guardian*, 16 February, http://politics.guardian.co.uk/Print/0,3858,4357383,00.html (accessed on 2.10.2002).

Crampton, R. (1997) *A Concise History of Bulgaria*, Cambridge: Cambridge University Press.

Czech Statistical Office (2001) *Cestat Statistical Bulletin*, 4, Prague: Czech Statistical Office.

Czech Statistical Office (2003) *Cestat Statistical Bulletin*, 4, Prague: Czech Statistical Office.

Davies, R. W. (1990) 'Gorbachev's Socialism in Historical Perspective', *New Left Review*, 179, 5–27.

De Mente, B. (1994) *Chinese Etiquette and Ethics in Business*, Lincolnwood, IL: NTC Business Books.

Djankov, S. and Pohl, G. (1998) 'The Restructuring of Large Firms in the Slovak Republic', *The Economics of Transition*, 6, 1, 67–85.

Dobák, M. (2003) 'The Role Executives Play in Transformational Processes', paper presented at the 6th Chemnitz East Forum, Chemnitz, March.

Doja, A. (2000) *Naître et grandir chez les Albanais*, Paris: L'Harmattan.

Dollar, D. (1999) 'The Transformation of Vietnam's Economy: Sustaining Growth in the 21st Century', in Litvack, J. and Rondinelli, D. (eds) *Market Reform in Vietnam, Building Institutions for Development*, Westport, CT: Quorum Books, 31–46.

Douw, L., Huang, C. and Ip, D. (eds) (2001) *Rethinking Chinese Transnational Enterprises: Cultural Affinity and Business Strategies*, London: Curzon/IIAS.

Dumitrescu, M.-F. (1997) 'Attitudes of Romanian Managers Towards Business, as Reflected by the Romanian National Culture. A Foreign Enterprise Perspective', unpublished MA dissertation, Chalfont St Giles: Buckinghamshire College of Higher Education/Brunel University.

Dyker, A. (1992) *Restructuring the Soviet Economy*, London and New York: Routledge.

EBRD (1998) *Annual Report 1997*, London: European Bank for Reconstruction and Development (EBRD).

EBRD (2001a) *Annual Report 2000*, London: European Bank for Reconstruction and Development (EBRD).

EBRD (2001b) *Transition Report 2001: Energy in Transition*, London: European Bank for Reconstruction and Development (EBRD).

*Economist, The* (2003) weekly, London: Economist Group.

Edwards, V. (2002) 'Managerial Evolution in Central and Eastern Europe: the Impact of Cultural Resources and Constraints', in Warner, M. and Joynt, P. (eds) *Managing Across Cultures, Issues and Perspectives*, 2nd edn, London: Thomson Learning, 124–36.

Edwards, V. and Foster, F. (1994) 'Meeting the Need for Management Development in Eastern Europe', *The International Journal of Educational Management*, 8, 1, 14–19.

Edwards, V. and Lawrence, P. (2000) *Management in Eastern Europe*, Basingstoke: Palgrave.

Edwards V., Polonsky, G. and Polonsky, A. (2000) *The Russian Province after Communism*, Basingstoke: Macmillan.

Ernst, M., Alexeev, M. and Marer, P. (1996) *Transforming the Core*, Oxford: Westview Press.

Evans-Pritchard, A. (2002) 'Euro Chiefs Press on with Big Bang Entry of 10 States', *Daily Telegraph*, 10 October, p. 10.

Fadahusni, A. and Smallbone, D. (1998) 'The External Environment for Small Business Development in Central and East European Transition Economies: a Literature Based Review', in Edwards, V. (ed.) *Proceedings of the Fourth Annual Conference on Convergence or Divergence: Aspirations and Reality in Central and Eastern Europe and Russia*, Chalfont St Giles: CREEB, 148–70.

Fahey, S. (1997) 'Vietnam and the "Third Way": the Nature of Socio-Economic Transition', *Tijdschrift voor Economische en Sociale Geografie*, 88, 5, 469–80.

Fforde, A. and Vylder, S. (1996) *From Plan to Market: the Economic Transition in Vietnam*, Boulder, CO: Westview Press.

Figes, O. (2003) *Natasha's Dance: A Cultural History of Russia*, London: Penguin.

Filatotchev, I., Wright, M., Uhlenbruck, K., Tihanyi, L. and Hoskisson, R. E. (2003)

'Governance, Organizational Capabilities, and Restructuring in Transition', *Journal of World Business*, 38, 4, 331–47.

*Finansovaja gazetta* (2002) No. 54, Moscow.

Fischer, S., Sahay, R. and Vegh, C. A. (1996) 'Stabilization and Growth in Transition Economies: the Early Experience', *Journal of Economic Perspectives*, 10, 2, 45–66.

Fogel, D. S. (1994) 'Lessons Learned', in Fogel, D. S. (ed.) *Managing in Emerging Market Economies, Cases from the Czech and Slovak Republics*, Boulder, CO: Westview Press, 225–33.

Forrester, P. L. and Porter, R. S. (1999) 'The Politics of Management in People's China: from CMRS to Modern Enterprise and Beyond', in Warner, M. (ed.) *China's Managerial Revolution*, London: Frank Cass, 47–72.

Freeman, N. J. (1998) 'Bust or Boom?', *The Vietnam Business Journal*, June, 58–9.

Fukuyama, F. (1992) *The End of History and the Last Man*, London: Penguin.

Gaddy, C. G. (1996) *The Price of the Past*, Washington, DC: Brookings Institution Press.

Galetić, L., and Tipurić, D. (1999) 'Organizational Differences between Small, Medium and Large Enterprises in Transition: an Empirical Study in Croatia', in Edwards, V. (ed.) *Proceedings of the Fifth Annual Conference on the Impact of Transformation on Individuals, Organizations, Society*, Chalfont St Giles: CREEB, 148–59.

Gavril, E. and Vatamanu, L. (1999) 'The International Transfer of Technology and Joint Ventures in the Process of Restructuring the Romanian Metallurgical Industries', in Edwards, V. (ed.) *Proceedings of the Fifth Annual Conference on the Impact of Transformation on Individuals, Organizations, Society*, Chalfont St Giles: CREEB, 257–66.

Gehmann, U. (1996) 'Corporate Culture in Transition – Aspects of Organizational Behaviour and Related Socioeconomic Consequences', in Lang, R. (ed.) *Wandel von Unternehmenskulturen in Ostdeutschland und Osteuropa*, Munich and Mering: Rainer Hampp Verlag, 209–26.

Goldman, M. (1997) *Revolution and Change in Central and Eastern Europe: Political, Economic, and Social Challenges*, New York: M.E. Sharpe.

Goodman, D. and Segal, G. (1996) *China Rising*, London: Routledge.

Gorynia, M. and Wolniak, R. (2001) 'The Competitiveness of Polish Firms on the Eve of Poland's Entry into European Union', in Liuhto, K. (ed.) *Ten Years of Economic Transformation*, Studies in Industrial Engineering and Management No 16, Lappeenranta University of Technology (3 vols), vol. II, 83–100.

Goskomstat (1999) *Annual Report*, Moscow: Goskomstat.

Goskomstat (2001) *Annual Report*, Moscow: Goskomstat.

Griffin, K. (ed.) (1998a) *Economic Reform in Vietnam*, Basingstoke: Macmillan.

Griffin, K. (1998b) 'Restructuring and Economic Reforms', in Griffin, K. (ed.) *Economic Reform in Vietnam*, Basingstoke: Macmillan, 1–19.

Griffin, K. (1998c) 'The Role of the State in the New Economy', in Griffin, K. (ed.) *Economic Reform in Vietnam*, Basingstoke: Macmillan, 37–55.

Gurkov, I. (2002) 'Mapping HRM in Russia: the Results of Repeated Surveys of CEOs', in Lang, R. (ed.) *Personalmanagement im Transformationsprozess*, Munich and Mehring: Rainer Hampp Verlag, 63–70.

Hashi, I. and Xhillari, L. (1997) 'Privatisation and Transition in Albania', Staffordshire University Business School Working Papers, http://netec.mcc.ac.uk/WoPEc/Papers/wukstafwp004.html (accessed on 14.10.2002).

Havlik, P. (1996) 'Stabilization and Prospects for Sustainable Growth in the Transition Economies', in Knell, M. (ed.) *Economics of Transition: Structural Adjustments and Growth Prospects in Eastern Europe*, Cheltenham: Edward Elgar, 25–48.

Havlik, P. (2002) 'Russian Economic Trends', *RECEP*, 11, 3, 2.

Heintz, M. (2002) 'East European Managers and Western Management Theories: an Ethnographic Approach of Romanian Service Sector Enterprises', *Journal for East European Management Studies*, 7, 3, 279–97.

Hertz, N. (1997) *Russian Business Relationships in the Wake of Reform*, Basingstoke: Macmillan.

Holland, D. and Pain, N. (1998) 'The Determinants and Impact of Foreign Direct Investment in the Transition Economies: A Panel Data Analysis', in Edwards, V. (ed.) *Proceedings of the Fourth Annual Conference on Convergence or Divergence: Aspirations and Reality in Central and Eastern Europe and Russia*, Chalfont St Giles: CREEB, 300–17.

Hosking, G. (1997) *Russia: People and Empire*, London: HarperCollins.

Hsu, R. C. (1991) *Economic Theories in China 1979–1988*, Cambridge: Cambridge University Press.

Illes, K. and Pataki, B. (2001) 'Hungarian Enterprises in the Global Market', in Liuhto, K. (ed.) *East Goes West, The Internationalization of Eastern Enterprises*, Studies in Industrial Engineering and Management No. 14, Lappeenranta University of Technology, 406–34.

Jaklič, M. and Zagoršek, H. (2002) 'Rationality and Slovenian Managers' Perception of Shareholder Value', *Economic and Business Review for Central and South-Eastern Europe*, 4, 1, 5–23.

Jin, D. and Haynes, K. E. (1997) 'Economic Transition at the Edge of Order and Chaos: China's Dualist and Leading Sectoral Approach', *Journal of Economic Issues*, 31, 1, 79–101.

Joynt, P. and Warner, M. (eds) (2002) *Managing Across Cultures: Issues and Perspectives*, 2nd edn, London: Thomson Learning.

Kaple, D. A. (1994) *Dream of a Red Factory: the Legacy of High Stalinism in China*, Oxford: Oxford University Press.

Kazakevitch, G. and Smyth, R. (2005) 'Shock Therapy versus Gradual Transition: Comparing the Experiences of Russia and China', paper presented at the conference 'Institutional Challenges for the Global China', Monash University, November [2003], *Asia Pacific Business Review* (in press) .

Kelemen, M. (1999) 'The Myth of Restructuring: "Competent" Managers and the Transition to a Market Economy: a Romanian Tale', *British Journal of Management*, 10, 199–208.

Kelemen, M. and Hristov, L. (1998) 'From Centrally Planned Culture to Entrepreneurial Culture: the Example of Bulgarian and Romanian Organisations', *Journal for East European Management Studies*, 3, 3, 216–26.

Khan A. R. (1996) 'Globalization, Employment and Equity: the China Experience', study undertaken as part of the ILO/EASMAT project, 'Strengthening the Capacity of the Social Partners for Effective Employment Strategies in the Context of Globalization and Liberalization' (ILO/EASMAT), Bangkok: ILO.

Khan, A. R. (1998) 'Integration into the Global Economy', in Griffin, K. (ed.) *Economic Reform in Vietnam*, Basingstoke: Macmillan, 21–35.

Khang, D. B. and Doan, N. (2000) 'Development Impacts of Small and Medium Enterprises: a Preliminary Survey of Ho Chi Minh City', in Quang, T. (ed.) *Vietnam: Challenges on the Path to Development*, Pathum Thani: SAV-SOM Joint Publishing, 161–78.

Khang, D. B. and Nga, H. D. N. (2001) 'Service Quality Management: Co-op Mart Nguyen Dinh Chieu', in Quang, T. (ed.) *Vietnam: Challenges on the Path to Development*, Pathum Thani: SAV-SOM Joint Publishing, 139–66.

Khang, D. B. and Thoai, L. T. (2001) 'Customer Service Quality in Manufacturing: Floor Tiles and Slab Company No. 1', in Quang, T. (ed.) *Vietnam: Challenges on the Path to Development*, Pathum Thani: SAV-SOM Joint Publishing, 167–89.

Khang, D. B. and Thuy, T. H. B. (2001) 'Productivity Improvement: Thanh Cong Textile and Garment Co.', in Quang, T. (ed.) *Vietnam: Challenges on the Path to Development*, Pathum Thani: SAV-SOM Joint Publishing, 277–96.

Kiezun, W. (1991) *Management in Socialist Countries: USSR and Central Europe*, Berlin: De Gruyter.

Kleinberg, R. (1990) *China's 'Opening' to the Outside World: the Experiment with Foreign Capitalism*, Boulder, CO: Westview Press.

Kolev, B. and Pencheva, B. (2001) 'Trade Liberalization with the Transition to a Market Economy: the Europe Agreement and the Development of Bulgarian Foreign Trade in 1996–2000', in Liuhto, K. (ed.) *Ten Years of Economic Transformation*, Studies in Industrial Engineering and Management No 16, Lappeenranta University of Technology (3 vols), vol. II, 375–99.

Koparanova, M. (1998) 'Danone-Serdika JS Co', *East European Economics*, 36, 4, 27–39.

Kornai, J. (1980) *The Economics of Shortage*, Amsterdam: North-Holland.

Kornai, J. (1992) *The Socialist System: the Political Economy of Communism*, Princeton, NJ: Princeton University Press.

Korzec, M. (1992) *Labour and the Failure of Reform in China*, London: Macmillan.

Kozarzewski, P. (2001) 'Corporate Governance Restructuring in the Course of Privatization in Poland', in *Enterprise in Transition*, Third International Conference on Enterprise in Transition (CD-Rom), Split – Hvar, 2053–74.

Kozarzewski, P. (2003) 'Corporate Governance Structures in Poland's Largest Enterprises', in *Enterprise in Transition*, Fifth International Conference, Split – Hvar, 2223–41.

Koźmiński, A. and Yip, G. (2000) *Strategies for Central and Eastern Europe*, Basingstoke: Macmillan.

Kraft, E. (1999) 'Ten years of Transition in Central and Eastern Europe: a Somewhat Opiniated Survey', *Economic and Business Review for Central and South-Eastern Europe*, 1, 1–2, 7–52.

Kume, V. and Llaci, S. (2000) 'Albania, an Ex-Communist Country in the Transition Period: Problems and Challenges', *Journal for East European Management Studies*, 5, 2, 103–29.

Kumssa, A. and Jones, J. F. (1999) 'The Social Consequences of Reform in Transitional Economies', *International Journal of Social Economics*, 26, 1/2/3, 194–210.

Lang, R. (1998) 'Führungskräfte im osteuropäischen Transformationsprozeß – Hauptfelder des wissenschaftlichen Diskurses und Konsequenzen für die Führungspraxis', in Lang, R. (ed.) *Führungskräfte im osteuropäischen Transformationsprozeß*, Munich and Mering: Rainer Hampp Verlag, 5–19.

Lang, R. and Müller, S. (2001) 'Privatization, Perception of Success and Attitudes of Managers in the East German Transformation Process', in Liuhto, K. (ed.) *Ten Years of Economic Transformation*, Studies in Industrial Engineering and Management No 16, Lappeenranta University of Technology (3 vols), vol. III, 391–407.

Lang, R. and Steger, T. (2002) 'The Odyssey of Management Knowledge to Transforming Economies: a Critical Review of a Theoretical Alternative', *Human Resource Development International*, 5, 3, 279–94.

Langer, J. (2001) 'Austria's Business Relations to Slovenia – Meeting with Another Culture', in *Enterprise in Transition*, Third International Conference on Enterprise in Transition (CD-Rom), Split – Hvar, 1105–14.

Lardy, N. R. (1994) *China in the World Economy*, Washington, DC: Institute for International Economics.

Lascu, D.-N., Ahmed, Z. and Vatasecu, M. (1997) 'Applications of the Marketing Concept Philosophy in Romania', in Stan, L., *Romania in Transition*, Aldershot: Dartmouth, 183–90.

Lau, L. J., Qian, Y. and Roland, G. (2000) 'Reform without Losers: an Interpretation of China's Dual-Track Approach to Transition', *Journal of Political Economy*, 108, 1, 120–43.

Lavigne, M. (1999) *The Economics of Transition: from Socialist Economy to Market Economy*, 2nd edn, Basingstoke and London: Macmillan.

Le, T. (2000) 'Top Three Investor Headaches Listed', *Vietnam Investment Review*, 449, 4–5.

Lee, G. O. M. and Warner, M. (2005) 'Epidemics, Labour-Markets and Unemployment: the Impact of SARS on Human Resources Management', *International Journal of Human Resource Management* (in press).

Lee, S. and Luthans, F. (2000) 'Management in Albania', in Warner, M. (ed.) *Regional Encyclopedia of Business and Management: Management in Europe*, London: Thomson Learning, 159–67.

Lee, S. and Trimi, S. (2001) 'Restructuring the Business Education Infrastructure for Economic Transformation in Albania – a Research Note', *Journal for East European Management Studies*, 6, 4, 454–9.

Li, D. (2000) 'Chinese State-Owned Enterprises under the Dual Influence of the Government and the Market', in Richter, F.-J. (ed.) *The Dragon Millennium: Chinese Business in the Coming World Economy*, London: Quorum Books, 3–12.

Li, J. Y. (1991) *Taxation in the PR China*, New York: Praeger.

Lieb-Doczy, E. (2001) *Transition to Survival*, Aldershot: Ashgate.

Lin, C. P. (1996) *PRC Tomorrow: Development under the Ninth Five-Year Plan*, Kaohsiung: National Sun Yat-Sen University.

Litvack, J. and Rondinelli, D. (eds) (1999) *Market Reform in Vietnam: Building Institutions for Development*, Westport, CT: Quorum Books.

Llaci, S. and Kume, V. (2002) 'Trade Unions in Transition Economies: New Roles and Challenges – the Case of Albania', in Lang, R. (ed.) (2002) *Personalmanagement im Transformationsprozess*, Munich and Mehring: Rainer Hampp Verlag, 183–9.

Long, G. Y. (1999) 'China's Changing Regional Disparities During the Reform Period, *Economic Geography*, 75, 59–70.

McGreal, I. (1995) *Great Thinkers of the Eastern World: the Major Thinkers and the Philosophical and Religious Classics of China, India, Japan, Korea and the World of Islam*, New York: HarperCollins.

Magris , C. (1997) *Danube*, London: The Harvill Press.

Makanin, V. (1995) *Baize-Covered Table with Decanter*, London: Readers International.

Mallon, R. (1993) 'Vietnam: Image and Reality', in Heath, J. (ed.) *Revitalizing Socialist Enterprise: a Race against Time*, London: Routledge, 204–21.

Marinov, M. and Marinova, S. (2001) 'Changes Caused by Privatization and Foreign Direct Investment in Central and Eastern Europe: the Case of Bulgaria versus the Region', in Liuhto, K. (ed.) *Ten Years of Economic Transformation*, Studies in Industrial Engineering and Management No 16, Lappeenranta University of Technology (3 vols), vol. II, 460–74.

Marr, R. (1994) 'Die Rolle der Führungskräfte im Prozeß der Transformation eines Wirtschaftssystems von der Plan- zur Marktwirtschaft', in Rosenstiel, L. v. (ed.) *Führung im Systemwandel – Untersuchungen zum Führungsverhalten beim Übergang von der Plan- in die Marktwirtschaft*, Munich and Mering: Rainer Hampp Verlag, 49–65.

Martin, R. (1999) *Transforming Management in Central and Eastern Europe*, Oxford: Oxford University Press.

Maruyama, M. (ed.) (1993) *Management Reform in Eastern and Central Europe: Use of Pre-Communist Cultures*, Aldershot: Dartmouth.

Maslow, W. (1998) 'Wertorientierungen und Stereotype beim Führungsverhalten von Managern in Russland', in Lang, R. (ed.) *Führungskräfte im osteuropäischen Transformationsprozeß*, Munich and Mering: Rainer Hampp Verlag, 27–35.

Maurice, M., Sorge, A. and Warner, M. (1980) 'Societal Differences in Organizing Manufacturing Units: a Comparison of France, West Germany, and Great Britain', *Organization Studies*, 1, 1, 59–86.

Michailova, S. (1996) 'Approaching the Macro-Micro Interface in Transitional Societies: Evidence from Bulgaria', *Journal for East European Management Studies*, 1, 1, 43–70.

Michailova, S. and Hollinshead, G. (1998) 'Developments in the Management of Human Resources in Eastern Europe – the Case of Bulgaria', CEES Working Paper No. 9, Copenhagen: Centre for East European Studies.

Mintzberg, H. (1973) *The Nature of Managerial Work*, New York: Harper & Row.

Mocearov, A. (2001) 'Is Joining the European Union Enough for the Central and Eastern European Countries to Escape from the Economic Periphery of Europe? – Romania's Prospects', in Liuhto, K. (ed.) *Ten Years of Economic Transformation*, Studies in Industrial Engineering and Management No 16, Lappeenranta University of Technology (3 vols), vol. I, pp. 441–62.

Montes, M. F. (1997) 'Vietnam: Transition as a Socialist Project in East Asia', *Working Paper No. 136*, Helsinki: Wider.

Moreno, R., Pasadilla, G. and Remolona, E. (1999) 'Asia's Financial Crisis: Lessons and Implications for Vietnam', in Leung, S. (ed.) *Vietnam and the East Asian Crisis*, Cheltenham: Edward Elgar, 31–54.

Muço, M. (1997) 'Economic Transition in Albania: Political Constraints and Mentality Barriers', http: //www.nato.int/acad/fellow/95–97/muco.pdf (accessed on 11.7.2002).

Naughton, B. (1995) *Growing Out of the Plan: Chinese Economic Reform, 1978–1993*, New York: Cambridge University Press.

Nee, V. (1992) 'Organizational Dynamics of Market Transition: Hybrid Forms, Property Rights, and Mixed Economy in China', *Administrative Science Quarterly*, 37, 1, 1–27.

Nee, V. and Stark, D. (eds) (1989) *Remaking the Institutions of Socialism: China and Eastern Europe*, Stanford, CA: Stanford University Press.

*Nekotorye primery uspeshnoj restruktualizacii predprijatij* (1997) Moscow TACIS Technical Dissemination Project, Brussels: European Commission.

Nguyen, M. D. (2000) 'Some Issues on Ownership in Vietnam', *Journal of Economics and Development*, 19, 4, 4.

Nicolescu, O. (2001) 'Romanian SMEs Evolution Challenges and Perspectives during Transition-Period' (*sic*), in Liuhto, K. (ed.) *Ten Years of Economic Transformation*, Studies in Industrial Engineering and Management No 16, Lappeenranta University of Technology (3 vols), vol. II, 162–81.

Nolan, P. (1995) *China's Rise and Russia's Fall*, Basingstoke: Macmillan.

Noronha, C. (2002) *The Theory of Culture-Specific Total Quality Management: Quality Management in Chinese Regions*, London: Palgrave and New York: St Martin's Press.

Nove, A. (1983) *The Economics of Feasible Socialism*, London: George Allen and Unwin.

Obolensky, D. (1971) *The Byzantine Commonwealth: Eastern Europe 500–1453*, London: Weidenfeld & Nicolson.

Olaru, A. (1998) 'The Attitude Towards Change of Romanian Managers in the Transition to Market Economy', in Lang, R. (ed.) *Führungskräfte im osteuropäischen Transformationsprozeß*, Munich and Mering: Rainer Hampp Verlag, 313–20.

Ondrcka, P. (2001) 'Ten Years of Transformation and Seven Years after the Split of the Former Czechoslovakia', in Liuhto, K. (ed.) *Ten Years of Economic Transformation*, Studies in Industrial Engineering and Management No 16, Lappeenranta University of Technology (3 vols), vol. I, 85–126.

Papava, V. (2002) 'Necroeconomics – the Theory of Post-Communist Transformation of an Economy', *International Journal of Social Economics*, 29, 10, 796–805.

Pavić, I. and Vidučić, L. (1999) 'Restructuring of Large Enterprises in Economies of Transition with Special Reference to Croatia', *Management*, 4, 1–2, 27–47.

Pavlik, P. (2001) 'Adaptation of the Czech Economy: Is the Transition Over?, in Liuhto, K. (ed.) *Ten Years of Economic Transformation*, Studies in Industrial Engineering and Management No 16, Lappeenranta University of Technology (3 vols), vol. I, 102–26.

Peev, E. (1999) 'Ownership and Control Transformation and Discretionary Managerial Behaviour: the Case of Bulgaria', in Edwards, V. (ed.) *Proceedings of the Fifth Annual Conference on the Impact of Transformation on Individuals, Organizations, Society*, Chalfont St Giles: CREEB, vol. I, 298–314.

Peev, E. (2002) 'Ownership and Control Structures in Transition to "Crony" Capitalism: the Case of Bulgaria', *East European Economics*, 40, 5, 73–91.

Peng, M. (2000) *Business Strategies in Transition Economies*, Thousand Oaks, CA: Sage.

Peng, M. W., Buck, T. and Filatotchev, I. (2003) 'Do Outside Directors and New Managers Help Improve Firm Performance? An Exploratory Study in Russian Privatization', *Journal of World Business*, 38, 4, 348–60.

Pipes, R. (1995) *Russia Under the Old Regime*, London: Penguin.

Poletaev, A. (ed.) (1998) *Obzor Rossijskoj Ekonomiky*, Moscow: Bureau for Economic Analysis.

Poletaev, A. (ed.) (2000) *Obzor ekonomicheskoj politiki v Rossii*, Moscow: Bureau for Economic Analysis.

Poletaev, A. (ed.) (2002) *Obzor Rossijskoj Ekonomiky*, Moscow: Bureau for Economic Analysis.

Polonsky, G. (1998) 'Small Business in the Russian Provinces: Case Study Evidence from Volgograd', *Communist Economies and Economic Transformation*, 10, 4, 519–38.

Polonsky, G. (ed.) (2002) *Ten Cases on Restructuring*, Moscow: TACIS.

Polonsky, G. and Clark, B. (1997) 'Integrating Russia into the Global Economy: FDI at any cost?, in Edwards, V. (ed.) *Proceedings of the Third Annual Conference on Central and Eastern Europe in a Global Context*, Chalfont St Giles: CREEB, 173–95.

Polonsky, G. and Iviozian, Z. (2000) 'Restructuring of Russian Industries: Is it Really Possible?', *Post-Communist Economies*, 12, 2, 229–40.

Porvaznik, J. and Stanek, P. (2001) 'Transformation of Slovak Economy to Market Conditions: Problems and Starting Points to Solutions for Future Period', in Liuhto, K. (ed.) *Ten Years of Economic Transformation*, Studies in Industrial Engineering and Management No 16, Lappeenranta University of Technology (3 vols), vol. I, 127–44.

Postelnicu, C. and Postelnicu, Gh. (2002) 'The Impact of Globalization on the Romanian Economy', in Sharma, S. and Galetić, L. (eds) *An Enterprise Odyssey: Economics and Business in the New Millennium*, International Conference, University of Zagreb, Graduate School of Economics and Business, Zagreb, 27–9 June, 469–80.

Privatization Authority and State Participation Administration (2001) 'LNM Holdings and the Authority for Privatisation and Administration of State Ownership (APAPS) Sign Agreement for the Privatisation of SIDEX', http://www.guv.ro/engleza/presa/communicate/200107/com-010725–apaps-semnaresidex.htm (accessed on 2.10.2002).

*Profit* (2003), 14 July.

Pučko, D. (2001) 'Restructuring Former Socially-Owned Enterprises in Slovenia: Findings and Lessons after a Decade of Transition', *Economic and Business Review for Central and South-Eastern Europe*, 3, 1, 5–24.

Pučko, D. (2002) 'Management in the Central and Eastern European Transitional Countries: Where Are We After Ten Years of the Transition', *Comportamento Organizacional e Gestao*, 8, 1, 75–82.

Pučko, D. and Edwards, V. (1999) 'The Restructuring of Slovenian Enterprises in the 1990s – Views from Two Sides', *Economic and Business Review for Central and South-Eastern Europe*, 1, 1–2, 67–89.

Pučko, D. and Lahovnik, M. (1998) 'Changes in Strategic Behaviour of Slovenian Small Businesses in the Transition Period – Convergence or Divergence', in Edwards, V. (ed.) *Proceedings of the Fourth Annual Conference on Convergence or Divergence: Aspirations and Reality in Central and Eastern Europe and Russia*, Chalfont St Giles: CREEB, 38–53.

Puffer, S. and McCarthy, D. (2003) 'The Emergence of Corporate Governance in Russia', *Journal of World Business*, 38, 4, 284–98.

Quang, T. (ed.) (2000) *Vietnam: Challenges on the Path to Development*, Pathum Thani: SAV-SOM Joint Publishing.

Quang, T. (ed.) (2001) *Vietnam: Gearing Up for Integration*, Pathum Thani: SAV-SOM Joint Publishing.

Quang, T. and Hanh, T. (2001) 'Strategy to Cope with Changes: Consulting and Research Company for Technology Transfer and Investment', in Quang, T. (ed.) *Vietnam: Gearing Up for Integration*, Pathum Thani: SAV-SOM Joint Publishing, 15–40.

Quang, T. and Hoa, T. (2001) 'Just-in-Time and Productivity: Coats Phong Phu Joint Venture', in Quang, T. (ed.) *Vietnam: Gearing Up for Integration*, Pathum Thani: SAV-SOM Joint Publishing, 251–75.

Quang, T. and Hoc, L. (2000) 'ISO 9000 Implementation in Vietnam: the Case Studies of Two Rubber Product Manufacturers', in Quang, T. (ed.) *Vietnam: Challenges on the Path to Development*, Pathum Thani: SAV-SOM Joint Publishing, 211–33.

Quang, T. and Huyen, P. (2000) 'Product Extension: the Case of BIVINA Beer', in Quang, T. (ed.) *Vietnam: Challenges on the Path to Development*, Pathum Thani: SAV-SOM Joint Publishing, 135–59.

Quang, T. and Nhut, Q. (2000) 'The Equitization of State-Owned Enterprises in the Mekong Delta: an Analysis of Constraints in the Implementation Process', in Quang, T. (ed.) *Vietnam: Challenges on the Path to Development*, Pathum Thani: SAV-SOM Joint Publishing, 81–106.

Quang, T. and Truong, D. (2001) 'Compensation of Top Managers: a Comparison between State-Owned and Equitized Companies', in Quang, T. (ed.) *Vietnam: Gearing Up for Integration*, Pathum Thani: SAV-SOM Joint Publishing, 119–37.

Quang, T. and Vuong, N. (2000) 'Management Style and Organizational Effectiveness in State and Non-state Sectors in Vietnam', in Quang, T. (ed.) *Vietnam: Challenges on the Path to Development*, Pathum Thani: SAV-SOM Joint Publishing, 57–77.

Radaev, A. (1994) *Voprosy malogo businesa*, Moscow: Nauka.

Rakovski, M. (1977) 'Marxism and Soviet Societies', *Capital and Class*, 1, 83–105.

Ralston, D. A., Holt, D. H., Terpstra, R. H. and Kai-Cheng, Y. (1997) 'The Impact of National Culture and Economic Ideology on Managerial Work Values: a Study of the United States, Russia, Japan, and China', *Journal of International Business Studies*, 28, 1, 177–207.

Ramachandran, N. and Duc, T. (2001) 'Activity-Based Costing Application: Huong Sen Hotel', in Quang, T. (ed.) *Vietnam: Gearing Up for Integration*, Pathum Thani: SAV-SOM Joint Publishing, 223–50.

Ramachandran, N. and Giang, N. (2001) 'Activity-Based Costing Application: Song Da No. 1 Construction Co.', in Quang, T. (ed.) *Vietnam: Gearing Up for Integration*, Pathum Thani: SAV-SOM Joint Publishing, 207–221.

Reeves-Ellington, R. (1998) 'Cooperative Learning for Business Change: a Bulgarian Example', in Edwards, V. (ed.) *Proceedings of the Fourth Annual Conference on Convergence or Divergence: Aspirations and Reality in Central and Eastern Europe and Russia*, Chalfont St Giles: CREEB, 94–114.

Riskin, C. (1988) *China's Political Economy: the Quest for Development Since 1949*, Oxford: Oxford University Press.

Robinson, I. and Tomczak-Stepien, B. (2000) 'Cultural Transformation at Enterprise Level: Case Study Evidence from Poland', *Journal for East European Management Studies*, 5, 2, 130–51.

Rondinelli, D. and Litvack, J. (1999) 'Economic Reform, Social Progress, and Institutional Development: a Framework for Assessing Vietnam's Transition', in Litvack, J. and Rondinelli, D. (eds) *Market Reform in Vietnam: Building Institutions for Development*, Westport, CT: Quorum Books, 1–30.

Rosser, J. B., Jr and Rosser, M. V. (1996) 'Endogenous Chaotic Dynamics in Transitional Economies', *Chaos, Solutions and Fractals*, 7, 12, 2189–97.

Rosser, M. V. (2002) 'Experiences of Economic Transition in Complex Contexts', *International Journal of Social Economics*, 29, 6, 436–52.

Roth, K. and Kostova, T. (2003) 'Organizational Coping with Institutional Upheaval in Transition Economies', *Journal of World Business*, 38, 4, 314–30.

Ruth, M. (1996) 'Evolutionary Economics at the Crossroads of Biology and Physics', *Journal of Social and Evolutionary Systems*, 19, 2, 125–44.

Samson, I. (2002) 'Russian Economic Trends', *RECEP*, 11, 3, 7.

Savitt, R. (1998) 'Evolving Management Practices in the Czech Republic: Restructuring and Market Orientation', *Journal for East European Management Studies*, 3, 4, 339–54.

Schlevogt, K. A. (2002) *The Art of Chinese Management: Theory, Evidence and Applications*, Oxford: Oxford University Press.

Scott, W. R. (2001) *Institutions and Organizations*, 2nd edn, Thousand Oaks, CA: Sage.

Scott, W. R. (2002) 'The Changing World of the Chinese Enterprise', in Tsui, A. and Lau, C.-M. (eds) *The Management of Enterprises in the People's Republic of China*, Norwell, MA: Kluwer, 59–68.

Senjur, M. (2002) 'Slovenija, rezervat poceni delavcev?', *Delo*, 6 April, sobotna priloga, 4–6.

Sheahan, J. (1986) *Alternative International Economic Strategies and Their Relevance for China*, Washington, DC: World Bank.

Sheldon, M. (1993) 'Agrarian Development Strategies in China and Vietnam', in Turley, W. and Seldon, M. (eds) *Reinventing Vietnamese Socialism*, Boulder, CO: Westview Press, 209–53.

Shen, R. (1997) *The Restructuring of Romania's Economy: a Paradigm of Flexibility and Adaptability*, Westport, CT and London: Praeger.

Slaveski, T. and Nedanovski, P. (2002) 'Foreign Direct Investment in the Balkans: the Case of Albania, FYROM, and Bulgaria', *East European Economics*, 40, 4, 83–99.

Slavik, Š. (2001) 'Strategic Management in Slovak Enterprises – a Survey Findings' (*sic*), *Journal for East European Management Studies*, 6, 1, 65–91.

Smallbone, D. and Rogut, A. (2003) 'From Transition to Accession: the Challenge for SMEs in Candidate Countries', in *Enterprise in Transition*, Fourth International Conference on Enterprise in Transition (CD-Rom), Split – Hvar, 205–25.

Smith, H. (1976) *The Russians*, London: Sphere.

Stanizikis, J. (1991) 'Political Capitalism in Poland', *East European Politics and Society*, 5, 1, 127–41.

Stark, D. (1992) 'Path Dependence and Privatization Strategies in East Central Europe', *East European Politics and Society*, 6, 1, 17–54.

Stark, D. and Nee, V. (1989) 'Towards an Institutional Analysis of State Socialism', in Nee, V. and Stark, D. (eds) *Remaking the Institutions of Socialism: China and Eastern Europe*, Stanford, CA: Stanford University Press, 1–31.

*Statistical Yearbook on Candidate and South-East European Countries* (2002) Luxembourg: Eurostat.

Stepien, B. and Robinson, I. (2001) 'Strategic Change Within Post-Socialist Polish Enterprises', in Edwards, V. (ed.) *Proceedings of the Seventh Annual Conference on Central and Eastern Europe: Whither transformation: successful evolution or fragmentation and decay?*, Chalfont St Giles: CREEB, 36–57.

Stiglitz, J. E. (2002) *Globalization and Its Discontents*, New York: Norton.

Studio Legale Tonucci e Economisti Associati (2002) *Guida agli Investimenti in Albania*, Tirana: Ambasciata d'Italia, http: //www.ambitalia-tirana.com/ commercio/guida-investimenti.pdf (accessed on 5.9.2002).

Swierczek, F. W. and Anh, T. (2000) 'Management Training Needs: an Assessment of Vietnam Saigon Plastics Association', in Quang, T. (ed.) *Vietnam: Challenges on the Path to Development*, Pathum Thani: SAV-SOM Joint Publishing, 237–60.

Swierczek, F. W. and Binh, N. (2001) 'Entrepreneurship Profile: Successful Factors of Small and Medium Enterprises in Ho Chi Minh City', in Quang, T. (ed.) *Vietnam: Gearing Up for Integration*, Pathum Thani: SAV-SOM Joint Publishing, 77–97.

Sysko-Romanczuk, S. and Lozano, A. (2002) 'Regional Partnership – Entrepreneurship Development Concept', in Sharma, S. and Galetić, L. (eds) *An Enterprise Odyssey: Economics and Business in the New Millennium*, International Conference, University of Zagreb, Graduate School of Economics and Business, Zagreb, 27–9 June, 1503–14.

Tang, J. and Ward, A. (2003) *The Changing Face of Chinese Management*, London: Routledge.

*The Europa World Year Book 2001*, 42nd edn (2001), London and New York: Europa.

*The Europa World Year Book 2002*, 43rd edn (2002), London and New York: Europa.

Thompson, P. and Smith, C. (1992) 'Socialism and the Labour Process in Theory and Practice', in Smith, C. and Thompson, P. (eds) *Labour in Transition: the Labour Process in Eastern Europe and China*, London: Routledge, 3–33.

Thuy, L. X. and Doan, N. (2000) 'Assessing International Joint Ventures in Vietnam', in Quang, T. (ed.) *Vietnam: Challenges on the Path to Development*, Pathum Thani: SAV-SOM Joint Publishing, 13–31.

Todeva, E. (1996) 'Dynamics of Management Practices in Eastern Europe: the Case of Bulgaria', *Journal for East European Management Studies*, 1, 4, 47–63.

Todeva, E. (2000) 'Management in Bulgaria', in Warner, M. (ed.) *Regional Encyclopedia of Business and Management*, vol. 4: *Management in Europe*, London: Thomson Learning, 184–92.

Tönnies, F. (2001 [1887]) *Community and Civil Society*, Harris, J. (ed.), Cambridge: Cambridge University Press.

Tse, E. (2000) 'Challenges of Competing in China for Multinationals', in Richter, F.-J. (ed.) *The Dragon Millennium: Chinese Business in the Coming World Economy*, London: Quorum Books, 93–106.

Unger, J. and Chan, A. (1995) 'China, Corporatism, and the East Asian Model', *The Australian Journal of Chinese Affairs*, 33, January, 29–35.

van Brabant, J. M. (1998) *The Political Economy of Transition*, London: Routledge.

Vatamanu, O. (1998) 'The Management of Transition in the Metallurgical Industry in the Light of Romania's Integration in the European Union', in Edwards, V. (ed.) *Proceedings of the Fourth Annual Conference on Convergence or Divergence: Aspirations and Reality in Central and Eastern Europe and Russia*, Chalfont St Giles: CREEB, 224–30.

Vatchkova, E. (2002) 'The Speed of Changes – Bulgarian Way to the Integrated European HRM', in Lang, R. (ed.) (2002) *Personalmanagement im Transformationsprozess*, Munich and Mehring: Rainer Hampp Verlag, 95–105.

Vlachoutsicos, C. (1999) 'Internal Barriers to the Transition of Enterprises from Central Plan to Market', *Economic and Business Review for Central and South-Eastern Europe*, 1–2, 1, 105–31.

Voinea, L. (2002) 'Revisiting FDI Patterns in Transition. The Case of Romania', paper prepared for EACES Conference, http://www.eaces.gelso.unitn.it/Eaces/work/Papers/Revisiting%20FDI.pdf (accessed on 16.10.2002).

Vojnić, D. (2001) 'Countries in Transition at the Beginning of the 21st Century – Transition, Integration, Globalization and Controversies of Market', in *Enterprise in Transition*, Third International Conference on Enterprise in Transition (CD-Rom), Split – Hvar, 5–32.

Wandycz, P. (1992) *The Price of Freedom: a History of East Central Europe from the Middle Ages to the Present*, London: Routledge.

Wang, X. L. and Zhang, L. J. (2000) 'The Future of Private Enterprises in China', in Richter, F.-J. (ed.) *The Dragon Millennium: Chinese Business in the Coming World Economy*, London: Quorum Books, 35–46.

Warner, M. (1995a) *The Management of Human Resources in Chinese Industry*, Basingstoke: Macmillan and New York: St Martin's Press.

Warner, M. (1995b) 'Managing China's Human Resources', *Human Systems Management*, 14, 3, 239–48.

Warner, M. (1999) (ed.) *China's Managerial Revolution*, London: Frank Cass.

Warner, M. (2003a) (ed.) *The Future of Chinese Management*, London: Frank Cass.

Warner, M. (ed.) (2003b) *Culture and Management in Asia*, London: RoutledgeCurzon.

Wei, X. (2003) 'Two Extreme Transition Economies: a Comparative Study of East German and Chinese Restructuring', in *Enterprise in Transition*, Fourth International Conference on Enterprise in Transition (CD-Rom), Split – Hvar, 101–20.

Whiteley, A., Cheung, S. and Zhang, S. Q. (2000) *Human Resource Strategies in China*, Singapore: World Scientific.

Williams, M. C. (1992) *Vietnam at the Crossroads*, London: Pinter.

Wiskemann, E. (1966) *Europe of the Dictators, 1919–1945*, London: Collins.

Wong, C. (1995) *Fiscal Management and Economic Reform in the PR China*, New York: Oxford University Press.

Woodward, R. and Kozarzewski, P. (2003) 'Enterprise Performance and Ownership Changes in Polish Management–Employee Buyouts', in *Enterprise in Transition*, Fourth International Conference on Enterprise in Transition (CD-Rom), Split – Hvar, 81–100.

World Bank (1988) *China: Finance and Investment*, Washington, DC: World Bank.

World Bank (1993) *The East Asian Miracle: Economic Growth and Public Policy*, Washington, DC: World Bank.

World Bank (1994) *China: Foreign Trade Reform*, Washington, DC: World Bank.

World Bank (1996) *World Development Report 1996: From Plan to Market*, Washington, DC: World Bank.

World Bank (1997) *China Engaged: Integration with the Global Economy*, Washington, DC: World Bank.

World Bank (2000) *World Development Report 1999/2000*, Washington, DC: World Bank.

World Bank (2002) *Transition – the First Ten Years: Analysis and Lessons for Eastern Europe and the Former Soviet Union*, Washington, DC: World Bank.

Wu, Y.-S. (1994) *Comparative Economic Transformations: Mainland China, Hungary, the Soviet Union and Taiwan*, Stanford, CA: Stanford University Press.

Yang, H. Q. (1995) *Banking and Financial Control in Reforming Planned Economies*, New York: St. Martin's Press.

Zhu, Y. (1998) 'The Challenges and Opportunities for the Trade Union Movement in the Transition Era: Two Socialist Market Economies China and Vietnam', http://www.ilo.org/public/english/bureau/inst/project/network/netresp/zhu.htm (accessed on 22.1.2003).

Zhu, Y. (2000) 'Globalization, Foreign Direct Investment and the Impact on Labour Relations and Regulations: the Case of China', *The International Journal of Comparative Labour Law and Industrial Relations*, 16, 1, 5–24.

Zhu, Y. (2002) 'Economic Reform and Human Resource Management in Vietnamese Enterprises', *Asia Pacific Business Review*, 8, 3, 115–34.

Zhu, Y. (2003) 'Culture and Management in Vietnam', in Warner, M. (ed.) *Culture and Management in Asia*, London: RoutledgeCurzon, 249–63.

Zhu, Y. and Campbell, I. (1996) 'Economic Reform and the Challenge of Transforming Labour Regulation in China', *Labour and Industry*, 7, 2, 29–49.

Zhu, Y. and Fahey, S. (1999) 'The Impact of Economic Reform on Industrial Labour Relations in China and Vietnam', *Post-Communist Economies*, 11, 2, 173–92.

Zhu, Y. and Fahey, S. (2000) 'The Challenges and Opportunities for the Trade Union Movement in the Transition Era: Two Socialist Market Economies – China and Vietnam', *Asia Pacific Business Review*, 6, 3–4, 282–99.

Zhu, Y. and Warner, M. (2000a) 'Changing Approaches to Employment Relations in the People's Republic of China', in Bamber, G. J., Park, F., Lee, C., Ross, P. and Broadbent, K. (eds) *Employment Relations in the Asia-Pacific: Changing Approaches*, Sydney: Thomson Learning, 117–28.

Zhu, Y. and Warner, M. (2000b) 'An Emerging Model of Employment Relations in China: a Divergent Path from the Japanese', *International Business Review*, 9, 345–61.

Zhu, Y. and Warner, M. (2002) 'Human Resource Management in China's "Frontier" Special Economic Zone: a Study of Selected Enterprises on Hainan Island', *International Journal of Employment Studies*, 10, 1, 75–104.

Zhu, Y. and Warner, M. (2004) 'HRM in East Asia', in Harzing, A. W. and Ruysseveldt, J. V. (eds) *International Human Resource Management*, 2nd edn, London: Sage, 195–220.

Zhu, Y. and Warner, M. (2004) 'Changing Patterns of Human Resource Management in Contemporary China: WTO Accession and Enterprise Responses', *Industrial Relations Journal*, 35, 4, 311–28.

# Index